WILLIAM INNES, CAPTAIN OF THE ROYAL BLACKHEATH CLUB, 1778

After the well-known painting by Lemuel Francis Abbott, R.A.   The painting itself is lost, but has been preserved in a mezzotint engraving by V. Green, from which this reproduction is taken.

THE CLASSICS OF GOLF

Edition of

A HISTORY OF GOLF

by
Robert Browning

Foreword by Herbert Warren Wind
Afterword by S. L. McKinlay

ISBN: 0-940889-05-6

Foreword

Perhaps the least celebrated of the truly first-class books on golf is "A History of Golf" by Robert Browning, which was published in this country in 1955. A Scot whose family came from the Glasgow area, Browning was the editor of Golfing *magazine, one of the best British golf periodicals, for a full forty-five years—from 1910 to 1955. A scholar who earned both his M.A. and LL.B. degrees, he was never happier, one gathers, than when he was hunting down the authenticity of the diverse claims to the game's origin and the many fascinating steps in its long evolution. One also gets the feeling that Browning was a happy, tireless researcher who carried on a large investigative correspondence for many years with golf writers, editors, and bibliophiles scattered the world over. He emerges also as an exceedingly modest man. Who else except a person of that nature would select as mild a title as "A History of Golf" for such a handsomely researched and written book? It is pleasant to learn from Browning's introduction to his chef-d'oeuvre that in 1918, when the British forces in France were preparing for the final attack, he was a young subaltern in temporary command of a battery in one of the battalions of the Fifty-first Scottish Division. One day, as he recounts, the commanding officer of that battalion happened to ask Browning what he had done in civilian life, "and this led to the discovery of a mutual interest in golf, and I learned I was talking to the son of that Captain J. C. Stewart of Fasnacloich who in partnership with George Glennie won the first championship ever played."*

One of my oldest Scottish friends, Sam McKinlay (who has kindly contributed the Afterword to this book), is the only person with whom I can remember ever discussing Browning. McKinlay, a golfer of Walker Cup class who did some writing and editing for the Glasgow Herald *and the Glasgow* Times *and who later became the editor of the* Times, *mentioned one day that Browning had to be a rather shy man, since one seldom ran into him in the press tent or inside the clubhouse at a tournament. However reclusive Browning might have been, he saw a great deal of competitive golf, and, among his contemporaries, perhaps only Bernard Darwin knew as much as he did about the game.*

"A History of Golf," written in clear, crisp, stand-up prose, is in a class by itself: it is far and away the finest one-volume history of golf. One of its virtues is that Browning does not spread a vast scholarly tapestry before the reader but presents his huge but brilliantly organized knowledge in thirty-five chapters, each devoted to a separate phase of this complicated game. If you have any questions about golf that you want the answer to, you will find it in Browning's history, and, more often than not, the information you seek is easy to locate because of the straight-forward titles that Browning has given his chapters. To cite some examples, "Why Golf Is Royal and Ancient"; "The Formation of the Clubs"; "The First Thirty Years of the Open"; "How Golf Came to England"; "The Amateurs Make a Fresh Start"; "The Beginning of Golf in the States"; "The Rising of the Amazons"; "America Steals the Picture"; "From Feathery to Rubber Core"; "From Baffing Spoon to Wedge"; "The Development of Golf Architecture"; "The Evolution of the Rules"; and "Golf As an International Sport." Whenever I am writing a golf article, it is the rare day that I do not consult Browning's history to confirm some fact. For me, the three most useful reference books are "The Encyclopedia of Golf", edited by Peter Ryde and Donald Steel;

"The World Atlas of Golf"; and Browning's "A History of Golf." The only danger, as I see it, is that once you have found the information you are seeking in Browning, there is a strong temptation to keep on reading for the sheer pleasure of it.

For example, let us say that a golfer wants to know when the Scots were first permitted to play golf on Sunday. Here is Browning on that subject:

> It would appear, however, that by the end of the sixteenth century the rigid sabbatarianism of John Knox and his followers had begun to place further restrictions on Sunday amusements. In 1618 we find King James VI declaring that 'with our owne eares wee heard the generall complaint of our people, that they were barred from all lawfull recreation and exercise upon the Sundayes afternoone, after the ending of all Divine service, for when shal the common people have leave to exercise, if not upon the Sundayes and holydayes, seeing that they must apply their labour, and winne their living in all working dayes?' He therefore rebuked the 'precise people' and declared his pleasure to be, 'that after the end of divine service, our good people be not disturbed, letted, or discouraged from any lawfull recreation—such as dauncing, either men or women, archerie for men, leaping, vaulting, or any such harmless recreation', but prohibiting 'the said recreations to any that are not present in the church at the service of God before going to the said recreations.'

Many such instances of Browning's wide-ranging knowledge come to mind. For example, whereas most golfers who read about the game are usually well informed about the wise and genial character of Old Tom Morris, for some forty years the beloved custodian of the links of St. Andrews, most readers know comparatively little about Allan Robertson, Old Tom's mentor and the first truly outstanding golfer produced at St. Andrews. Moreover, they are apt to have their reservations about him. In most books, Allan's skill as a golfer is brought out but it is not described in interesting detail. He comes across as a dour and dislikeable man who, because his family had for generations made feather golf balls, tried to stop the introduction of the gutta-percha ball. The reader of Browning's history is accorded a much fuller picture of Allan Robertson. The chapter entitled "The First of the Invincibles" begins as follows: "Professional golf as we understand it may be said to have begun with the appearance on the stage of the great Allan Robertson." Browning then devotes some seven pages to Robertson, and brings him arrestingly to life. For example, consider these two excerpts:

> The strength of his game lay in the avoidance of mistakes. Below the middle height, thickset and short-necked, he was an example of the perfect golfing temperament, a mixture of imperturbable pluck and good humour. He had above all the same capacity for pulling out the little extra bit in a crisis as you find among modern golfers in such 'bonny fighters' as Walter Hagen and Ben Hogan.

> Allan's lasting contribution to the game was his introduction of the use of iron clubs for approach play. Although he had resisted the introduction of the gutta-percha ball, under the impression that it would take away the ball-makers' livelihood, he was quick to realize the difference the less lively ball made in the technique of the game. 'Before Allan's day,' says Dr. Macpherson, 'the baffing spoon was the weapon of approach to the hole if a bunker intervened ... But Allan introduced the deadly "iron" which he wrought with marvelous accuracy.' In the days of the feathery, the iron clubs—cleeks and niblicks—had been designed for hacking the ball out of bad lies. Their greater angle of loft, however, made them especially adapted for use with the 'guttie,' which had to be 'clipped' up to get it into the air. The abandonment of the wooden putter must also be attributable to Allan, who set the example of using the cleek for long green approaches, only reverting to his wooden putter when he had some specially precarious putt to hole.

Browning had the talent of the born raconteur. When he is writing of the first English golf clubs and turns to

the Royal North Devon Club, which is situated at Westward Ho! on the north coast of Devonshire, he works
into his narrative that the English novelist, Charles
Kingsley, happened to be living in the house of one of
the club's most enthusiastic members, one Captain
Molesworth, while he was writing his renowned novel
"Westward Ho!" from which both the golf course and
the village it was in took their name. A bit later on,
Browning introduces some of the well-known golfers
who learned the game at Westward Ho!:

> Horace Hutchinson was only a schoolboy of sixteen
> when he won the Scratch Medal of the Club Autumn
> Meeting. A few years later he played at the head of the
> Oxford team in the first University match, and a few
> years after that when the Amateur Championship was
> inaugurated, he reached the final in each of the first
> three years, and won two of them.

> In the days when young Master Hutchinson was able
> to play golf at Westward Ho! when he came home on
> vacation from Oxford, he had as his caddie a little
> flaxen-haired laddie from Northam village who was
> employed as house-boy in the Hutchinson home. The
> boy was destined to become the most famous of all the
> golfing sons of Westward Ho! His name was John Hen-
> ry Taylor, the first English professional to beat the Scots
> at their own game and win the Open Championship,
> which he has held five times in all. So you see that the
> first English amateur to win the Amateur Champion-
> ship and the first English professional to win the Open
> Championship both came from this little corner of De-
> von.

For Browning, the young subaltern during the First
World War, the men who had made him so enthusiastic
about golf were the Great Triumvirate of Harry Vardon, J. H. Taylor, and James Braid who dominated
British golf during the twenty years before the war and
who, just as important, were four-square men as well as
remarkable champions. Nevertheless, Browning, like
most British golfers, was quick to appreciate the man-

ifold abilities of *Walter Hagen* and the other members of the American invasion in the 1920s. For example, take this excerpt:

> The older heroes of the game were all distinguished for their skill with heroic weapons. Braid was the mighty driver, Vardon the perfect iron player, Taylor the master of the mashie. Hagen stands out as the wizard of the niblick and the putter. And though every golfer will admit that the shots from the bunker and on the green are just as much a part of golf as the long game, yet it is only natural to imagine that the player who owes his success to his power of getting down from sand or rough with a niblick shot and a putt cannot really be a player of the highest class, in spite of all his victories. But the people who used to think of Hagen as gaining his championships by incredible recoveries after still more incredible mistakes were forced to recognize an immense change that 'Sir Walter' affected in his play in the four years that intervened between the winning of his second and third championships. The man who played the record second round of 67 at Muirfield in 1929, the lowest round ever returned in the final stages of a British Open Championship up to that date, did so by well-nigh perfect golf. He was hitting the ball almost along a chalk line from tee to pin all the way, his only real mistake being a drive pushed out into a bunker on the difficult eighth. There never was a more convincing round.

I think that you will find that Browning's "A History of Golf" is a superlative chronicle of the game's development nicely laced by the author's gift for the appropriate and lifting anecdote. For example, I had never heard of how "Calamity Jane," Jones' putter, got its name until Browning explained it at the end of a passage in which he informs us that at one time it was common for champions to give their favorite clubs colorful names.

> The original 'Calamity Jane' was an historical personage, a notorious female cattle-rustler of the bad old days in the Far West. In a film of her life-story, when one of her admirers is represented as inquiring why she was given the name, she replies: 'Oh! I guess it's because

of what happens to my enemies!' However, I have witnessed too many examples of the good nature with which Emperor Jones treats his opponents to imagine for a moment that the name was chosen as a hint of what was going to happen to his opponents. As a matter of fact it was not he who gave the putter its name. What happened was that Bobby had putted badly in the match in which he was rather heavily beaten by Francis Ouimet in the U.S. Amateur Championship of 1921, and on the following day he went over to Nassau, Long Island, to visit Jimmy Maiden, the brother of Stewart Maiden, the professional of Bobby's home club at East Lake. Jimmy presented his visitor with a rusty old putter to which he had given the name of 'Calamity Jane,' and with this Bobby holed so many long putts in the course of the day that the thing became a joke. No one at that stage could forsee that 'Calamity Jane' was to become one of the most famous clubs of all time.

Browning occasionally refers in his history to the years after the Second World War, but it is clear that, however much he appreciated the amazing technique of his contemporaries, his heart belonged to the earlier eras of the century. "Modern golf," he states near the end of his history, "is a stiffer test of a player's skill, but it has robbed the game of something of its charm as an adventure of the spirit." He may have something there.

Herbert Warren Wind

CONTENTS

CHAP.		PAGE
	INTRODUCTION	V
I.	WHY GOLF IS ROYAL AND ANCIENT	I
II.	GOLF AS A CROSS-COUNTRY GAME	7
III.	THE ARGUMENT OF THE PICTURES	14
IV.	THE ARGUMENT OF LANGUAGE	20
V.	'IN TYME OF SERMONIS'.	29
VI.	THE FORMATION OF THE CLUBS	35
VII.	WINING AND DINING IN THE BRAVE DAYS OF OLD .	45
VIII.	ELECTION BY COMBAT	52
IX.	WHY EIGHTEEN HOLES MAKE A ROUND	59
X.	THE EVOLUTION OF THE CADDIE	64
XI.	THE FIRST OF THE INVINCIBLES	69
XII.	THE START OF THE CHAMPIONSHIPS	75
XIII.	THE FIRST THIRTY YEARS OF THE OPEN . . .	81
XIV.	HOW GOLF CAME TO ENGLAND	89
XV.	THE START OF THE UNIVERSITY MATCH	95
XVI.	THE AMATEURS MAKE A FRESH START	101
XVII.	THE FATHER OF ENGLISH GOLF	107
XVIII.	THE BEGINNING OF THE GAME IN THE STATES . .	113
XIX.	WOMEN'S GOLF BEFORE WATERLOO	120
XX.	THE RISING OF THE AMAZONS	124
XXI.	AMERICA STEALS THE PICTURE	129
XXII.	FROM FEATHERY TO RUBBER CORE	135
XXIII.	FROM BAFFING SPOON TO SAND WEDGE . . .	143
XXIV.	A SCIENCE INSTEAD OF AN ART	150
XXV.	PUTTING A GIRDLE ROUND THE GLOBE	157
XXVI.	THE DEVELOPMENT OF GOLF ARCHITECTURE . . .	165
XXVII.	THE EVOLUTION OF THE RULES	170
XXVIII.	METHODS OF SCORING	178
XXIX.	BETWEEN TWO WARS	186
XXX.	SEX EQUALITY ON THE LINKS.	192
XXXI.	HISTORIC TROPHIES AND MOUNTING PRIZE-MONEY .	198
XXXII.	GOLF AS AN INTERNATIONAL SPORT	204
XXXIII.	HISTORY'S DEBT TO GOLF	207
XXXIV.	GOLF AS A ROYAL GAME AGAIN	214
	APPENDIX: CHRONOLOGICAL TABLE	221
	INDEX	229

INTRODUCTION

THE game of golf has during the last sixty or seventy years produced a wealth of literature such as no other sport or pastime can rival, but though the triumphs of the modern masters have again and again been chronicled with eager enthusiasm and every detail of their methods analysed with anxious care, no serious effort has yet been made to present a co-ordinated account of the earlier history of the game, which came into popular favour in Scotland more than five hundred years ago. The nearest approach to such an attempt has been Robert Clark's *Golf: a Royal and Ancient Game*, first published in 1875, which includes extracts from an immense variety of ancient documents bearing on the history of the game, and to which every writer on this phase of golf must acknowledge his indebtedness. But Clark's compilation is incomplete and scrappy, a collection of documentary odds and ends. He made no attempt to weld them into a logical whole; and his own scanty comments are the merest surface observations, unsupported by any critical examination. Most of the writers of occasional chapters on the history of golf in books dealing with the game are only interested in golf and quite uninterested in history, and the result is that they continually fail to collate the most important golfing developments with the historical events that gave rise to them. It is unforgivable, for instance, that so many writers blindly follow Clark in speaking of James IV going out in 1503 to play golf in defiance of his own edicts, without realizing that that date coincided with his marriage to his Tudor princess and with a peace treaty that made these edicts obsolete.

'To write the history of golf as it should be done,' declared Andrew Lang in the first chapter which he wrote for the Badminton *Golf* in 1890, 'demands a thorough study of all Scottish Acts of Parliament, Kirk Sessions records, memoirs and in fact of Scottish literature, legislation, and history from the beginning of time. . . . A young man must do it, and he will be so ancient before he finishes the toil that he will scarce see the flag on the short hole at St Andrews from the tee.' Lang, however, could not foresee that the amazing interest in the game on both sides of the Atlantic would lead to scores of ardent investigators contributing scraps of information to this research. My own work as editor for nearly half a century of one of the oldest periodicals connected with the game has made it easy for me to keep track of such items of knowledge. I wish particularly to mention the help I have derived from three good friends and former contributors to my own magazine: Eric Oswald, who compiled for *Golf Illustrated* an elaborate and exhaustive survey of the records of the Open Championship up to the First World War; the late J. Bruce Kerr, who was responsible for some important additions to my notes on the start of golf at Oxford and Cambridge; and the late J. A. Brongers, the editor of the Dutch *Golf*, with whom I had a long and pleasant controversy regarding the claim for a Dutch origin of the game. I also want to thank another old friend, Dean O. M. Leland of the University of Minnesota, for the important discovery of the seventeenth-century painting of the game of *chole* by the Flemish artist Paul Bril, discussed in Chapter II, and for much valuable comment on this and other aspects of golf history.

It is impossible for me to acknowledge the sources of all the items of useful information which have come to me—often in the most unexpected way. For instance, when the British forces in France were gradually assembling for the final advance in the late summer of 1918, the Commanding Officer of one of the battalions of the famous Fifty-first Scottish Division on its way up to the line turned his horse aside to make some casual inquiry from a young subaltern in temporary command of a battery in position near the road. The familiar query regarding my occupation in civil life led to the discovery of a mutual interest in golf, and I learned that I was talking to the son of that Captain J. C. Stewart of Fasnacloich who in partnership with George Glennie won the first championship ever played. I think Colonel Stewart was rather pleased to find that I was familiar with that stage of golf history. But here was a direct link with the start of championship golf in 1857—and who would have thought to find it in the battle front of the Somme?

A few years after the First World War the newly appointed custodian of the Golf Museum of the James River Country Club,

Newport News, Virginia, the late John Campbell, called at the office of *Golfing* in London to ask the editor's help in obtaining interesting material for the museum, to discover that he was renewing an old friendship, for Jack and I had known one another as boys, our fathers being partners in a firm of fine art publishers in Glasgow, and Jack more than repaid the help I gave him by letting me have photostats of various duplicates of historical documents from both sides of the Atlantic in the custody of the museum.

A mild controversy over the date of the start of golf in Ireland led to an informative correspondence with Brigadier-General Sir David Kinloch, of Gilmerton, who was in the start of things at Oxford University and in Dublin. I have even in some cases found myself profiting from my own mistakes, as when a too ready acceptance of early information from the archives of the Worcestershire Golf Club at Malvern, the pioneers of the game in the midlands, led to my receiving still earlier information from the late Colonel R. Prescott-Decie, the original founder of the Club.

Where I have made use of information derived from some earlier work I have tried to make a point of acknowledging the source in the text, but if in any instance I have inadvertently failed to do so, I should like to apologize in advance. Where I am putting forward my own conjectures or opinions on points that are dubious or in dispute I have tried to make it plain that I am doing so, and take credit for avoiding the use of the word 'tradition' which has been dragged in to bolster up some wild guesses in the past. Not many years ago a Scottish daily paper which ought to have known better published an article containing a reference to a 'tradition' that golf was introduced into Scotland by the Dutch workmen brought over by King Robert Bruce after the Battle of Bannockburn to commence the building of St Andrews Cathedral. It would be difficult to cram a greater number of chronological inexactitudes into a single sentence, but inaccuracies will attach themselves to the best regulated traditions. What the writer failed to explain was how a 'tradition' so apropos had escaped all reference in print until as late as the twentieth century.

Some of the other 'traditions' that have passed into general acceptance have no better foundation. A frequent problem for the historian is created by doubtful claims to seniority. Even in my own wanderings round English Clubs it has been a common experience to be assured by some 'oldest surviving member' that his Club is 'the oldest in Blankshire.' When a polite inquiry elicits the exact date of the Club's formation, and I point out that another Blankshire Club claims to have come into existence a year earlier, the almost invariable reply is: 'Ah! Yes. But golf was played on our course for two or three years before the Club was actually formed.' I do not retort by asking how many years golf was played on the rival course before *their* Club was formed, because the enthusiasts who make these claims do not want to go into that. There is to be one criterion for them and another for the rest of the world. In my own account of the formation of the earlier Clubs, I have adopted as my criterion the date of the Club's first competition. If anyone prefers another criterion there is no reason why they should not do so, provided they work out the date by their method for the other Clubs as well as for their own.

Acknowledgment is also due to the proprietors of *Golfing* for permission to make use of my own historical articles and notes from that magazine, and of the photographs and illustrations that appeared along with them.

In conclusion I should like to emphasize that this is a history of golf and not of golfers, so that if any of my readers feel inclined to complain that less than justice has been done to the exploits of their own heroes or heroines, they must understand that the others have been selected only as examples of the historical development of the game.

1955   R. B.

ILLUSTRATIONS

WILLIAM INNES, CAPTAIN OF THE BLACKHEATH CLUB,
   1778 .   .   .   .   *Frontispiece*

THE FIRST INTERNATIONAL FOURSOME .   .   .   *facing page* 12
                  (see note, page xii)

THE FIRST GOLFING PRINCE OF WALES, 1595 .   ,, ,,   17

THE FIRST ROYAL GOLFERS .   .   .   .   .   ,, ,,   24

CHARLES I PLAYING GOLF AT LEITH. .   .   .   ,, ,,   25

THE GAME OF CHOLE   .   .   *Four pages between* 32 *and* 33

FROM A BOOK OF HOURS OF 1530 .   .   .   *facing page* 40

FROM A FLEMISH BOOK OF HOURS .   .   .   ,, ,,   41

KOLVEN ON THE ICE IN 1668 .   .   .   .   ,, ,,   48

AN AMSTERDAM KOLVEN COURT (1761) .   .   ,, ,,   56

KOLVEN ON THE ICE. .   .   .   .   .   ,, ,,   57

'THE KOLFER GIRDS HIS ICE-SPURS ON' .   .   ,, ,,   72

A REMBRANDT ETCHING OF 1654 .   .   .   ,, ,,   73

THE FIRST GREEN AT ST ANDREWS, 1798 .   .   ,, ,,   80

WILLIAM ST CLAIR OF ROSLIN .   .   .   .   ,, ,,   81

'IN TYME OF SERMONIS' .   .   .   .   .   ,, ,,   89

A NORTH BERWICK FOURSOME IN THE 1840'S .   ,, ,,   104

THE GOLDEN AGE OF GOLF UNIFORMS. .   .   ,, ,,   112

NORTH BERWICK LINKS 1835 .   .   .   .   ,, ,,   113

A GROUP OF OLD MASTERS AT ST ANDREWS .   ,, ,,   120

THE OLDEST CHAMPIONSHIP TROPHY .   .   .   ,, ,,   121

GOLF AT BLACKHEATH IN 1863 . . . . . *facing page* 136

BLACKHEATH *v.* LONDON SCOTTISH, 1873 . . . ,, ,, 137

'OLD TOM' MORRIS AT ST ANDREWS, 1898 . . . ,, ,, 152

JOHN BALL *v.* JOHN E. LAIDLAY, 1890 . . . ,, ,, 153

HAROLD HILTON *v.* JOHN L. LOW, 1901 . . . ,, ,, 168

HARRY VARDON . . . . ,, ,, 169

WALTER HAGEN AT ROYAL ST GEORGE'S, 1928 . ,, ,, 177

THE APPLE-TREE GANG, 1888 . . . . . . ,, ,, 180

A DRIVE BY BOBBY JONES . . . . . . ,, ,, 181

KING GEORGE VI PLAYING IN AN EXHIBITION
MATCH . . . . ,, ,, 184

WHERE THE FIRST GREAT BRITAIN *v.* U.S. MATCH WAS
PLAYED . . . . ,, ,, 185

THE LINKS OF THE HONOURABLE COMPANY AT MUIR-
FIELD . . . . ,, ,, 200

THE SPORT OF PREMIERS AND PRESIDENTS . . . ,, ,, 201

TWO QUEENS OF THE LINKS . . . . . . ,, ,, 204

MRS MILDRED ('BABE') ZAHARIAS . . . . ,, ,, 205

THE HOME OF THE FIRST ROYAL GOLF CLUB . . ,, ,, 208

THE FIRST INTERNATIONAL FOURSOME

Two English noblemen, who, during their attendance at the Scottish Court, had, among other fashionable amusements of the period, occasionally practised golf, were one day debating the question with His Highness the Duke of York (afterwards James II), whether that amusement were peculiar to Scotland or England; and having some difficulty in coming to an issue on the subject, it was proposed to decide the question by an appeal to the game itself; the Englishmen agreeing to risk the legitimacy of their national pretensions as golfers, together with a large sum of money, on the result of a match, to be played with His Highness and any Scotsman he could bring forward . . . . The person recommended to him for his purpose was a poor man, named John Patersone, a shoemaker, who was not only reputed the best golf-player of this day, but whose ancestors had been equally celebrated from time immemorial . . . .

The match was played, in which the duke was, of course, completely victorious.

A HISTORY OF GOLF
The Royal and Ancient Game

CHAPTER ONE
(1502–1688)

Why Golf is Royal and Ancient

THE Royal and Ancient Game of Golf has ample justification for its historic title. During nearly two hundred years, from the Peace of Glasgow in 1502 to the Revolution of 1688, every reigning monarch of the Stuart line—two kings and one queen of Scotland, four kings of the United Kingdom—was a golfer. Yet golf is something more than the favourite pastime of the Scottish royal house; it is the outward and visible symbol of the union of England and Scotland. As long as the two countries continued to engage in internecine war with one another, the Scottish game had to be banned in its native land in the interests of military training. The peace treaty of 1502 set the Scots free to indulge in their national diversion. A hundred years later a Scottish king brought the game with him to London, and started a movement which has put a girdle round the globe.

The first golfer of whom any record has come down to us, is King James IV of Scotland, called 'James of the Iron Belt,' the king who died fighting on foot with his spearmen round him on the stricken field of Flodden. The accounts of the Lord High Treasurer for the year 1502 contain an entry:

> Item: The xxi day of September, to the bowar (bowmaker) of Sanct Johnestown (i.e. Perth) for clubbs.   xiiijs.

and more than a year later appear a couple of items:

> The third day of Februar, to the King to play at the Golf with the Erle of Bothuile, iij Franch crowns.   sumena, xlijs.
> For Golf Clubbis and Ballis to the King that he playit with.   lxs.

These, however, are not the first references to the game in the Scottish records. Half a century earlier the Fourteenth Parliament

1

of King James II—the Scottish James II that is, 'James of the Fiery Face,' who was killed by the bursting of one of his own primitive cannon at the siege of Roxburgh Castle—had in March 1457 issued its oft-quoted decree that 'the futeball and golfe be utterly cryed downe and not to be used.' A similar enactment was passed early in the following reign, and in 1491 the Third Parliament of James IV renewed the ban imposed by his father and grandfather: 'It is statute and ordained that in na place of the Realme there be used Fute-ball, Golfe, or uther sik unproffitable sportis,' which were contrary to 'the commoun good of the Realme and defense thereof.'

All these enactments make it clear that the ban on golf was imposed purely in the interests of military training, for the discomfiture of Scotland's 'auld enimies of England.' Accordingly modern essayists, skimming the surface of history, have been content to follow Robert Clark in his unconsidered comment that when the king went out to golf with the Earl of Bothwell, he was 'breaking his own behest.' It does not seem to have occurred to any of them to inquire whether any change of circumstances had taken place in 1502 to account for the new attitude to sport. And of course any historian would realize that there had been a very big change indeed. On 22nd February 1502, on the altar of Glasgow Cathedral, James had ratified a treaty of perpetual peace with England and of his marriage with Princess Margaret, daughter of the English king, Henry VII, who had himself signed the treaty at Richmond on 24th January. The marriage took place with resplendent ceremony at Holyrood on 9th August 1503. *That* was the change that made it possible for the king and anybody else to go to golf with a clear conscience.

There is even some indication that this royal marriage, and the peace which it was intended to guarantee, brought the Scottish king's favourite sport into temporary fashion in England. A letter written by Catherine of Aragon, the first wife of Henry VIII, to Cardinal Wolsey, contains the following passage: 'And all his [i.e. the king's] subjects be very glad, Master Almoner, I thank God, to be busy with the golf, for they take it for pastime.' It is always dangerous to assume that any mention of golf in early documents refers to the Scottish game and is not merely a slipshod translation of the name of one of the continental sports, but I imagine that Queen Catherine would know what she was talking about. We have evidence that Henry VII and Henry VIII were both fond of tennis. The preference of their Scottish relation by marriage for an entirely different type of ball game was not likely to escape remark in the family circle. Moreover, the phrase 'they take it for pastime' certainly suggests that the vogue of the game was new. The letter is dated 13th August 1513; Flodden was still undreamt of; and it is quite conceivable that the Scottish game had achieved a brief popularity on the other side of the border.

It is true that the roseate visions of perpetual peace between the two countries proved to be ahead of their time. The English overtures, which had been perfectly genuine on the part of Henry VII, developed under Henry VIII into a policy of keeping Scotland neutral while England joined Spain in the Holy League's plan for the encirclement of France, and James went to war against his English brother-in-law in an effort to create a demonstration on the other side. Flodden was Scotland's last fling on behalf of 'the auld alliance,' and in the years that followed golf became firmly established along with football as the Scottish national sport. James V, 'the guid-man of Ballengeich,' is said to have played golf frequently at Godford, and every youthful student of history knows that one of the charges brought against his daughter, the beautiful and ill-fated Mary Queen of Scots, was that within a few days of the murder of her husband, Darnley, she had been seen 'playing golf and pall-mall in the fields beside Seton.' The monarch whose example did most for golf, however, was James IV's great-grandson, James VI. When he succeeded to the English throne as James I he took his clubs with him, and thus the marriage of James IV and Margaret Tudor brought peace and golf to both countries after all.

In Scotland James VI and I had learned the game on the historic North Inch (anglice 'island') of Perth, and later had appointed William Mayne, 'bower burges of Edinburgh,' to be the royal clubmaker 'during all the dayes of his lyif-tyme.' He had brought up both his young sons to play golf, and that the game was played by the princes in London we know from an anecdote of his elder son, Henry, Prince of Wales, recorded by the anonymous author of a manuscript in the Harleian Library at Oxford: 'At another time,

playing at Goff, a play not unlike to Palemaille, whilst his school-
master stood talking with another, and marked not His Highness
warning him to stand further off, the Prince, thinking he had gone
aside, lifted up his Goff-club to strike the ball; meantyme one
standing by said to him, "Beware that you hit not Master Newton,"
whereupon the Prince, drawing back his hand, said, "Had I done so,
I had but paid my debts."' This is the anecdote which the barrow-
boys of Fleet Street have made the basis of a 'tradition' that James VI
and I introduced the game at Blackheath in 1608, the argument
apparently being that as Blackheath, even in the middle of the nineteenth century, was still the only course in London it must have been
on Blackheath that Prince Henry played. Such reasoning, of
course, is entirely fallacious. Golf in the sixteenth century did not
involve any permanently established course, and I have no doubt
that Prince Henry's games were played in the park of the royal
manor at Greenwich.

This young man, one of the most promising princes of the
unpredictable House of Stuart, was carried off by typhoid at the
age of eighteen, and his place was taken by his brother Charles, who
came to the throne as Charles I. Charles, who had apparently first
tried his hand at the game as a boy in his native Dunfermline, appears
as a golfer on two occasions. He was playing a round on the links
of Leith when a dispatch was brought to him reporting the breaking
out of the rebellion of the Irish Catholics under Sir Phelim O'Neale,
which was the beginning of all his troubles. According to one
account the king immediately called for his coach and drove off in
great agitation to Holyrood, but Woodrow prefers another version
which states that Charles insisted on playing out the match, in the
very manner of Drake finishing off his game of bowls with the
Spanish Armada signalled. It is a trifle hard on Charles that in this
matter he has received no sort of fair play from the historians, being
accused of cowardice by those who prefer the one version and
rebuked for levity by those who adopt the other. Even Sir W. G.
Simpson, who accepts the story of his abandoning the game, can only
suggest that the king 'acted on this occasion with his usual cunning
—that at the time the news arrived he was being beaten, and that he
hurried away to save his half-crown rather than his crown.' Poor
Charles! The next time we hear of him playing golf, it is as a

prisoner in the hands of the Scots, amusing himself with a round on the Shield Field, outside the walls of Newcastle-upon-Tyne.

Charles II's experience of golf was of a nature to give him what the Scots call a 'scunner' against the game for the rest of his life. When the Scots in defiance of Cromwell crowned him as king after the death of his father, the self-righteous Scottish ministers treated their king very much as if he had been committed for a term to an approved school. 'The Don Juan of Jersey,' declares Trevelyan in *England Under the Stuarts*, 'was not permitted in his northern kingdom to "walk in the fields" on the Sabbath, or to indulge in "promiscuous dancing." He partook of the sober vanity of golf in the company of staid persons.' What golfer ever learned to enjoy the game who had to take to it merely for the sake of exercise—especially in the company of staid persons, whose presence would make it impossible to indulge in adequate verbal relief when a long drive found a cuppy lie?

By far the happiest of the Stuarts in his golfing associations was James II, who as Duke of York played frequently at Leith while resident in Edinburgh during the years 1681 and 1682 as commissioner from the king his brother to the Scottish Parliament. As a result of a dispute between the duke and two English noblemen at the Scottish court concerning the origin of the game, it was proposed to decide the matter by a match over Leith links in which the Englishmen would play against the duke and any Scottish partner he liked to produce. The partner recommended to the duke by the Leith worthies was a poor shoemaker named John Patersone, and it is not difficult to guess that the presence of this local artisan champion was the factor that decided this first international match. The duke and his partner were victorious and the shoemaker was dismissed with an equal share of the very considerable stake wagered on the result. With this money he built himself a house in the Canongate of Edinburgh, upon the wall of which the duke caused an escutcheon to be fixed, bearing the arms of the Patersone family surmounted by a crest in the form of a dexter hand grasping a golf club, with the motto, 'Far and Sure.' The house, long known locally as 'The Golfer's Land,' is still standing. The Latin inscription, as I have seen for myself, bears out the above account as far as a Latin inscription can be expected to bear out anything, and the

additional motto which the inscription bears, 'I hate no person'—
an anagram on the name 'John Patersone'—also serves to confirm
the traditional story.

One of the saddest results of the Revolution of 1688 was that
neither Dutch William nor any of the 'wee, wee German lairdies'
who came after him had any interest in the game, and the golf boom
in England was set back for another couple of hundred years. The
golfing story of the Scottish royal line fades out with the picture
of Bonnie Prince Charlie relieving the boredom of exile in Italy
by knocking a ball about in the Borghese gardens.

CHAPTER TWO
(1421–1624)

Golf as a Cross-country Game

O F the history of golf prior to the famous Act of Parliament of 1457 in which we find it coupled with football as one of the two great national sports of Scotland, nothing certain is known. As a similar Act of the previous reign, passed in 1424, refers to football but not to golf, it has been conjectured that the rise of golf to popular favour must have taken place during the intervening quarter of a century, but its origin is lost in the mists of antiquity.

Sir Walter Simpson in his *Art of Golf* draws a fanciful picture of a shepherd idly striking a round pebble with his crook and accidentally knocking it into a rabbit scrape, essaying to repeat the stroke, and calling a companion to join in the new game. But this guess at the origin of golf has nothing to support it beyond a pleasing plausibility —hardly even that, for I cannot imagine that the game began from the wrong end, with the holing out. That, I fancy, would be devised as an extra touch, when two players in a cross-country game had reached their goal in an equal number of strokes and were looking for some amusing method of deciding the tie.

On the other hand there actually is some vague evidence in favour of the idea that golf may have been an offshoot of the older game of hurley or shinty, the equivalent of the English hockey, and may have originated in a form of 'practice' indulged in by hurley players journeying across country. When the Aonach Tailteann, the Irish Olympic Games, were revived some years ago, golf was included on the score of this supposed Celtic origin. An epic account of Cuchullain, one of the heroes of Ulster legend, is quoted to show him amusing himself with golf on his journey. 'The boy set out then, and he took his instruments of pleasure with him; he took his hurly of creduma and his silver ball, and he took his massive Clettini ... and he began to shorten his way with them. He would give

7

the ball a stroke of his hurly and drive it a great distance before him; and would cast [? swing] his hurly at it, and would give it a second stroke that would drive it not a shorter distance than the first blow'; —using the same club or hockey-stick as both driver and brassie, so to speak.

The Hon. Ruaraidh Erskine of Marr, in an article in *Golfing*, drew attention to a passage to somewhat similar effect in the Gaelic tale of Gaisgeach na Sgeithe Deirge, in which the 'Hero of the Red Shield' meets three of his foster-brothers, and they 'go out in the morning to drive the ball.' The hero pitted himself against the three, and 'he would put a half-shot down and a half-shot in on them.' Apparently what is meant is that without putting out his whole strength he could defeat the three, but precisely how is not quite so clear. It is possible that the reference is only to some sort of scrambling game of shinty with one player against three. But it is at least equally possible that what is meant is that he played the best ball of the three at some primitive form of golf, and giving them half a stroke could still beat them—probably only in point of distance covered, for we have no reason to suppose that at this stage there was any 'holing out.'

A half-way stage between hockey and golf is represented by the game of *chole,* which still survives in Belgium and, under the name of *soule,* in various departments of Northern France. The game, however, is very old. The earliest references to golf and to the Dutch *kolven* both date back to the middle of the fifteenth century, but Mr Andrew Lang, in the first chapter of the Badminton *Golf,* mentions that Ducange, in his *Lexicon of Low Latin,* quotes various references to *chole* from legal documents of 1353, 1357, etc.—dates earlier by a century than any of the references to the other two games. A missal of 1504, also referred to in the Badminton *Golf,* shows peasants engaged in playing *chole* with clubs with heads of a steely blue that would seem to indicate that they were of iron. This is consistent with the modern practice, for in the game as now played in Belgium the ball is of beechwood and the club a quaintly shaped lofting iron.

Zola, in *Germinal,* has a somewhat flamboyant description of the game as played by the French miners, but a better idea of it can be gleaned from M. Charles Deulin's tale of 'Le Grand Choleur,' in his

Contes du Roi Gambrinus, a translation of which, by Mrs Anstruther Thomson, was published in *Longmans' Magazine* (June 1889) under the title of 'The Devil's Round.' The tale, which describes how St Peter and St Anthony came to the wheelwright of the hamlet of Coq, near Condé-sur-l'Escaut, to have a club reshafted for a match they were to play on Shrove Tuesday, and rewarded his good nature and skill in repairing it by granting his wish to become the greatest golfer (*choleur*) in the world, is quite fantastic, but there is no reason to question the references to the technique of the play.

The general idea of the game is not in doubt. The two opponents (or the two opposing sides into which the players have divided themselves, if there are more than two players) begin by agreeing upon a goal to which they are to play, a cemetery gate, a church door, or the like. This mark may be as much as two, three, or even four leagues distant from the starting point. Then the opponents 'bid' the number of 'turns' (of three strokes each) in which they will undertake to reach the goal, always remembering that after each 'turn' of three strokes the other side is entitled to a stroke in which to *dechole*, i.e., to strike the ball backward away from the goal, or into a difficult place. The side which bids the smallest number of turns is 'in' and strikes off, and after each three strokes the 'out' side, the *decholeurs*, have their chance to hit the ball back or into any 'hazard' they can find. (It is difficult to avoid translating the technical terms into those of golf, but, of course, each game has its own glossary.) Inasmuch as we have here the idea of attack and defence, with both sides playing the same ball, *chole* retains some of the elements of hockey, but in its general conception it is a sort of cross-country golf.

A good idea of the game can be obtained from the picture by the Flemish artist Paul Bril, reproduced after page 32. This picture, painted in Rome in 1624, is the property of the Institute of Arts of Minneapolis, Minnesota, and the credit for recognizing its value as evidence of the similarity between *chole* and golf belongs to my friend Dean O. M. Leland, of the University of Minnesota. Dean Leland, who has a large golf library and museum, has made an intensive study of the game, and it is to him that I am indebted for this photograph of the painting and also for the other three photographs following immediately after it, which are reproductions on a larger scale of details from the same picture, designed to emphasize particular points common to the two games.

The first thing that surprises me in the painting is the number of players. No fewer than five different couples seem to be playing, or about to play, at one time, and the landscape is nearly as congested as the Braid Hills on a Saturday afternoon! In part, doubtless, this is due to the anxiety of the artist to get as much as possible into his canvas, but it is consistent with the description of the game in 'Le Grand Choleur': 'For my part, I do not know a more amusing game; and when the country is almost cleared of the harvest, men, women, children, everybody drives his ball as he pleases, and there is nothing cheerier than to see them filing on a Sunday like a flight of starlings across potato-fields and ploughed lands.'

It must not be supposed, however, that the five couples depicted in the painting are following the same course. The player teeing up in the left of the picture, for instance, cannot be intending to play towards the doorway in the left centre which appears to be the goal of three of the other couples. None of the references to *chole* fit in with the idea of 'holes' as short as this would imply. Presumably the players on the left are merely setting out on their travels to some mark in the far distance while the others are playing out a 'hole' in the reverse direction on their return journey.

Closer examination of the picture brings out striking resemblances between seventeenth-century *chole* and modern golf. That the player in the left-hand bottom corner of the picture is seen teeing up his ball for the start of the game is in accordance with expectation, for in his great match against the wheelwright of Coq, Beelzebub started by teeing the ball on a heap of frozen snow. More surprising is the presence of two entirely different kinds of clubs, a mallet-headed type as used in the kindred game of pall-mall and a second type with a long slender shaft and a small round head. None of the references to the game contain any suggestion that the *chole* player used more than one club. The miraculous club which 'Le Grand Choleur' obtained from St Peter was 'only a bad little iron head attached to a wretched worn-out shaft,' and there is no hint that he needed more clubs than one. At the extreme right of the painting, in the door of the clubmaker's shop, stands a man with a club which shows an unmistakable cavity in its head apparently designed to facilitate a lofting stroke. This, rather than the mallet type, is the traditional weapon of *chole*. However, none of the players in the picture appears to possess more than one club, and it is possible that the different types were designed to suit different players rather than different shots. It is true that the 'caddie' who accompanies the couple in the left-hand corner of the picture is shown carrying a spare mallet, one of the long-shafted spoons, and a bag of spare balls. I think it probable that the supposed 'caddie' is not in attendance on this particular match (for none of the other couples appear to have a caddie), but is an employee of the club-maker's shop shown in the right bottom corner of the picture, and has come to offer some of his wares to the couple just starting out. In that case the spare balls and the mallet would be for sale as replacements, and the 'long spoon,' if I may so describe it, may not be a club at all, but merely an instrument for retrieving balls from inaccessible places, like the 'landing nets' which golf clubs still provide for retrieving our golf balls from burns and ditches. (We know that 'unplayable lies' were recognized in *chole*.)

Dean Leland points out that each of the two players in this particular group has his own ball, as in golf, and suggests that this represents a variation from the traditional form of the game, but I am inclined to assume that the player shown teeing up is the player who has won the auction and that the other, though he has a ball in his hand ready to tee up if he had been 'in,' is in fact the *decholeur*.

A matter for surprise is the pit in the centre of the foreground, in which one of the players appears to be trapped. As the door in the background is presumably the goal at which the players are to 'hole out,' we have here a suggestion of a cross hazard guarding the hole! It is tempting to suppose that it may at one period have become a recognized refinement of the game to select a final mark covered by just such a hazard or hazards, which would lend excitement to the finish, since if the *decholeurs* could put the ball into a hazard so bad that the 'in' side would use up their 'turn' of three strokes in getting clear, the *decholeurs* might then pop them back into it when it became their turn to *dechole*, and so waste one or more turns for the attackers.

I have always understood that in the modern game of *chole* the main idea was of hitting out for distance, and that it was not necessary with the final shot actually to strike the chosen mark, but only to get beyond it. This, however, is not borne out by the attitude of the players in the picture, who are clearly concerned with the actual striking of the door, nor is it consistent with the story of 'Le Grand Choleur's' match against the devil, which he won by striking the door of the cemetery of Condé with his fifth stroke.

It would be pleasing to imagine that golf may have been an offshoot of *chole,* and I have discovered some faint support for the idea in a most unlikely place—a Scottish account of the Battle of Baugé. This is from the *Liber Pluscardensis,* a history of Scotland written during the reign of James II and quoted in Dr Agnes Mure Mackenzie's *Scottish Pageant.*

Henry V's invasion of France, which began so auspiciously for England with the victory of Agincourt, had by 1420 made him master of the whole of Normandy, and in that year the French king, Charles VI, sent an embassy to ask for help from the Scots. A contingent of 7,000 men was promptly sent, but arrived too late to prevent the Peace of Troyes and the marriage of Catherine of France to the English king. The war seemed to be petering out, with the Dauphin putting up a half-hearted resistance to the English mopping-up operations.

By Easter, 1421, the English king's brother, Thomas, Duke of Clarence, was laying siege to the fortified town of Baugé, which still held out for the Dauphin, when he found himself threatened by the arrival of a relieving force of the Scots under the Earl of Buchan, who took up his quarters in the neighbouring town of Le Lude, eight miles away. A truce until after Easter week was broken by the English commander attempting a surprise attack late on the afternoon of Easter Saturday, when the Scots were taking advantage of the truce by 'playing ball and amusing themselves with other pleasant or devout occupations.'

'But by God's mercy,' continues the chronicler, 'some men of note were playing close to the crossing of a certain river' and caught sight of the English standards advancing under cover of the woods. They sent one of their number haring back to warn Buchan; and the handful of Scots who had turned out to watch the play prepared to dispute the crossing of the river. In his eagerness to snatch the advantage of surprise Clarence had outmarched his archers, who

The First International Foursome, by Allan Stewart. *(By permission of the British Art Co., Ltd.)*

could have covered the crossing, and when the Scottish cross-bowmen opened a desultory fire on his horses, the English knights had to dismount and fight their way across. The resultant delay gave the rest of the Scots time to draw together. Clarence himself was killed at the first onset; with him fell the Earls of Kent and of Ross and Lord Grey, while the Earls of Somerset and of Huntingdon were among the long list of prisoners captured in the first serious defeat inflicted on the English arms since Agincourt.

The point of interest to the golf historian, however, is the question what game it was that took these Scots so far from their camp at Le Lude down towards the river crossing. When the chronicler speaks of the Scots taking advantage of the truce to play ball, it may be assumed that several different ball games are intended, but one does not go away out into the fields to play tennis, and pitches for football or shinty could no doubt be found close to the Scottish lines. It is, I think, a fair assumption that it was some form of cross-country game that took this particular group so far from the camp. More-over, 'men of note' would not be so likely to be found joining in the *mêlée* of football or shinty; and in any case the form of the wording suggests few players rather than many. Few indeed they were, for the description of the beginning of the battle gives us their names: Hugh Kennedy, who later became the leader of the Garde Écossaise fighting under the victorious banner of Joan of Arc, Robert Stewart, of Ralston, and John Smale, from Aberdeen. I would like to think that there was a fourth member of the foursome, who was given the less heroic task of dashing away to get the rest of the army together while the three already mentioned, 'with their men'—i.e. the handful of spearmen and cross-bowmen who had come out to watch their leaders' play—took up the defence of the bridge.

It is conceivable that the little party which wandered out towards Baugé were playing golf, but there is no proof of that. Some form of cross-country ball game, however, it must have been, and I think the best guess is that the Scots had taken up the game of *chole*. If they learned it in this campaign, brought it back to Scotland, and transformed it into golf, the dates would fit. The *chole* of 1421 might easily have developed into golf in time to become widely popular by 1457.

CHAPTER THREE
(1530–1668)

The Argument of the Pictures

O F all the theories of the origin of golf, there is none which appeals so strongly to the popular imagination as that which derives it from the Dutch game of *het kolven*.   The resemblance between the words golf and *kolf* (though *kolf* is the name of the club and not of the game) is such as to catch the attention even of the dullest.   The seventeenth-century Dutch pictures of *kolven* on the ice are in themselves so attractive, the superficial resemblance between this game and golf is so striking, that every editor of golf history is tempted to toy with the theory, if only to provide himself with an excuse for reproducing some of the Dutch pictures!

The fact that the Flemish picture of *chole* and the Dutch pictures of *kolven* on the ice have no parallel of similarly early date in English or Scottish pictures of golf, is evidence of nothing except the superior artistic sense of the Continent, for it is a remarkable fact that up to the middle of the seventeenth century the art of painting made no appeal to English taste.   The point is emphasized by G. M. Trevelyan in his *England Under the Stuarts*: 'The only pictures in these English homes were the portraits.   In the early days of Dutch art our writers found fault with Holland, because there "every man's house is full of pictures, a vanity that draweth on a charge."   Diaries and guide-books of travel in Italy, written by scholars and men of cultivation, describe the treasures of palaces and churches, and above all the monuments of antiquity; but scarcely a word is wasted on the pictures, even in detailed accounts of Florence or the Campo Santo of Pisa.'

The myth of the Dutch origin of golf originated at the beginning of the golf boom in England.   Too many travellers from this country, themselves but recently acquainted with golf, imagined themselves the 'discoverers' of these paintings in the Dutch museums, and assumed without investigation that the Dutch pictures were older than the Scottish game. In fact the earliest of these paintings, a water-colour by Hendrick Avercamp, was painted about 1625, and could scarcely be evidence of Dutch origin for a game that had been played in Scotland nearly two hundred years before that.

The idea of such a link between *kolven* and golf does not stand up to closer examination, for *kolven* is still played in some parts of Holland, and it has little resemblance to golf. It is not a field game at all, but is played in a walled space or covered court. In the provinces of Friesland and North Holland where the game is still in favour, the *kolf-bann* or court is commonly attached to some inn, as bowling-greens are at the present day in the north of England. The club used has a straight brass face and is larger and more crudely made than any modern golf club, but the biggest difference is in the ball, which is about the size of a cricket ball and weighs nearly a couple of pounds. Two posts are set up at opposite ends of the court at anything from 40 to 130 feet apart, and the object of the game is to play the ball from one end of the court so as to strike the post at the far end and if possible to rebound so as to leave an easy shot at the nearer post with the next stroke. The side which succeeds in striking the two posts in the fewest strokes is the winner.

Clearly there is little in common between the Scottish golf and this game of shoving heavy balls about a wooden floor or a paved courtyard, and supporters of the theory of the Dutch origin of the former game are forced to fall back on the contention that the *kolven* on the ice, which forms the subject of the seventeenth-century Dutch pictures, was a game of an entirely different character. Detailed examination of these same pictures, however, fails to bear this out. In some of them, notably the print by Romayn de Hooge reproduced on another page, the characteristic 'post' is prominently visible, and the huge size of the balls suggests that the game was precisely the same as at the present day. The crowded state of the ice in most of the Dutch pictures does not seem consistent with any idea of striking out for distance; the players never seem to have room to try anything like a full shot without the risk of murdering somebody. Moreover, the grip of the club with the hands well apart, which is adopted by many of the players, is more consistent with the *shoving* stroke of the modern *kolven* than with anything resembling a golf swing.

Earlier references to *kolven* seem to me only to confirm the established character of the game. For instance, an edict issued by the town of Naarden about the year 1456 forbids the playing of it (*doen mit kolven*) in the churches and in the churchyards. In the Middle Ages, of course, the body of a church was clear of seats; the main part of the congregation had to stand; and the available space would be quite suitable for *kolven* if it were substantially the same game as it is to-day. In the same way *kolven* could be played in the old churchyards, where the tombstones were laid flat. But it is difficult to visualize any game resembling golf being played either in a churchyard or inside a church.

The Dutch writer J. A. Brongers, who has been indefatigable in collecting evidence to support the theory of a link between the two games, has drawn my attention to an edict of 1398 by Albert, Duke of Bavaria, conferring on the citizens of Brielle the right of playing *kolven* outside the ramparts of the town, and would like to argue from this that *kolven* in the fourteenth century must have been a cross-country game. Taken in conjunction with some of the later references to the game, however, I am inclined to imagine that the permission to play *kolven* outside the ramparts was given merely in order to stop the *kolven* players from making a nuisance of themselves in the town. One of the early references to *kolven* in the Dutch American colonies is a record of *kolven* players being fined for playing the game in the streets.

To my mind the mere fact that *kolven* could be played on the ice is one of the reasons for believing that it was never in the least like golf. Just consider for a moment what golf would be like if we were to try to play it on the ice as shown in the Dutch pictures. On one occasion at Wimbledon Park when the lake adjoining the eighteenth hole was frozen over, a golfer hooked his drive on to the frozen surface. The ball ran the whole length of the lake, 600 yards, and only came to a stop because it reached the limits of the ice. Golf on the ice would be an impossibility, because the distances the ball could travel would be fantastic.

A more difficult problem is presented by other Dutch pictures of the same period showing children holding clubs that are obviously

HENRY FREDERICK, ELDEST SON OF JAMES VI AND I, AT THE AGE OF TWO

From a painting in Holdenby House, 'traditionally believed to be a portrait of one of the Royal Family of Scotland' (1595).

A YOUNG DUTCH (BOY) GOLFER OF THE SEVENTEENTH CENTURY

From the painting by Albert Cuyp (1650)

Reproduced by courtesy of Country Life Ltd from 'A Golfer's Gallery of Old Masters,' in which, however, both pictures are described as of little girls.

too slender in the shaft and too slim in the head for *kolven*, and balls that closely resemble the old featheries. But a picture by Pieter de Hooch, which shows two children on a typical *kolf* court, suggests that these clubs were used in a childish version of the game as played in summer.

The earliest of all these pictures of golfing children is the portrait of 'A Child with a Golf Club' which hangs in Holdenby House, and is traditionally asserted to be a portrait of one of the Royal Family of Scotland. The tradition is probably correct, for unless I am very much mistaken this is a portrait of Henry Frederick, the eldest son of James VI and I. The portrait bears the date 1595, and the legend 'Aetas 2.' Now Prince Henry was born on 19th February 1593 (old style, of course) and if the portrait were painted for his second birthday or thereabouts it would of course be dated 1595. The portrait is by an unknown artist, but if he were Dutch that would not in any way invalidate the tradition, for the infant prince was in a sense a protégé of the Dutch Protestant states, which were united to Scotland by the bond of a common religion at a time when England was wobbling from one religion to the other with each successive reign. At his christening, which took place in the Chapel Royal of Stirling Castle, on 30th August of the same year, and at which he was in usual form created Prince and Great Steward of Scotland, Duke of Rothesay, Earl of Carrick, Lord of the Isles, and Baron and Knight of Renfrew, the ambassadors of Holland and Zeeland presented him with 'two fair and large cups of gold' and a golden coffer in which was contained 'a letter of obligation' superscribed by the two ambassadors and 'divers other chief Governors, to pay the Prince yearly during his lifetime 5,000 guelderings,' esteemed equal to £500 sterling at that day and equivalent, according to Dr Agnes Mure Mackenzie, to £10,000 a year in modern money. So it was Holland and Zeeland that undertook to keep the prince in pocket-money; and the portrait may quite conceivably have been commissioned on their behalf.

Earlier by nearly a century than the Dutch paintings is an illustration in an exquisite little *Book of Hours*, believed to have been prepared at Bruges, in 1530, for the Emperor Charles V of Germany, whose device it bears on its cover. The book, which consists of 183 vellum leaves, well written in a bold Gothic hand, includes ten beautifully painted full-page miniatures of the Ghent-Bruges school, and forty-nine borders. Many of the illustrations are of biblical scenes: for instance, the principal figures on the left hand of the double page in our reproduction are easily identifiable as Ruth and Naomi. Many of the others introduce various games and rustic scenes, which fits in well enough with the story of the book's origin, for Charles V was a lover of every kind of sport. Various forms of ball games, play with tops and with hoops, figure in the borders. And the first impression of the border shown on the right-hand page of the illustration is that here, unmistakably, is golf. The kneeling child on the right of the foreground is obviously putting at a hole; the figure on the left might be attempting a run up; the player in the middle distance of the right-hand border appears to be taking a full swing for a long shot 'through the green.' If this is not golf, what is it?

The snag is that no other border in the *Book of Hours* is devoted to any single game. I had an opportunity of examining this *Book of Hours* when it came up for sale as part of the Chester-Beatty collection, before the Second World War. (In fact I had a commission to buy it for America, but was outbidden by a German collector.) One of the points that struck me was that each border appeared to depict three or more different forms of sport. Thus, on the left-hand page of the illustration you have an archer with a long-bow, another with a cross-bow, and a child playing at what looks like a primitive form of croquet. If the right-hand page represents *chole, kolven,* and some child's putting game we are back very much where we were before.

Special interest attaches to the two pictures of children putting, in the one case into a hoop, in the other into a shallow hole not much larger than the ball. In neither case is the player's attitude suggestive of golf, but the pictures make it clear that the idea of *holing out* had developed in more games than one.

By far the oldest pictorial representation of what might conceivably be golf is to be found neither in Holland nor in Flanders, but in England, in Gloucester Cathedral. In one of the medallions of the great stained glass east window built for Sir Thomas Brad-stone between the years 1340 and 1350, in memory of his comrades who fell in the battle of Crécy, is a figure swinging some sort of club in very convincing and workmanlike style. The window has suffered a little with the passage of the centuries; the upper part of the player's head and a space immediately above it are gone and have been replaced by a blank of clear glass, but the glass is otherwise intact and the swing can be examined in detail. It is true that the club bears a much closer resemblance to a modern hockey stick than to a golf club, but the player's attitude seems to me to be more consistent with a deliberate and controlled swing at a stationary ball than with a blow at a moving one.

However, all these attempts to trace out resemblances between other games and the Scottish golf are beside the mark. The idea of hitting a ball with a crooked stick—as, for instance, in the simplest form of pall-mall, where the rivalry consists merely in seeing which player can send the ball furthest—is so primitive as to be common to all countries. Yet the simple fact remains that it was the Scots who devised the essential features of golf, the *combination* of hitting for distance with the final nicety of approach to an exiguous mark, and the independent progress of each player with his own ball, free from interference by his adversary. In the translation by Layamon (1155–1200) of Wace's *Roman de Brut*, composed about the time when Saxons and Normans began to adopt a common language, the account of the sports at King Alfred's coronation in 872 refers to players 'driving balls wide over the fields.' But to label these players as golfers or to translate the name of some foreign game as 'golf' is to beg the whole question. How far people are prepared to go with this sort of conjecture is illustrated by another stained-glass window—a much more modern one—in St Cuthbert's Church, Philbeach Gardens, Kensington, in which the saint is represented in the act of striking a ball with what might quite well be an ancient golf club. This does not mean, however, that there is any ground for believing the saint to have been a golfer. The only justification for the picture is a tradition that the saint as a child 'playde atte ball with the children that his felloes were'—and it is hardly likely that the children's game of ball was golf!

CHAPTER FOUR

The Argument of Language

ALTHOUGH the editors of the *Oxford Dictionary* decline to commit themselves on the subject, I see no reason to doubt the derivation of *golf* from the German *kolbe*, which also means 'club.' The *Etymologisches Wörterbuch der deutschen Sprache*, quoted in the Badminton *Golf*, attributes *Kolben*, Old High German *Cholbo*, Icelandic *Kolfr*, to a hypothetic Gothic word *Kulban* meaning a knobbed stick. If this line of argument is correct, *golf*, *chole*, and *kolf* all mean 'club,' and each of them is in its own fashion the game of the club. The relationship between the words is in accordance with Grimm's Law; but the operation of this law does not carry with it any implication that the words are derived from one another. To short-circuit the argument into a contention that *golf* is derived from the Dutch *kolf* comes into the category not of Grimm's law, but of Grimms' Fairy Tales!

The law which takes its name from Jacob Grimm, though it was originally discovered by Rasmus Rask, the Danish philologist, provides a key to the relationship existing between the Indo-European, Low German, and High German groups of languages. The Greek *DH* or *TH* as in *Thugater*, shifts in English (Low German) to *D* as in *Daughter*, and in German (High German) to *T* as in *Töchter*, the three words having the same meaning. In the same way the Greek or Latin *GH* or *CH* is modified in Low German to *G* and in High German to *K*, so that you have French *Chole*, English *Golf*, and Dutch *Kolf* corresponding to one another in the expected form. I must emphasize, however—for it is a point which the philologists have failed to make sufficiently clear to the casual reader—that the relationship thus indicated is only an illustration of the process by which the European languages were developed through the ages from a common root. 'It is wrong,' Goldberg points out (*The Wonder of Words*, by Isaac Goldberg, New York,

1939), 'to regard the Teutonic languages as being derived from one another. They are sister-tongues, all stemming from primitive Germanic.' So when you find words like *golf*, *chole*, and *kolf* conforming to Grimm's Law, the fact is *prima facie* evidence that the words are *not* derived from one another, but only from a common ancestor. Still less, of course, does the similarity of the words indicate any relationship between the games themselves. On the contrary, the difference in the words is precisely what Grimm's Law would lead us to expect if the games were entirely independent. If golf, for instance, had been developed from the Dutch game of *kolven*, one would have expected the Dutch consonants to have been retained unaltered.

Attempts to establish a Dutch derivation for some of the technical terms of the game are for the most part forced and unconvincing, and in one or two notable cases appear to be based on a misconception of the original significance of the golfing terms. We have seen that in the game of *chole* the player placed his ball on a small heap of earth or of frozen snow for his initial stroke, and a well-known engraving in a book by Jan Luyken, *Des Menschen Begin, Midden en Einde* (The Beginning, Middle, and End of Human Life), shows a player striking off with his ball poised on just such a heap, which was called a '*tuitje*. The suggestion, of course, is that this gave us our word 'tee.'

In golf, however, the word tee does not seem originally to have any reference to the pinch of sand or the peg on which the modern golfer poises his ball, but only to the *place* from which the player was entitled to strike off. In one of the earliest codes of rules known to us, framed for the Honourable Company of Edinburgh Golfers in 1775, Rule 2 lays down that 'Your Tee must be upon the ground.'[1] Rule 1 of the same code enacts that 'You must tee your Ball not nearer the Hole than two Club lengths, nor further distant from it than four.' The putting green, that is to say, was also the teeing ground, and the player had to tee in the space between two imaginary circles drawn round the hole. This presents an obvious similarity

---

[1] Mr H. S. C. Everard, the historian of the Royal and Ancient Club, seems to have been astonished to be assured by a veteran of an elder day that this rule simply meant what it said and was a prohibition of the use of artificial aids to raise the ball from the ground.

to the *tee* in curling, though there the tee is the centre of the con-
centric circles which curlers call 'the house,' and which is the target
in which they try to bring their stones to rest.   The curling *tee* is
almost certainly from the Gaelic *tigh*, meaning a house, and I
imagine that the golf tee is the same.

A similar sort of difficulty arises with the attempts to connect our
putt with the Dutch verb *putten*.   It is wasted ingenuity, for in golf
the word 'putt' had originally no connection with the idea of holing
out.   Oh yes, I grant you that in the modern parlance of the game
the terms 'putt,' 'putter,' and 'putting green' all have reference to
the rolling shots near the hole, but this restricted application of these
terms is entirely modern.   Even the term 'putting green' was not
known in old golf.   The word 'green' meant the whole course,
and still survives in this sense in the phrases 'Green Committee,'
'greenkeeper,' and 'through the green.'   Even yet the English Golf
Union uses the word in its old sense in official announcements that
'next year's Championship will be played on the *green* of such and
such a Club.'   A minute of the Royal and Ancient Club in 1789,
dealing with the even then vexed question of the stymie, refers to
the prepared area round the tin as 'the hole green.'   In the days of
the feathery ball the golfer had two putters, a driving putter for
playing low shots along the fairway, especially into the wind, and
a green-putter for use nearer the hole.   The former is alluded to
in *Golfiana* (1823):

> There, to the left, I see Mount-Melville stand
> Erect, his *driving putter* in his hand;
> It is a club he cannot leave behind,
> So well it works the ball against the wind.[1]

And nearly half a century later, James Ballantine could wind up
one of his golfing songs with the exhortation

> Then don your brilliant scarlet coats
>   With your bright blue velvet caps, boys,
> And some will play the *rocket shots*
> And some the *putting paps*, boys,

[1] It is recorded that when Mr O'Brian Peter, of Kirkland, won the Gold Medal
of the Royal and Ancient Club in 1851, with a score of 105, playing in a gale, he
used his driving putter throughout the round.

which I take to be a reference to the choice between a pitch shot and a 'pitch and run' in approach play.

In my opinion the words 'putt' and 'putting' were originally used in golf in precisely the same sense as in the sport of 'putting the weight.' Any shot that aimed at keeping the ball low was a putt. The golfer of the feathery days holed out with his putter because its straight face made it the ideal club for the low shot by which the ball was tossed towards the hole. The modern idea of the putt as a shot in which the ball is *rolled* into the tin was not entirely applicable, because greens in the early days were not specially tended and prepared, and a purely rolling shot could not always be trusted to roll straight.

An extreme instance of the lengths to which misplaced ingenuity can go in searching out the history of words is the suggested derivation of 'driver' from a Norse word of similar sound. We have already seen that the expression 'driving balls over the fields' is as old as Layamon. So the word is essentially English. But in any case the words 'drive' and 'driver' were not in use in early golf. Even when H. B. Farnie set himself to write the first book of golf instruction ever published, *The Golfer's Manual,* which appeared in 1857, the club with which the golfer struck off from the tee was the 'play-club'; and he did not drive towards a selected landmark, he 'played upon it.' It is recorded of Old Sutherland, one of the 'keen hands' of the middle of last century, that towards the close of a match at St Andrews with Captain Kinloch, the latter was about to drive off, when a boy appeared on the bridge over the Swilcan. Old Sutherland shouted out 'Stop! stop! don't play upon him' (nowadays we would say 'don't drive into him'), '*he is a fine young golfer.*' The warning shout was too late to stop the stroke, but it did not matter much, because Kinloch was so convulsed with laughter over the idea that only fine young golfers were to be spared that he nearly missed the ball altogether.

The word 'driver' is actually used in Farnie's *Manual,* but apparently only in a generic sense, to cover what we now call the distance clubs. The golfer of that day had two drivers in his set, the play club (driver) and the grassed driver (brassie).

'Spoon,' 'cleek,' and 'bunker' are taken from names familiar to Scottish domesticity, and 'mashie,' though comparatively modern, is the same. The mashie does not specially resemble the utensil employed to mash potatoes; it took the name from its effect upon the ball when entrusted to unskilful hands. But 'niblick' and 'stymie' present an insoluble problem. My own guess is that niblick is a corruption of 'neb laigh,' i.e. a broken nose, and refers to the short face of the club, originally designed for playing out of ruts.

'Stymie' possibly comes from the old word 'styme,' which appears as early as 1300, usually in the phrase 'not to see a styme,' i.e. not to be able to see at all. Burns has the lines

> I 've seen me daez't upon a time
> I scarce could wink or see a styme.

Apparently, therefore, the golf term refers to the 'blinding' of the one ball by the other as it lies between it and the hole; the further ball has to peer or 'styme' round the other. A trifle fanciful, perhaps, but at least more convincing than the suggested derivation from hypothetical phrases in Gaelic or in Dutch—the Gaelic *Stigh mi,* meaning 'inside me,' or the Dutch *Stuit mij*, 'it stops me.'

Even the golfer's warning shout of 'Fore' has been pressed into service by the believers in the Dutch origin of the game, who produce a Dutch 'voor' as an equivalent. But there is no evidence that 'voor' was a recognized warning cry in *kolven*, and lacking that the argument is meaningless, for you could produce a plausible Dutch equivalent for almost any word of Anglo-Saxon origin in our language. However, there is no need to hunt out any far-fetched etymologies in this particular case. Dr Neilson, a keen student of Scottish history and literature, discovered a passage in the works of John Knox which, shorn of the eccentricities of sixteenth-century spelling, reads as follows: 'One among many comes to the East Port [i.e. gate] of Leith, where lay two great pieces of ordnance, and where their enemies were known to be, and cried to his fellows that were at the gate making defence: "Ware before!" and so fires one great piece, and thereafter the other.' The cry of 'Beware before'—'Look out in front!'—was, of course, the signal for the defenders of the gate to drop to the ground in order that the guns might be fired over them. The situation is not dissimilar to that of the golfer intending to drive over the head of someone on the

THE FIRST GOLFER of whom any written record has come down to us: King James IV of Scotland, from a portrait by an unknown artist in the possession of the Scottish National Portrait Gallery.

The first lady golfer mentioned in history: Mary Queen of Scots, who is said to have played golf and pall-mall in the meadows of Seton House.

Charles I, while playing golf on Leith links, receiving news of the outbreak of the Irish Rebellion. (After the well-known picture by Sir John Gilbert.)

fairway in front, and the way in which the military signal 'Ware before!' might in the course of time be cut down to ''Fore!' needs no explaining. 'Look out in front!' It is the most democratic of shouts, which no one dares to let pass unheeded. During an Open Championship at Sandwich many summers ago, I saw a future King of England scurrying apologetically off the fairway in response to a distant bellow of 'Fore!' from one of our less distinguished professionals.

A term that has given rise to a certain amount of controversy even in its native land is the word 'links.' There is a modern tendency to restrict this term to the natural seaside golf country among the sand-dunes, and it is frequently suggested that the word has always been applied only to courses of this traditional type. But I can find no support for this contention. The noble expanse of turf on which the Royal Eastbourne course is laid out was known as 'The Links' long before anyone thought of playing golf over it, and it is high up on the downs. A similar stretch of down at Cambridge was long known as 'The Links' although nobody ever thought of playing golf there. Sir Walter Scott in *Redgauntlet* puts a definition into the mouth of the English Darsie Latimer:

'I turned my steps towards the sea, or rather the Solway Firth, which here separates the two sister kingdoms, and which lay at about a mile's distance, by a pleasant walk over sandy knolls, covered with short herbage, which you call *links*, and we English *downs*.'—LETTER III.

Another definition from the same source is:

'They sat cozily nitched into what you might call a *bunker*—a little sand-pit, dry and snug, and surrounded by its banks, and a screen of whins in full bloom.'—LETTER X.

In spite of a muddled passage in the preface to *The Surgeon's Daughter*, which may quite probably have been due to hasty proof-reading, there seems to be no doubt that Sir Walter was himself a golfer. The fact appears to be sufficiently established by his letter to John Cundell, the editor of 'Some Historical Notices Relative to the Progress of Golf in Scotland' which was included in the little volume of the *Rules of the Thistle Golf Club* published in Edinburgh in 1824, in which Scott declares himself to be 'still an admirer of that manly exercise, which in former days I occasionally practised.'

In that letter Scott expresses an opinion regarding the origin of the name of the game itself, which seems to me to go right to the heart of the matter. 'I should doubt much,' he says, 'the assertion that the word "Golf" is derived from the verb "to gowff," or strike hard. On the contrary, I conceive the verb itself is derived from the game, and that "to gowff" is to strike sharp and strong as in that amusement. If I were to hazard a conjecture, I should think the name Golf is derived from the same Teutonic expression from which the Germans have "colb," a club, and the Low-Dutch "kolff," which comes very near the sound of "golf."'

Apart from his own interest in the game, Scott could scarcely fail to have some acquaintance with a recreation which was especially favoured by the legal profession of Edinburgh from whom so many of his characters are drawn. Thus in *The Heart of Midlothian*, when the sitting magistrate of the day is about to begin the examination of Butler regarding the incidents of the Porteous riot, we are told that 'Mr Middleburgh had taken his seat, and was debating in an animated manner, with one of his colleagues, the doubtful chance of a game of golf which they had played the day before.'

Again in *Redgauntlet*, when the elder Fairford explains to his son that his first appearance in the Court of Session—in the famous case of *Peebles* v. *Plainstanes*—has been arranged, 'All that,' exclaims the old lawyer, 'is managed for ye like a tee'd ball.'

The same simile, curiously, is employed by Robert Louis Stevenson in another novel of that period, that is also not without a certain legal flavour. In *Catriona* he makes David Balfour say of the flattery and attention he received from the young lawyers who fluttered round Prestongrange: 'Seeing me so firm [i.e. so much in favour] with the Advocate, and persuaded that I was to fly high and far, they had taken a word from the golfing green and called me *the tee'd ball*.' Earlier in the same story, Charles Stewart, the Jacobite lawyer, exclaims on his hard fate in having to appear for all sorts of disaffected persons who claim his services in the name of the clan. 'For my private part I have no particular desire to harm King George; and as for King James, God bless him, he does very well for me across the water. I'm a lawyer, ye see; fond of my books and my bottle, a good plea, a well-drawn deed, a crack in the

Parliament House with other lawyer bodies, and perhaps a turn at the golf on a Saturday at e'en.'

I have already pointed out the trap for the unwary that lies in the gradual transmutation of some of the accepted golf terms. Almost up to the end of the nineteenth century, the 'green' meant the whole course. The word 'course' which has entirely replaced 'green' in this sense in the modern vocabulary of the game, originally had the same meaning as 'fairway,' and is defined in the Badminton *Golf* (1890) as 'that portion of the links on which the game ought to be played, generally bounded on either side by rough ground or other hazard.' Here again you have another golfing expression which has completely changed its meaning, for 'rough ground,' shortened into 'rough,' is now used especially of long grass and heather—neither of which is a hazard.

A further complication arises from the tendency for accepted terms to develop different meanings on opposite sides of the Atlantic. A 'foursome' originally meant a match between two sides of two players each, each side playing only one ball, the partners driving off at alternate tees and thereafter playing alternate shots on the way to the hole. And the word is still used in that sense both in the Rules of Golf and in the colloquial speech of British golfers. But in the United States and Canada this is commonly referred to as a 'Scotch foursome,' the word foursome being reserved for the commoner form of play in which each of the players on the opposing sides plays his own ball, but in each pair the better of the two scores for each hole counts as the score of the partnership for that hole. On the eastern side of the Atlantic, however, the latter form of the game is termed a four-ball match, usually shortened to 'a four-ball.'

More unfortunate is the divergence in the use of the term 'bogey.' In British golf the 'bogey' of a hole was the par figure, the score which a first-class golfer might be expected to take. But as standards improved 'bogey' figures were not tightened up sufficiently rapidly, and there was a tendency for the 'bogey' scores to be one stroke more than par at three or four holes out of the eighteen, on the majority of courses. Unluckily this seems to have given American golfers the idea that 'bogey' is one over par at every hole, with the result that on the western side of the Atlantic 'bogey' has become a term of contempt. In reports of big tournaments in the

States and Canada, a player who drops a stroke at any hole is said
to have 'bogeyed it.'   If he takes a 6 at a hole where he ought to
have got a 4, he is said to have 'double-bogeyed' it.   To the
English handicap golfer, accustomed to preen himself on the number
of 'bogeys' he achieves in the course of his round, the American
use of the word naturally appears the rankest blasphemy.

CHAPTER FIVE

(1502–1736)

'In Tyme of Sermonis'

BETWEEN 1502, when the Peace of Glasgow set the Scots free to play their national pastime, and 1744, when the Leith golfers held the first competition for the Silver Club, our knowledge of the progress of the game is derived in the main from incidental references in household accounts, kirk registers, and the like. But the registers of the kirk sessions from 1580 onwards bear testimony of the popularity of the game in all parts of Scotland. There are records of golfers being charged with playing on Sunday, 'tyme of fast and precheing' at St Andrews, at Perth, at Leith, at Stirling, at Cullen, and at Banff. But it cannot be sufficiently emphasized that these were cases of players going to golf *instead of going to church.* The charge against them was always of playing 'in tyme of sermonis' or 'in time of the preaching after noon on the Sabbath.' The offence consisted, not in playing golf, but in being absent from church, and walking about the streets in sermon time was as much a breach of the kirk law as playing golf.

Some years ago I received a letter from an American Golf Club asking me to decide a wager laid to back the assertion that in Scotland in the fifteenth and sixteenth centuries the golfer caught playing on Sunday was liable to be beheaded or hanged, and that this law had never been definitely repealed! I was happy to be able to assure my correspondents that neither 'heading nor hanging' had at any time been the penalty for playing golf even on the sabbath. But in Reformation times fines were frequently imposed for this sort of transgression. Forty shillings (Scots) would appear to have been the usual penalty imposed. In 1592 the town council of Edinburgh made a proclamation against playing 'at ony pastymes or gammis within or without the toun upoun the Sabboth day, sic as Gof.' Again, in 1593, the same council proclaims that 'dyvers inhabitants of this burgh repaires upoun the Sabboth day, to the toun of Leyth, and in tyme of sermonis are sene vagant athort the streets, drynking in tavernis, or otherwayes at Golf, aircherie, or other pastymes upoun the Links, thairby profaning the Sabboth day.' All such are warned to desist, 'under the payne of wairding thair persounis quhill thai pay ane unlaw of fourty shillings, and otherwayes be punist in thair persouns at the discreation of the Magestrates.'

It would appear, however, that by the end of the sixteenth century the rigid sabbatarianism of John Knox and his followers had begun to place further restrictions on Sunday amusements. In 1618 we find King James VI declaring that 'with our owne eares wee heard the generall complaint of our people, that they were barred from all lawfull recreation and exercise upon the Sundayes afternoone, after the ending of all Divine service, for when shal the common people have leave to exercise, if not upon the Sundayes and holydayes, seeing they must apply their labour, and winne their living in all working dayes?' He therefore rebuked the 'precise people' and declared his pleasure to be, 'that after the end of divine service, our good people be not disturbed, letted, or discouraged from any lawfull recreation—such as dauncing, either men or women, archerie for men, leaping, vaulting, or any other such harmless recreation,' but prohibiting 'the said recreations to any that are not present in the church at the service of God before their going to the said recreations.'

King Charles I in 1633, 'out of a like pious care for the service of God, and for suppressing of any humors that oppose trueth, and for the ease, comfort, and recreation of our well-deserving people,' ratifies and anew publishes 'this our blessed father's declaration,' and commands 'our justices of assize' 'to see that no man doe trouble or molest any of our loyall and duetiful people, in or for their lawfull recreations, having first done their duetie to God.'

Even from the earliest times golf was a game for all classes. That it was as popular with the nobility and gentry as with the tradesmen and apprentices who were summoned to answer before the kirk sessions for playing on Sunday, is proved by all sorts of odd references. Apart from King James IV and the Earl of Bothwell, the first golfer we hear of by name is Sir Robert Maule (1497–1560), who is described in the *Registrum de Panmure* as being 'ane man of comlie behaviour, of hie stature, sanguine in collure both of hyd and haire, colarique of nature and subject to suddane anger. . . . He had gryt delyght in haukine and hountine. . . . Lykewakes he exercisit the gowf, and ofttimes past to Barry Lynks, quhan the wadsie [wager] was for drink. . . . This was the yeer of God 1527, or there abouts.' Barry Links, where the Scots defeated the Danes in a great battle in 1010, is close to the modern Carnoustie.

Gavin Hamilton, who was Bishop of Galloway from 1610 to 1612, is mentioned as being at golf on the Links of Leith, 'for he lovid that all his life-tyme verie much,' when he was seized with the illness from which he died. We get a glimpse of Andrew Melvill as a golfer during his fourth year at St Andrews University in 1574; he records that his father allowed him bow and arrows, club (? only one) and balls, but no pocket-money for catchpall (? rackets) and tavern. The great Marquis of Montrose was a golfer, as his father the earl had been before him. We have notes of the former's expenses for golfing visits to St Andrews and Leith as well as for play on his 'home course' at Montrose. On 9th November 1629, the day before his marriage to 'sweet Mistress Magdalene Carnegie,' we find him buying golf balls in order to play against his brother-in-law, Sir John Colquhoun, the Laird of Luss, and nine days after the wedding the young bridegroom is sending a messenger to St Andrews for six new golf clubs, repairing some old ones, and for a further supply of golf balls. The fact is sometimes quoted with a hint of censure, but as Montrose was only seventeen and his bride a year younger, I don't imagine that the boy's fondness for golf in any way marred their youthful romance. The golfing items in the accounts of Sir John Foulis, of Ravelstoun, for 1672, show that his usual companions at golf were the Duke of Hamilton, the Lord Chancellor (the Duke of Rothes), the Lord Register (Sir Archibald Primrose), the Master of Saltoun, Sir John Baird of Newbyth, and Sir Peter Wedderburn, of Gosfoord, the last two being both Lords of Session.

Unfortunately not all the famous folk who figure in the annals of golf were as 'douce' as those I have mentioned, and scenes of violence on the links were not unknown. It is amusing to find that the earliest references to *chole* in documents of the fourteenth century are for the most part the result of summonses for assault by one player on another.   Tempers, to be sure, would be more easily roused in a game where both sides played the same ball, and three triumphant strokes by the *choleur* might be nullified in the most exasperating way by the *decholeur* knocking the ball into some particularly horrible spot.   That sort of thing was not so likely to happen at golf, with each side playing its own ball, but worse things than that were done on the links if we are to accept a tradition preserved in the family of the Marquis of Ailsa, that an ancestor of theirs once played a match on 'the linkes atte Air' against a monk of Crossragruel, the stake on the result being the monk's nose. If there is any foundation for the story, the match was probably part of the campaign of intimidation by which the then Earl of Cassilis[1] in 1570 forced Allan Stewart, commendator of the abbey of Crossraguel, to sign a conveyance of the abbey lands to the earl. The luckless commendator was somehow prevailed upon to visit the earl at Culzean, was later conveyed to the lonely tower called the Black Vault of Dunure (the ruins of which still stand), and there roasted over a slow fire until he agreed to sign the deeds.

The *Historie of the Kennedys*, which was published about 1600, also records that Kennedy of Bargany (who had a family feud with Kennedy of Cassilis) had a 'laigh,' i.e. a flat, or broken, nose, due to 'ane straik of ane goiff ball on the hills of Air in recklesnes.'

In the family of the Logans of Restalrig there is a legend, recorded in Chambers's *Traditions of Edinburgh*, that Halbert Logan of that ilk was playing golf at Lochend when a messenger from the Privy Council arrived to summon him to appear before them to answer for his supposed part in the Gowrie Conspiracy.   Despising the summons and being heated by the game, which presumably was going the wrong way, Logan 'used some despiteful language to the officer,' who hastened to make his report to the court and came back with a warrant for the arrest of Logan for high treason.   This put a different complexion on the matter; Logan flung down his clubs, mounted a fleet horse, and fled to England.

---

[1] The title of Marquis of Ailsa is a comparatively modern creation: the ancestors of the Kennedy family were earls of Cassilis and lords of Culzean. An account of the ill-treatment of Stewart in the Black Vault of Dunure is given in Scott's *Tales of a Grandfather*.

THE GAME OF CHOLE

From a painting by the Flemish artist, Paul Bril, painted in Rome in 1624, and now the property of the Minneapolis Institute of Arts.

The Game of Chole

A larger reproduction of the left-hand corner showing a *chole* player teeing the ball and what appears to be a caddie carrying two spare clubs and a bag of balls.

THE GAME OF CHOLE

From the right-hand bottom corner. The door of the shop of the club- and ball-maker, showing a remarkable variety of types of clubs.

THE GAME OF CHOLE

A reproduction on a larger scale of the centre foreground showing the pit apparently guarding the approach to the door chosen as the goal for which the players are making.

The first press notice of a game would appear to be that of 'a solemn match at golf' played in 1724 between Alexander Elphinstone, a younger son of Lord Balmerino, and Captain John Porteous of the Edinburgh City Guard, for what was in those days the considerable stake of twenty guineas a side. The match was attended by the Duke of Hamilton, the Earl of Morton, and a great concourse of spectators, Elphinstone proving the winner. Porteous, who had been appointed to command the City Guard after the Jacobite rising of 1715, afterwards became notorious by his high-handed action at the execution of a smuggler named Wilson in 1736. When the mob attempted some sort of demonstration on behalf of the condemned man, who had earned popular favour by helping a fellow prisoner to escape from the Tolbooth, Porteous ordered the City Guard round the scaffold to fire on the crowd, and appears also to have fired on them with his own hand. For this outrage he was tried and sentenced to death, and when some rumour of an intended reprieve went round, a body of the incensed citizens, armed and disguised, broke into the Tolbooth, seized Porteous, and hanged him on a signpost in the street. The episode forms one of the chief scenes of Scott's novel, *The Heart of Midlothian.*

Elphinstone, the victor in the golf match, was more fortunate, although he also within a few years after it had blood upon his hands. In 1729 he fought a duel on the golf links with Lieutenant Swift, of Cadogan's Regiment, and mortally wounded his antagonist, but though he was indicted before the High Court of Justiciary, the case was never pressed, and three years later he died peaceably in his bed.

It is a relief to turn from these lawless scenes to Smollett's account of Leith links as he saw it thirty years after the Porteous Riots:

I never saw such a concourse of genteel company at any races in England, as appeared on the course at Leith. Hard by, in the field called the Links, the citizens of Edinburgh divert themselves at a game called golf. Of this diversion the Scotch are so fond, that, when the weather will permit, you may see a multitude of all ranks mingled together in their shirts, and following the ball with the utmost eagerness. Among others, I was shown one particular set of golfers, the youngest of whom was turned of fourscore. They were all gentlemen of independent fortunes, who had amused themselves with this pastime for the best part of a century, without having ever felt the least alarm from sickness or disgust ; and they never went to bed without having each the best part of a gallon of claret in his belly.   Such uninterrupted exercise, co-operating with the keen air of the sea, must, without doubt, keep the appetite always on edge, and steel the constitution against all the common attacks of distemper.

CHAPTER SIX
(1743–1787)

The Formation of the Clubs

THE modern history of golf begins with the formation of the first Golf Clubs in the middle of the eighteenth century. To arrive at any proper understanding of the change which then took place, it is necessary to clear our mind of any assumption that the existence of a links and of a community of golfers playing over it implied the existence of any authority to look after the course or to regulate the play. Courses in those days were wholly natural; the only green-keepers were the rabbits. Clubs and competitions—apart from private matches—were alike unknown. Nobody had thought of the idea of keeping a score by counting the number of strokes taken for the round. And though it is probable that each community had its own unwritten code of rules, these were simple and few and framed to meet local conditions.

In these early days, according to the *Statistical Account of Scotland*, 'the greatest and wisest of the land were to be seen on the Links of Leith mingling freely with the humblest mechanics in pursuit of their common and beloved amusement. All distinctions of rank were levelled by the joyous spirit of the game. Lords of Session and cobblers, knights, baronets, and tailors might be seen earnestly contesting for the palm of superior dexterity, and vehemently but good-humouredly discussing moot points of the game, as they arose in the course of play.' But this Arcadian simplicity, comments the learned author of *The Golf Book of East Lothian*, 'was too fine to last; the Club system made an end of it at Leith as it has done elsewhere.'

Even in these Arcadian days, however, the prowess of the leading players would be a matter of popular discussion in their own community. You have good evidence of this in the first book on golf

35

ever written, Thomas Mathison's mock-heroic epic of *The Goff*,
published in Edinburgh in 1743:

> North from *Edina* eight furlongs and more
> Lies that fam'd field, on *Fortha's* sounding shore,
> Here Caledonian Chiefs for health resort,
> Confirm their sinews by the manly sport.
> *Macdonald* and unmatched *Dalrymple*, ply
> Their pond'rous weapons and the green defy;
> *Rattray* for skill and *Crosse* for strength renown'd,
> *Stuart* and *Leslie* beat the sandy ground,
> And *Brown* and *Alston*, Chiefs well known to fame,
> And numbers more the Muse forbears to name.
> Gigantic *Biggar* here full oft is seen
> Like huge Behemoth on an Indian green;
> His bulk enormous scarce can 'scape the eyes,
> Amaz'd spectators wonder how he plies.
> Yea, here great *Forbes*, patron of the just
> The dread of villains, and the good man's trust,
> When spent with toils in serving humankind,
> His body recreates and unbends his mind.

In the first edition of the poem the names of the different players
referred to were represented by blanks. Presumably the 'points'
of the local cracks were so well known that Mathison could leave his
golfing readers to fill in the familiar surnames for themselves. The
intimacy of the common bond thus indicated is incontestable. Yet
the poem contains no hint of the existence of anything in the nature
of a Club. The community of golfers playing over Leith Links
in 1743 had neither office-bearers nor meeting place. The argument frequently put forward, that the Honourable Company of
Edinburgh Golfers must have been in existence prior to 1744,
because in that year we find the golfers of Leith petitioning the town
of Edinburgh to provide a trophy for open competition, involves
a complete *non sequitur*. At this date the supposed Club had not
even a name. For some years to come we find the Leith golfing
community vaguely alluded to as 'the Gentlemen Golfers of
Edinburgh,' 'the Leith Society,' 'the Golfing Company,' with all
sorts of variations.

This state of things appears less surprising if we remember that prior to the reign of Charles II, Clubs of any kind were quite unknown in England. Probably the first Clubs were the political Clubs that came into being in the hectic years that followed Titus Oates's denunciation of the Popish Plot. When the Green Ribbon Club was formed in 1675, with its headquarters in the King's Head Tavern on the west side of the lower end of Chancery Lane, opposite the Inner Temple, and its name taken from the new party colour that had superseded the 'Presbyterian true blue,' the idea was a complete innovation. 'Before the Club was founded,' declares G. M. Trevelyan in his *England Under the Stuarts*, 'no party in England ever had a local habitation, beyond such as was afforded by the private hospitality of individual chiefs.'

It was only by a slow and gradual process that the Club idea was extended to apply to sport. In the case of golf the creation of the Clubs was the indirect and unforeseen result of the first attempt to run an Open Meeting. In 1744 'several Gentlemen of Honour, skilfull in the ancient and healthfull exercise of Golf,' petitioned the City of Edinburgh to provide a Silver Club for annual competition on the Links of Leith. The magistrates agreed to provide the trophy, though they inserted into the conditions of the gift a canny provision that 'upon no pretence whatsoever the City of Edinburgh shall be put to any sort of expense upon account of playing for the said Club annually, except to intimate by Tuck of Drum through the City the day on which it shall be annually played for, and to send the Silver Club to Leith upon the morning appointed for the match.' The magistrates also adopted the 'Scroll' of conditions for the competition drawn up by the golfers. The competition was to be an open one, open to 'as many Noblemen or Gentlemen or other Golfers, from any part of Great Britain or Ireland' as should send in their entries during the eight days preceding the date fixed for the competition. The winner was to be called 'the Captain of the Golf'—as we would nowadays say, the Champion Golfer—and was to be the arbiter of all disputes touching the game.

In one respect this first of all golf competitions was a complete failure; the entry was purely local. The majority of the twelve golfers who put down their names to play are mentioned in Mathison's poem. Only ten actually took part, and the winner was John Rattray, an Edinburgh surgeon—the 'Rattray for skill renowned' of the poet's opening lines. As he repeated his victory in the following year, one may believe the encomium well deserved.

But challengers for the trophy from other parts of Great Britain or Ireland continued to be conspicuous by their absence, and in 1764 the Captains of the Golf—i.e. the previous winners of the competition—successfully petitioned the City of Edinburgh for authority 'to admit such Noblemen and Gentlemen as they approve to be Members of the Company of Golfers,' and to restrict the competition for the Silver Club to these members. In other words, they decided to form themselves into a Club and make the contest for the trophy a Club competition. As the power to impose conditions of membership is surely inherent in the conception of a Club, the date, 1764, would appear to the modern golfer to be the legal date of the formation of the Honourable Company. But in the eighteenth century, as I shall presently show, the first step in the formation of almost every Golf Club was the presentation of a trophy for competition. The first competition for the Silver Club in 1744 to my mind represents the beginning of the Honourable Company, which I believe to be the oldest Golf Club and the example for all the rest.

Ten years later the example of the Leith golfers was followed by the St Andrews men. On 14th May 1754 twenty-two 'Noblemen and Gentlemen, being admirers of the ancient and healthful exercise of the Golf,' met together to subscribe for a Silver Club, to be the trophy of what we would now call an Open Scratch Competition, similar to the competition for the Silver Club of the City of Edinburgh. Only four players actually took part in this first competition, the winner being Bailie William Landale, merchant, St Andrews. As at Leith, the 'open' character of the contest failed to attract outside competition, and the Club in 1773 decided to restrict the competition to members of their own or the Leith Society.

In all this there was nothing of what to modern eyes would seem the normal process of the formation of a Club. The Rules of Golf Committee some years ago laid it down that the test of what constitutes a recognized Golf Club is whether it has duly elected office-bearers. The St Andrews meeting of 1754 elected no office-bearers. The only office-bearer in those early years was the captain, and he was not elected; he was the winner of the annual competition. The winner of the competition did not become the captain of a hypothetical Club; he became the holder of a local championship!

Prior to 1835 the Club was without any local habitation of its own, its occasional meetings being held at Bailie Glass's or at the Black Bull Tavern, but in that year the inauguration of the 'Union Club' on part of the ground afterwards occupied by the Grand Hotel provided a suitable place of meeting for both the golfers and the St Andrews Archers' Club. The establishment of the St Andrews Golf Club was therefore a much more gradual process than would be visualized by modern golfers, accustomed to start off with a name and a constitution and a formal election of office-bearers. Nevertheless the fact remains that in those early days the first step in the process was the inauguration of a competition, and therefore 14th May 1754 may be taken as the date of the beginning of the Royal and Ancient Golf Club, even as 7th March 1744 is the birthday of the Honourable Company of Edinburgh Golfers.

The date of the formation of the Blackheath Golf Club does not seem to me to admit of any doubt. It began exactly as the first Scottish Golf Clubs had done with the presentation of a trophy for competition among the local players. The trophy in this case took the form of a Silver Driver, which is still preserved in the present clubhouse at Eltham. The head of the club bears the inscription: 'August 16, 1766, the gift of Mr Henry Foot to the Honourable Company of Golfers at Blackheath.' The wording of the inscription is itself sufficient indication that the Blackheath *Club* did not then exist. As in the case of the Scottish Clubs, the formation of the Blackheath Club was the incidental result arising out of the holding of the competition. I have no doubt that the date above given, 1766, is the true date of the formation of the first Golf Club outside of Scotland.

An error frequently made by those who want to believe in an earlier date for the origin of the Club is the assertion that the Blackheath Club was 'originally known as the Knuckle Club.' The blame for this error rests with Mr Andrew Lang, who observes in the first chapter of the Badminton *Golf* that 'in 1822 it was proposed to alter the mystic[1] name of "Knuckle Club" to "Blackheath Golf Club."' But this is a misconception; we know all about the formation of the Knuckle Club from the Blackheath minute book. The Blackheath Club was a summer Club, limiting its season to the period from the first Saturday in April to the first Saturday in November of each year. The Knuckle Club was formed on 17th January 1789 to supplement the old arrangement by meeting weekly on Saturday *during the winter months,* and dining together, with 'a dish of soup and *knuckles*' as part of the fare. In 1825 the name of this body was changed to the Blackheath *Winter* Golf Club, and it became merged in the parent Club in 1844. It is this change to 'the Blackheath Winter Golf Club' which Lang misconstrued as a change to the 'Blackheath Golf Club.'

The Musselburgh (now, of course, Royal Musselburgh) Golf Club came into being in 1774 when Mr Thomas McMillan, of Shorthope, presented 'the Musselburgh Golfers'—again there is no reference to a Club—with a Cup for competition. He himself was the first winner of it, and the Rev. Dr Carlyle of Inveresk was the victor in the following year. 'The Minutes of the Club for the first ten years of its existence,' says Robert Clark, 'are unfortunately amissing, but the medals attached to the quaint old Cup, which severally bear the name of the winner for the year, satisfactorily carry back its existence as a Club' to the date given. I quite agree as regards the sufficiency of the evidence, but I am amused at the reiterated assumption that 'the Minutes have gone astray.' It seems to me perfectly clear that in every one of these cases it was the holding of the competition that marked the beginning of the Club's activities. The minutes are missing because no minutes were kept; the necessity for electing office-bearers and keeping proper records was only realized after the competition had been held for a number of years.

Although the Edinburgh Burgess Golfing Society (now the

[1] The only mystery about the Knuckle Club is the reason for the decision to destroy the first four pages of its minute book. The Club started off with an initiation ceremony and an elaborate ritual; the winner of the Gold Medal, for instance, was styled the 'Grand Knuckle.' Probably the whole thing was too puerile to stand the test of use.

A double page of a Book of Hours of 1530 showing archery (with long-bow and cross-bow) and a form of croquet in the left-hand border, and various games resembling golf on the right. (See page 17.)

A page from a Flemish Book of Hours, showing players in a typical *kolven* court apparently putting at a hole.

Royal Burgess Golfing Society of Edinburgh) appears to date from 1773, it has long put forward a vague and shadowy claim to have existed from 1735, though no evidence to support the selection of that particular year appears to be available. The claim, moreover, is not borne out by the wording of the Society's own Petition in 1800 to be made a Body Corporate, for the Petition sets forth that the Society had existed as a Club or Society for upwards of twenty years, which would fit reasonably well with a foundation in 1773 but scarcely with one in 1735. The Society were not *then* claiming to have existed from the earlier date. Admittedly the minute of 1773 indicates a resuscitation of an older 'Society of Golfers in and about Edinburgh,' but there is no reason to suppose that the earlier body represented anything more than a fraternity of Bruntsfield players who were in the habit of dining at the same tavern.

The clue, I believe, is to be found in a minute of the Bruntsfield Links Golf Club, dated 10th June 1787, which begins 'This Society having been formerly, by general consent, instituted into a Club ...' The historian of the Royal Burgess Golfing Society, Mr J. Cameron Robbie, appears to consider that this means that a 'Society' and a 'Club' were the same thing, but if that were so why go out of the way to put it on record that the Bruntsfield golfers had changed from the one into the other? It is no doubt true that *nowadays* a Golf Club and a Golfing Society mean the same thing; if there is a distinction it lies in a tendency to reserve the term Society for those nomad bodies which possess no course of their own but hold their meetings by permission on the courses of other Clubs. But in the middle of the eighteenth century the term Society seems to have been used to refer to any *community* of golfers who had not yet taken steps to organize themselves into a Club.

Mr Robbie himself touches the root of the matter when he observes that 'in Scotland by the end of the seventeenth century, the inhabitants of many places had prescriptive right of playing golf on certain areas. Already possessing this right there was no need to associate themselves in order to obtain it. . . . But obviously congenial society and private matches at specified times were essential for complete enjoyment. The players would dine together at a convenient inn, where as regular clients they would be regarded as a society of golfers, and be given the personal attention

usually accorded to consistent customers.' And he quotes Allan
Ramsay's lines:

> When we were wearied at the gowff
> Then Maggie Johnstone's was our howff;
> Noo a' our gamesters may sit dowff,
>   Wi' hearts like lead.
> Death wi' his rung reached her a yowff,
>   And sae she's dead,

to prove that the same state of things existed in 1711.

This in fact would be the position of affairs at every recognised
golf centre. Little cliques of habitual opponents would be in the
habit of dining together after their matches. Well-known players
would from time to time agree on one or two new local rules, which
would be accepted by all the rest. But, as Mr Robbie says, there
was no need for them to form themselves into any sort of association
to do this. The need for forming such an association only became
apparent when the community of golfers decided to hold a competition. This last was the start of things at Leith, at St Andrews, at
Blackheath, and at Musselburgh. There is no evidence of any
similar activity on the part of the Edinburgh Burgess golfers in
1735, or even in 1773. Possibly the retention of the name 'Society'
at the latter date was a recognition of the fact that it had not yet
attained the status of a Club, in respect that it possessed no trophy
for competition. The Society's early competitions (from 1773 to
1816) seem to have taken the form of some sort of sweepstake in
which the players took the value of their winnings in golf balls, and
even at one period in cash.

In the same way the Bruntsfield Links Golf Club claims to have
existed as a Society from 1761 and to have risen to the status of a
Club in 1787, which seems likely enough.

The oldest Club in the west of Scotland is the Glasgow Club,
which modestly claims 1787 as the date of its formation. I say
'modestly' because it is almost certainly a few years older than that.
In 1780 the town council gave official permission for the playing of
the game on Glasgow Green, and a directory of 1783 gives a list of
members of 'the Silver Golf Club,' which suggests that in this case

also the competition for the trophy led to the formation of the Club. Another directory gives a list of the members in 1787 to the number of twenty-two, and the membership in these early days does not appear at any time to have greatly exceeded this.

The course on the Green was of seven holes, as at Leith, three rounds of the course being played in the annual competition for the Silver Club. But golf had been played over the Green long before the town council gave the game their official sanction. A poem published in 1721 under the title of *Glotta, or The Clyde*, by James Arbuckle, a student at Glasgow University, who later became a contributor to the *Edinburgh Miscellany* and enjoyed the friendship of Alian Ramsay, contains this description of golf on the Green:

> In winter, too, when hoary frosts o'erspread
> The verdant turf, and naked lay the mead,
> The vig'rous youth commence the sportive war,
> And, arm'd with lead, their jointed clubs prepare:
> The timber curve to leathern orbs apply,
> Compact, elastic, to pervade the sky:
> These to the distant hole direct they drive;
> They claim the stakes who thither first arrive.
> Intent his ball the eager gamester eyes,
> His muscles strains, and various postures tries,
> Th' impelling blow to strike with greater force,
> And shape the motive orb's projectile course.
> If with due strength the weighty engine fall,
> Discharged obliquely, and impinge the ball,
> It winding mounts aloft, and sings in air;
> And wond'ring crowds the gamester's skill declare.
> But when some luckless wayward stroke descends,
> Whose force the ball in running quickly spends,
> The foes triumph, the club is cursed in vain;
> Spectators scoff, and ev'n allies complain,
> Thus still success is followed with applause;
> But ah! how few espouse a vanquished cause!

The Green in winter, however, was no more than a rushy haugh, apt in bad weather to degenerate into a miry swamp, and the list of captains of the Club indicates a period of 'suspended animation' between 1795 and 1809 and again between 1836 and 1869. The first gap coincides with the period of the Napoleonic wars, and it is easy to conjecture that the claims of volunteer training may for the time have superseded any thought of golf. The second hiatus was probably due to the growth of the city itself, which made the Green no longer a convenient or satisfactory rendezvous. When the Club was resuscitated in 1870, it played over a nine-hole course at Queen's Park.

The same gap in the Napoleonic war period appears in the case of the Royal Aberdeen Club, which claims 1815 as the year of its formation. This was certainly a resuscitation, for the ballot-box (still preserved in the clubhouse at Balgownie) in which the Club placed their votes for the election of new members bears a brass plate with the year 1780.

CHAPTER SEVEN
(1766–1850)

Wining and Dining in the Brave
Days of Old

IT must be remembered that in the days when the Silver Club
competitions were inaugurated at Leith and St Andrews all golf
was played on what would now be called public courses. There
were no private Clubs and consequently no clubhouses. The
Golf House at the south-west corner of Leith links was erected in
1768, but prior to that date the Leith golfers had been accustomed to
seek refreshment at a neighbouring tavern known as Luckie Clephan's. The institution of the annual competition for the Silver
Club, however, soon gave rise to the custom of the competitors
dining together after the game, and as early as 1753 a minute in the
Honourable Company's record book indicates that 'The Captain
and his Councill, considering that Mr David Lyon, ane eminent
Golfer, after subscribing and engaging himself to play for the Silver
Club this day, has not only not started for the Club, but has, contrary to the duty of his allegiance, withdrawn himself from the
Captain and his Company, and has dined in another house after
having bespoke a particular dish for himself in Luckie Clephan's,
the Captain therefore, with advice of his Councill, appoints the
Procurator-Fiscall to indyte the said David Lyon for his above
offence . . . and hereby orders the culprit to be cited to answer here
on Saturday next.'

In 1766 we find a number of the St Andrews players engaging to
meet once every fortnight and to dine together at Bailie Glass's,
each 'to pay a shilling for his dinner, the absent as well as the
present.' The Blackheath golfers of 1787 met in 'the Chocolate
House' and later removed to the Green Man Hotel. In 1792 the
Edinburgh Burgess Club secured a lease of a house (later to become
known as the 'Golf Tavern') and sublet it to a landlady. But even
there the golfers were customers rather than Club members, as is

shown by a quarrel with the landlady which led to the Club remov-
ing for a while (1827–30) to Gorrie's Tavern at the west end of the
links and starting the round from that end. An early minute of
the Society records an arrangement for a boy to be engaged to call
on each member every Saturday and take the names of those who
proposed to dine that day—not, you will observe, to play golf that
day, for all those old minute books made it abundantly clear that at
this stage the functions of the Clubs were far more intimately concerned with the dining than with the golf.

It was an age of good living and hard drinking. The minutes
of the Royal Aberdeen Golf Club on more than one occasion record
with simple pride that the consumption of liquor at dinner exceeded
three bottles per man. But both food and liquor were comparatively cheap. A minute of the Musselburgh Club, of December
1785, resolves that 'in order to remedy the inconvenience that has
been found in collecting the eightpences for the dinners . . . the
company resolve that each member shall pay into the treasurer's
hand six shillings sterling to pay for the dinners of the nine meetings
of the ensuing year . . . the overplus to remain in the treasurer's
hands.' Ah, me! what sort of dinner would you get for eightpence
in these modern days of austerity? There would be small chance
of the treasurer giving himself a headache through worrying how to
dispose of the overplus!

In the case of courses further out in the country, where the
resources of the local inn might be insufficient for the needs of a
big meeting, it was not unusual for the rations to be supplemented
by the generosity of individual members. The Rev. John Kerr,
the chronicler of golf in East Lothian, records that the North
Berwick golfers, who were famous for the sumptuousness of their
fare, were the possessors of two marquees in which to lunch at their
meetings. The secretary of the Club, Mr George Wauchope,
usually supplied the cook to prepare the feast, and the crystal was
provided by Mr George Sligo of Seacliffe. It was the North
Berwick golfers' far-sighted practice for each member present at
one meeting to intimate some contribution for the dinner at the next.

At the first meeting, for instance, there was 'a competition in mutton'
between Sir David Baird and Mr Sligo. 'Bass mutton,' 'mutton ham,'
'saddle of mutton,' are occasional variations. Of beef little is heard,

the reason perhaps being that it was possible to get this at North Berwick. 'A round of beef stewed in hock' is on one occasion sent by Mr Hay of Rockville, and on another the same is gifted by the Hon. H. Coventry, while 'Shetland beef,' in 1836, is contributed by Sir D. Kinloch. . . . 'Venison,' 'haunch of venison,' and 'venison pasty' are the favourite gifts of the Duke of Buccleuch.   The Earl of Eglinton, as an apology for his absence as captain at one of the 1839 meetings, sends 'a fine buck'! 'Reindeer's tongue' is the gift of Captain Keith.   'Green-goose' and 'gosling' figure on various occasions, and 'turkey' is also conspicuous. . . . Of rarer occurrence are such as the following: ducks, pheasants, part-ridges, grouse (generally from Whittingehame), capons, grouse-pie, guinea-fowl, *pâté de foie gras*, and *gâteau napolitain*.   Pigeon pie was a standing dish for which Sir Adam Hay and Mr Annesley were responsible, the former sometimes giving sheep's-head pie as a change.   The secre-tary, Mr Wauchope, seldom failed to provide a speciality called Perigord pie or *Perigueux pâté*.   In the fish department we find Mr Craigie Halkett promising, in 1833, 'to send salmon every meeting as long as the Club lasts'—a rash promise, which, however, seems to have been fulfilled so long, at least, as the giver himself lasted.   Captain Brown, being on the spot, furnished such luxuries as a fishing village could afford—lobsters, crabs, crabs' claws, and sand-eels; Captain Buckle, anchovies; Mr Halkett, cod sounds; Major Buchanan, sardines and cucumbers; Captain Keith, Lochleven trout; and turbot on occasions, at the instance of various members, graced the board.   The truly aldermanic reputation of the dinner may be proved by the prominent position occupied by the 'turtle' which seldom failed to introduce the proceedings.

That abundant provision was made for the golfers to 'synd doun' the solid portion of the dinner is also evident from the old Minutes. . . .   Sir David Baird presents the Club at the start with 'three dozen champagne,' a quantity which seems to have been adopted as a standard by the Club in imposing a fine on any member.   For the first Meeting in 1833, Campbell of Glensaddell and Macdonald of Clanranald each send six bottles of highland whisky. . . .   Mr Whyte-Melville on numerous occasions sends 'shrub.'   Once his gift is entitled 'rum for shrub' and at another time 'rum for punch.'   Major Pringle is also a frequent donor of rum.   Mr Sligo has a favourite drink donation entitled 'Bishop' and sometimes 'German Bishop,' which so far as we know has quite gone out of fashion. . . .

The practice on medal days at North Berwick was to decide the competition by three rounds of the course—at this time of seven

holes only—followed by lunch at three o'clock.   The afternoon
was devoted to foursomes, or sometimes to a sweepstake competition, and the day wound up with a dinner at seven o'clock, this time
in the local inn.   Golf at North Berwick was obviously far more of
a social function than at any other of the great golf centres.   There
was no railway communication with North Berwick until 1850 and,
although the membership of the Club was limited to fifty, the little
fishing town of the 1830's had no means of accommodating such an
incursion of players, but each country house within driving radius
had its contingent of visitors, who drove down in great style on the
morning of the meeting.   North Berwick is the only Club in these
early days, so far as I have been able to discover, in which ladies
were regularly present at the meetings, not of course as players, but
at least as participants in the mid-afternoon lunch.

An important feature of these eighteenth-century Golf Clubs
was the choice of a Club uniform, for if these were the golden days
of dining they were also the days of dressing up.   A minute of the
Royal and Ancient Club dated 4th August 1780 records that:

The Society took into their consideration that their Golfing Jackets
are in a bad condition.   Have agreed that they shall have new ones, viz.
Red with yellow buttons.   The undermentioned gentlemen have likewise agreed to have a Uniform Frock, viz. a Buff Colour with a Red Cap.
The Coat to be half lapelled, the Button White.

(Sgd.) BALCARRES (and ten others).

Four years later, however, they adopted a change of fashion and
made their uniform a red coat with a dark-blue velvet cape, with
white plain buttons, with an embroidered club and ball of silver on
each side of the cape, with two large buttons on the sleeves.

There is a general idea, based on the analogy of the red jackets
whose use is still enforced on one or two of the London public
courses laid out on commons, that these early golfing uniforms were
designed for the safety of the other users of the links, but this idea
has no foundation.   'Uniforms' for all sorts of other Clubs besides
Golf Clubs were in vogue in the eighteenth century.   The great
Pickwick, as you doubtless remember, designed a special one for
members of the Pickwick Club, complete with the inevitable 'club

A FROST SCENE: 1668

(After the picture by Adriaen van de Velde in the British National Gallery.)   Note the post in the middle distance
towards which the player is putting.

button.' It is true that the golfers in the majority of cases chose jackets of a military scarlet—neat without being gaudy, as the devil said when he painted his tail pea-green. But the choice was by no means universal. Prior to 1854 the uniform of the Innerleven Golfing Society was of the 'Prince Charles tartan.' The Glasgow golfers chose to appear in grey. And the Aberdeen Golf Club went one better than the rest by having *two* uniforms. In the clubhouse at Balgownie are still preserved a number of the red jackets the members wore while playing, and the equally resplendent blue jackets they changed into for dining. Unquestionably those were the days!

The wearing of the Club uniform was obligatory. The record book of the Honourable Company of Edinburgh Golfers, under the date of 16th November 1776, bears witness that:

This day Lieutenant James Dalrymple, of the 43rd Regiment, being convicted of playing five different times at Golf without his uniform [i.e. of course, his golfing uniform] was fined only in Six pints, having confessed the heinousness of his crime.

And twelve years later (31st May 1788) we find the same body unanimously agreeing 'that every Member of the Society shall dine in his uniform at every public meeting of the Club, and that the Members of the Club shall appear in the uniform when they play upon the Links.' (The signature of this minute is that of Lord Elcho.)

The Bruntsfield golfers were a bit late in coming into line with the rest of the world in this respect. On 12th June 1790 the Edinburgh Burgess Golfing Society resolved 'that in future the members of this Society shall wear an uniform as is universally done by other Societies of Golfers, and that the uniform be a scarlet jacket, black neck, and badge, as presently worn by some of the members.' At the end of July in the same year the Bruntsfield Links Golf Club likewise approved a design for a uniform, the feature of which was the Club button showing two clubs crossed with four balls, with the motto *Inde Salus*. The tendency during the next half-century appears to have been to make uniforms more and more elaborate. In 1837 members of the Burgess Society had to provide themselves with 'a dress coat, colour dark claret, with black velvet collar, double-breasted and lined in the skirts with white silk or satin, prominent buttons on cuffs of coat and also on the flaps, dress vest colour primrose with smaller buttons to correspond with those on the coat,' for wear on all special occasions.

The dates I have quoted show that the era of uniforms extended right through the first half of the nineteenth century. I fancy that the volunteer movement helped to maintain the popular taste for bold colours in sporting wear. But in the second half of the nineteenth century the pendulum swung to the opposite extreme and a blight of dowdiness descended upon the links. The tight 'uniform' jackets, like that which Mr William Innes of Blackheath is shown wearing in Abbott's famous picture, cannot have been conducive to freedom or power in the swing. By way of reaction, the Victorian golfer achieved a sort of freedom by wearing his oldest and 'easiest' suit; if a seam had given way here and there, so much the better. The thing became a fad and then a fashion. The better the player, the more disreputable and moth-eaten a jacket he was entitled to wear.

The pendulum began to swing back again at the end of the nineteenth century with the vogue of Norfolk jacket and knickers, which in turn were superseded after the First World War, when the Duke of Windsor, then Prince of Wales, helped to set the mode of 'plus fours' and Fair Isle jumpers. During the war the prince was an officer in the Guards, and his presence drew universal attention to their service uniform in which their nether habiliments were arranged to hang down over the knee in a manner more distinctive than decorative. It is even said that the name of 'plus fours' was derived from an army instruction that in the uniform of the Guards the trouser was to fold down over the knee 'plus four inches,' but I think this derivation is too good to be true. Handicaps of plus 4 on the links were at that time not wholly unknown and I incline to believe that the name only meant that as the plus 4 man represented the peak of golfing success, so the garb of 'plus fours' was the extreme limit of golfing swank.

The Fair Isle jumper had a thousand years of history behind it. In long past centuries the Moorish invaders brought to Spain the art of knitting these arabesque patterns; Spain in her turn prepared an Armada to bring the same designs to England, but her defeated galleons blundered northward on a broken wing to wreck on the remotest isles of Scotland, and the cloaks of the half-drowned survivors suggested fresh patterns to their Caledonian rescuers.

During this period amateur golfers vied with one another in the startling colours of their garb, and as for the professionals, even Solomon in all his glory was not arrayed like one of these!   Then came another reversion, and the Universities set the fashion of play in fishermen's jerseys and voluminous flannel bags.   But the vogue of slovenliness never lasts long.   To-day we have not indeed got back to the military 'uniforms' of the eighteenth century, but the tendency if not towards uniforms is at least towards uniformity. And the international teams of the United States and Great Britain go out to battle in Walker Cup and Ryder Cup matches in a uniform of a sort, though it takes no more startling guise than is provided by dark blazers, white shirts, and smartly creased slacks.

CHAPTER EIGHT

(1767–1855)

Election by Combat

ONE of the results of the development of the convivial side of Golf
Club activities was the gradual abandonment of the practice of
deciding the captaincy by the result of the annual competition. The
captain, naturally, was also the president at the Club gatherings,
and as the gifts of successful chairmanship do not necessarily go with
skill on the links, Clubs everywhere tended to abandon the old idea
and made the captaincy elective, though at St Andrews, at any rate,
the original procedure is still in theory maintained.

Every year at the Autumn Meeting of the Royal and Ancient
Club, the captain-elect plays himself into office at an unconscionably
early hour in the morning by driving a ball from the first tee before
the day's play begins. This traditional ceremony has been imitated
by countless Clubs in different parts of the world, newly elected
captains celebrating their election to office by 'playing themselves
in' in the same way. It is a little bit of ritual that I should like to
see adopted everywhere, and I hope I shall not be spoiling anybody's
pleasure in the idea if I point out that the legal fiction behind the St
Andrews ceremony is a little different from what most of its imitators
imagine. When the captain-elect of the Royal and Ancient Club
drives the first ball of the meeting he is not celebrating his accession
to office; in theory at least he is taking part in a competition to
decide who shall be the new captain! But he is the only competitor, and as soon as he takes part in the competition by hitting
that first shot from the tee, he automatically becomes the winner of
the Silver Club, which carries with it the captaincy for the ensuing
year.

In the early years of the competitions for the Silver Clubs at
Leith and St Andrews, when both were open to golfers from any
part of Great Britain and Ireland, the 'captaincy' was purely

52

competitive, and presumably remained so at least as long as the competitions remained 'open.'

When the Leith golfers in 1764 petitioned the City of Edinburgh to allow them to restrict the competition to their own members, the signatories to the petition were the Captains of the Golf—the holder of the trophy and the previous winners. Up to that point they had no other office-bearers. If the same state of things existed at St Andrews it would explain the origin of the curious system by which the choice of captains is determined up to the present day. The new captain is not elected by the Club, but by the past-captains sitting in solemn conclave.

Exactly at what stage the office of captain ceased to be competitive and began to be decided by nomination it is impossible to say. Dr James Grierson, in his *History of St Andrews*, published in 1807, observes that although the Silver Club was played for apparently every year, yet the dignity of 'Captain of the Company' was really elective. 'It is always fixed before proceeding to the field who is to return victorious for this honour . . . and though it is entered on the records of the Society that such a gentleman on such a day and in such a party, won the Silver Club by striking the ball into the hole in a certain number of strokes, this part of the record is fictitious, and well known to be no test of good play. That there might be a proper test and a real record of the best players, the Society in 1806 purchased a Gold Medal to be played for annually.' The learned author of *A History of the Royal and Ancient Golf Club*, who scouts the accuracy of Dr Grierson's statement, apparently assumes that it is intended to describe the state of things from the beginning and to mean that the supposed scores were bogus. But I do not think this is what Dr Grierson intended to convey. He was referring to the state of affairs that had come to exist in 1806 and which led to the institution of the competition for the Gold Medal, and as he was writing immediately after the event it is unlikely that he got his facts wrong. Nor are his remarks to be taken to mean that the *scores* were fictitious; they presumably represented the new captain's actual returns for the day. The fiction lay in the pretence that the score was the winning return in a general contest and to that extent 'a test of good play.' Already the office had become elective; the theory was still maintained that the captain-elect qualified for office by winning the Silver Club, but he was the only player regarded as competing for it.

Among the Blackheath golfers at this time, which is about the earliest date for which their minutes are still in existence, the captaincy would seem to have been decided by a combination of election and competition. In 1800, the first year for which records are available, two candidates for the office of captain were nominated, but the choice between them was not decided by vote; they were set to play against one another for the Silver Club, the winner taking the trophy and the chair. From 1801 to 1807 the captaincy was decided by the wishes of the members, which perhaps means only that in those years the choice was unanimous. In 1808 two candidates played off for the honour; in 1809 three; and this method of 'trial by ordeal' continued until 1823 when the office was made purely elective. A Gold Medal was provided as the principal prize for future Spring Meetings, and the Silver Club was played for no more.

The idea of making the captaincy competitive, however, proved too fascinating to be lightly abandoned by some of the later English Clubs. But the plan had its own disadvantages. The late Mr Horace Hutchinson has put it on record that at the mature age of sixteen he committed the 'blazing indiscretion' of winning the Scratch Gold Medal of the Royal North Devon Club, which carried with it the captaincy and the duty of presiding at all Club meetings for the next twelve months, a state of things which the greybeards of the Club so little approved that in the following year they made the office elective. The last Club to forsake the competitive plan must, I think, have been the Minehead Club, which up to 1930 still maintained their early custom that the winner of the scratch prize at the Summer Meeting became the captain for the ensuing year.

What sort of golfers were they, these earliest winners of the Club Championships and Gold Medals? For the earliest contests of all, which were decided by holes and not by strokes, we have no records whatever, and even after 1759, when score play came into vogue, we can only judge the best players by one or two outstanding performances.

The first of these almost legendary figures was William St Clair of Roslin, whose skill at archery and golf was so notable as to be attributed by vulgar superstition to his knowledge of the Black Art. St Clair was the last to occupy the office of Hereditary Grand Master of the Freemasons of Scotland, a dignity which he voluntarily resigned, becoming the first elected Grand Master. He was born in 1700, so that he was already in middle age when the competitions for the Silver Clubs were instituted, but he won the Silver Club of the Honourable Company in 1761, 1766, 1770, and 1771, and that of the St Andrews golfers in 1764, 1766, and 1768. He was the last winner over the twenty-two-hole round at St Andrews, with a score of 121—equivalent to 99 for an eighteen-hole round, a first-rate score for those days. It will be seen that the first of his golfing triumphs was gained when he was already over sixty, the last when he had passed man's allotted bogey of threescore years and ten.

At St Andrews the score of 94 returned by James Durham, of Largo, in the competition for the Silver Club in 1767, remained unequalled for eighty-six years, until the Autumn Meeting of 1853, when Captain J. C. Stewart of Fasnacloich won the King William IV Gold Medal with a total of 90. George Glennie's 88 in 1855 was not beaten until twenty-four years later, when William J. Mure returned a card of 86 to win the Silver Cross at the May Meeting. It is recorded of George Glennie that even in his student days at St Andrews he was so much better than his fellows that they decided to handicap him by allowing him to use only one club. Nor was that left to his own choice; a much battered old mid-spoon was assigned to him for this purpose, and even with this—equivalent perhaps to a modern No. 3 iron—he proved too strong for the field. Later on he and the Captain Stewart above mentioned were the successful Royal Blackheath pair in the first championship ever held.

It must be appreciated, however, that the era before the coming of the championships was the golden age of foursome play, and public interest was more excited over matches for high stakes between partnerships of well-known amateurs than by the contests for the Silver Clubs or the stroke play competitions that succeeded them. The well-known painting by Charles Lees, R.S.A., of 'A Great Golf Match at St Andrews, 1850: Sir David Baird and Sir Ralph Anstruther versus Major Playfair and John Campbell, Esq.,

of Saddell,' gives some indication of the sort of gallery attracted by
the meeting of four such crack golfers, as famous in their more
restricted field as the Open Champions of to-day.   The scene in
the picture is the fifteenth green on the Old Course, Major Playfair
has just putted.   Sir David Baird is bending forward with his club
in his hand to watch the fate of the stroke, while Sir Ralph Anstruther, bareheaded, is drawing himself up as if in unconscious
prayer that the ball should draw up too.   Major Playfair's partner,
Campbell of Saddell, is shown standing with his club over his
shoulder, well back on the right, in the detached attitude of the
man who has no doubt of his partner's ability to put the ball
down.

All four of the players engaged in this famous foursome were
members of the North Berwick Club as well as of the Royal and
Ancient, and are among the heroes whose poetical portraits appear
in *Golfiana,* which George Fullarton Carnegie wrote for the delecta-
tion of the golfers of the two Clubs.   Of Major Playfair, afterwards
Sir Hugh Lyon-Playfair, Carnegie wrote:

> There's Major Playfair, man of nerve unshaken,
> He knows a thing or two or I'm mistaken.
> And, when he's pressed, can play a tearing game,
> He works for *certainty* and not for *Fame;*
> There's none—I'll back the assertion with a wager—
> Can play the *heavy iron* like the Major.

That was written in 1833, and in *Another Peep at the Links,*
ten years later, we find it recorded that 'Still Major Playfair shines, a
star at golf,' but in after days his greatest claim to fame was the
immense improvements which as Provost of St Andrews he brought
about in the 'old grey city by the sea.'

His partner, Campbell, of Glensaddell, in Kintyre, had been one
of the Knights at the Eglintoun Tournament, and is described by
Robert Clark as being 'a sort of Magnus Apollo with the fashion-
ables of his day.'   'He was a great sporting man and though a
heavy-weight rode remarkably well to hounds.   He went in a
balloon from Heriot's Hospital to Fife when such a thing was
considered a bold feat.   He was a noble-looking man, pompous in
his manners, and very irascible! . . .'   In spite of a somewhat

Looking out on the
Kolven Court from the
Sun Inn in Amsterdam
(1761)—from the draw-
ing by the Dutch artist,
S. Fokke, in the Museum
of the North Manchester
Club.

The border shows a
player at pall-mall.

Kolven on the ice as depicted in a seventeenth-century painting by Aert van der Neer.

ponderous swing, he was a long driver; another player is described as being able at times to hit

> . . . a stroke
> Whose distance Saddell's envy might provoke.

Apparently he knew it too, for one of Carnegie's portraits describes:

> Saddell, dress'd in blue coat plain,
> With lots of Gourlays, free from spot or stain,
> He whirls his club to catch the proper *swing*,
> And freely bets round all the scarlet ring;
> And swears by *Ammon*, he 'll engage to drive
> As long a ball as any man alive.

Ten years later:

> Still Saddell walks, superb, improved in play,
> Though his blue jacket now is turned to gray;
> Still are his golf balls rife and clean as wont—
> Still swears by Ammon and still bets the *blunt*—
> Still plays all matches—still is often beat—
> And still, in iced punch, drowns each fresh defeat.

Sir David Baird, of Newbyth, invariably played in a tall hat. (This may appear a handicap to modern golfers, but if perhaps some of them were to try it, they might find themselves more successful in the effort to keep their heads still!) He was the moving spirit in the creation of the North Berwick Club in 1832, and its first captain, and as an instance of his keenness for golf it is recorded of him by Willie Dunn that on a drenching wet day he drove down from Newbyth to Musselburgh, played eight rounds of the nine-hole links, and drove back to Newbyth 'without changing a stitch.' He used to put his favourite sports in the following order: (1) golf, (2) salmon-fishing, (3) deer-stalking, (4) fox-hunting. Campbell of Saddell had the same tastes, and in his old age could exclaim on one occasion after holing a tricky and curling long putt: 'What a splendid putt! In my time I have had the best grouse-shooting in Scotland, and the best salmon river and the best deer-stalking, and I have kept the best hunters at Melton; but I am thankful to say I can now dream about a putt!'

Of the fourth player, Sir Ralph Anstruther, of Balcaskie, who was interested in politics, Carnegie wrote:

> Were he but once in Parliament, methinks,
> And working *there* as well as on the *links*,
> The burghs, I 'll be bound, would not repent them
> That they had such a man to represent them.
> There's *one thing* only, when he 's *on the roll*
> He must not lose his *nerve*, as when he 's near the hole.

Of the four players Major Playfair appears, from an account of a handicap competition at North Berwick, to have been slightly the best, for he gives a stroke to Baird and Anstruther, who in turn are three strokes better than Campbell. But this no doubt was one of the attractions of foursome play. In matches between players of approximately equal skill, it was usual to strike a balance by the giving of odds in the betting rather than by conceding a stroke or two in the round. And in foursome play any minor difference could be adjusted in the arrangement of the partnerships, as in the present case, in which the strongest player and the weakest combined against the other two, with the added interest, which is still a feature of foursome play, that it is not always the strongest players who make the strongest partnerships.

So pronounced was the taste for foursome play at this epoch, that when the first attempt to hold a championship meeting was made, it was by foursomes, as we shall presently see, that it was decided.

CHAPTER NINE
(1552–1764)

Why Eighteen Holes make a Round

DURING the half-century which succeeded the formation of the first Golf Clubs, the course at Leith was 'the metropolitan links of Scotland and of the world,' and the Honourable Company of Edinburgh Golfers set the mode for all the rest. Its membership included players from all parts of the northern kingdom, and the number of distinguished jurists in its ranks qualified it to take an unquestioned lead in framing the rules of the game. That the Honourable Company failed to retain this proud position must be attributed to the gradual deterioration of the Leith links, which faded out of popularity as the fame of St Andrews grew.

'The old grey city by the sea'—where in early days St Regulus founded his church for the conversion of the 'bloody, savage and barbarous Pights,' where friar and priest, archbishop and cardinal waxed fat and kicked, where the four Maries landed from France, and where the beautiful monuments of the older faith have even to this day preserved some vague ruin of their former glory to shame the vandalism of Genevan reformers—had the advantage in beauty of situation as well as in the quality of its turf, and early in the nineteenth century the St Andrews Club began to supersede the Honourable Company as the glass of golfing fashion and the arbiter of form. To-day the old cathedral city enjoys a fame unequalled by any other in the world of sport and is almost as great a place of pilgrimage as Mecca or Jerusalem or Rome. Of its ancient pride and privilege the University alone remains, but though

> St Andrews! they say that thy glories are gone,
> That thy streets are deserted, thy castles o'erthrown.
> If thy glories be gone, they are only, methinks,
> As it were, by enchantment, transferred to thy links.

And it is surely no small thing, even for what was once the

ecclesiastical capital of Scotland, that it should now have become the golfing capital of the world.

The earliest documentary evidence of the playing of golf at St Andrews takes the form of a licence dated 25th January 1552, granted by John Hamilton, 'by the mercie of God archebischop of Sanctandros, *primat et legat natie* of the haill realme of Scotland,' to the community of the city to rear rabbits 'within the northe pairt of their commond linkis next adjacent to the Wattir of Eddin,' and confirming the 'rycht and possessioun, propirtie and communite of the saidis linkis in . . . playing at golff, futball, schuteing at all gamis with all other maner of pastime . . . without ony dykin or closing of ony pairt thairof fra thame or impediment to be maid to thame theirintill in ony tyme coming.' It will be noted that this is not an original grant, merely a confirmation of rights already established by long usage. Thirty years later the register of St Andrews Kirk Session shows the two sons of Alexander Miller, in defiance of their father's orders, along with Nicholl Mane, William Bruce, 'and utheris, thair complices,' being brought up for playing 'in the golf feildis, tyme of fast and precheing, aganis the ordinances of the Kirk.'

Ratifications similar to those by Archbishop Hamilton were granted by Archbishop Gladstanes in 1614, and by James VI a few years later. The subsequent history of the links is easily traced by the various Instruments of Sasine, from which it appears that in 1797 the lands of Pilmor and Pilmor Links were sold under the powers contained in a bond in favour of Robert Gourlay and John Gunn, merchants in St Andrews, and passed from the possession of the town into that of Mr Thomas Erskine, of Cambo. The price was £805. The ground to the eastwards of the Swilcan was reserved from the disposition, and there was a declaration that the proprietor should be bound not 'to plough up any part of said golf links in all time coming,' but to reserve them 'as it has been in times past for the comfort and amusement of the inhabitants and others who shall resort thither for that amusement.'

That above everything else is the amazing thing about St Andrews. For more than four hundred years every golfer in the world who cared 'to resort thither for that amusement' enjoyed a legal right to play over the course. It was already the world's golf heritage centuries before it became the headquarters of the game.

This Arcadian state of things still existed even within my own recollection. At the beginning of the present century a younger brother and I took advantage of a school 'Spring Holiday' to go through to St Andrews to make our first acquaintance with the classic course. It was not a holiday at St Andrews, and on our way down from the railway station to the links we found the city strangely quiet and deserted. However, we came across a solitary policeman and asked him to tell us just what we had to do to be allowed to play over the course. His answer, 'Ye 've nothing to dae and nothing to pay; ye just tee up and drive off,' still seems to me the acme of golfing hospitality!

It is true that in more recent times the visitor who wishes to play over the Old Course has to pay a green fee just as he would elsewhere, and during the four summer months has to take his chance in a ballot for starting times, and that during August and September certain times are reserved for the members of the Royal and Ancient Club. But these restrictions were only introduced in order to provide some method of regulating the increasing traffic the course was being called upon to bear, and it took a special Act of Parliament to legalize them.

One of the first and most important results of the substitution of St Andrews for Leith as the recognized capital of golf was the adoption of eighteen holes as the recognized round. In the first half of the nineteenth century the rules still varied to some extent on different courses, and even in such matters as the number of holes in the round there was no recognized practice, the figure varying from the five of the original Leith lay-out to the twenty-five of Montrose. If Leith had remained the chief centre of the game, golf might have become a sterner and more monotonous business than it is to-day, for the Leith course was primarily a test of hard hitting; its five holes measured 414, 461, 426, 495, and 435 yards; three turns of the five holes made the recognized round, and holes in five with a feathery ball were almost as rare as holes in one to-day. The round at Blackheath was laid out in imitation of that at Leith, and when the Leith course was extended to seven holes, Blackheath in 1844 followed suit, the length of the seven holes being 170 yards, 335, 380, 540, 500, 230, and 410, a total of 2,565 yards, equivalent to close on 6,500 yards on an eighteen-hole round. The five-hole course had avoided the gravel pits, which in those days, Mr Hughes tells us, were still being worked; in the seven-hole course every hole except the sixth called for a carry over one or other of the pits before the green was reached.   The course as laid out in 1844 remained practically unchanged until play on the Common was abandoned and the Royal Blackheath Club, by amalgamation with the Eltham Club, removed to its present beautiful home at Eltham.

At this time North Berwick also had seven holes, and when the London Scottish Volunteers in 1865 obtained permission from Earl Spencer to lay out a course on Wimbledon Common, they at first followed the example of Blackheath.   Seven would have been in a fair way to being established as the 'correct' number of holes for a first-class course, had it not been for the example of St Andrews.

At St Andrews itself the adoption of the round of eighteen holes was purely arbitrary and even purely accidental.   Originally both St Andrews and Prestwick, its great rival of the west, had twelve holes.   The round dozen, in fact, seems a natural number to adopt for such a purpose, but the 'round' worked out very differently at the two places, owing to the difference in the lay-out of the ground. At Prestwick the shape of the course was vaguely circular, in the sense that it worked round to the point from which the game started. Three rounds of the links, or thirty-six holes, provided a good day's golf, and later became the test adopted for the first years of the Open Championship when it was instituted at Prestwick.

At St Andrews, however, the twelve holes were laid out in a strip along the shore, running out to the Eden.   The golfers struck off from beside the home hole and played eleven holes out to the far end of the course, then turned and played eleven holes home, playing to the same holes as on the outward journey, but in the reverse direction, and finished off by holing out at the home hole from which they started.   At this time, therefore, the round at St Andrews consisted of twenty-two holes.   In 1764, however, the Royal and Ancient Club passed a resolution that the four first holes should be converted into two, and as this change automatically converted the same four holes into two on the road in, the 'round' was reduced from twenty-two holes to eighteen.

It was not until long afterwards that the St Andrews golfers discovered the advisability of having separate fairways and greens for the outward and homeward journeys.   Indeed it is to the peculiar arrangement of the famous course that we owe the familiar phrases 'out' and 'home.'   In the case of the modern inland course laid out in two 'loops' of nine holes the words 'out' and 'home' are not particularly appropriate to the two halves of the round.   But at St Andrews in the old days the terms were perfectly applicable. The 'Long Hole Out' then traversed the same fairway as the 'Long Hole In'—the ground occupied by the present fourteenth.   And the same at all the other holes.   One would think that there must occasionally have been 'wigs on the green' when two matches arrived simultaneously at the same holes from opposite directions. But players were fewer in those days, and four-ball matches, perhaps happily, unknown.

CHAPTER TEN
(1681–1833)

The Evolution of the Caddie

ONE of the few golfing terms whose derivation appears to admit of no dispute is the title given to the henchman who carries our clubs. The word 'caddie' is merely the Scottish spelling of the French *cadet*, meaning a little chief, a title originally given to the younger sons of the French nobility who came to Edinburgh as pages in the train of Mary Queen of Scots. Later on the designation was applied by Scottish sarcasm to the hangers-on who in the eighteenth century loafed about the streets of Edinburgh, ready to run errands or do any sort of odd jobs; and so 'caddie' came to mean a porter, long before its application began to be restricted to the particular kind of porter who carries the golfer's clubs.

The first caddie whose name has come down to us was one Andrew Dickson, who caddied for the Duke of York, afterwards James II, in 1681 and 1682, when the duke was residing in Edinburgh, and was wont to beguile the cares of state with a round on the Links of Leith. 'I remember in my youth,' says Mr Tytler, of Woodhouselee (*Transactions of the Society of Antiquaries of Scotland*, p. 504), 'to have often conversed with an old man named Andrew Dickson, a golf club maker, who said that when a boy he used to carry the Duke's golf clubs, and to run before him and announce where the balls fell.'

If Dickson was the duke's regular caddie, it is more than probable that he assisted in the famous first International foursome, when the duke and John Patersone, the Edinburgh shoemaker, defeated the two English noblemen. At any rate, there seems little reason to doubt that he is the same Dickson who is honoured in Mathison's poem of *The Goff*, published in 1743:

> Of finest ash, *Castalio's* shaft was made;
> Pondrous with lead, and fenced with horn the head,
> (The work of *Dickson*, who in *Letha* dwells,
> And in the art of making clubs excels).

64

'Letha,' it need hardly be explained, is the mock-heroic version of Leith.

In the seventeenth century the caddie was merely 'the boy who carried my Lord's clubbes to the field.' He is so described in the household accounts of 'the Great Marquess' of Montrose, in 1628, and similarly in the accounts of Sir John Foulis, of Ravelston, for 1672, in which we find an item recording the payment of four shillings 'to the boy who carried my clubs.' It seems an extravagant sum for those days, but the accounts are, of course, in Scots money, so that the caddie's fee was equivalent to fourpence.

Caddies' fees, as a matter of fact, were not raised very noticeably during the next century or so. The minutes of the Royal and Ancient Club, under date 27th June 1771, record that 'the captain and company agree and appoint that in time coming the caddies who carry the clubs or run before the players, or are otherwise employed by the gentlemen golfers, are to get fourpence sterling for going the length of the hole called The Hole of Cross, and if they go further than that hole they are to get sixpence, and no more. Any of the gentlemen transgressing this rule are to pay two pint bottles of claret at the first meeting they shall attend.'

In between those two dates, 1672 and 1771, 'the boy who carries the clubs' had become 'the caddie.' But even now, to the purists of golfing speech there is no verb 'to caddie.' Your henchman at St Andrews does not undertake to 'caddie' for you, but to 'carry' for you. The word 'carry,' however, is used in the same purely technical sense, as is shown by the famous retort of the caddie whose employer had left a jacket in the clubhouse and wanted his caddie to go back for it: 'Go back for it yersel'! I'm paid to carry—no' to fetch and carry!'

The caddie in golf occupies a position accorded to the attendants in no other game and paralleled only by the relationship of squire to knight in the lists. The caddie is recognized by the rules of the game as part of the 'side.' He is the only person from whom the 'side' may ask advice as to the club to take, or the shot to play, and on the other hand his sins of omission or commission—accidentally interfering with an opponent's ball, or the like—involve the same penalties as if they had been committed by the player himself.

In the golden age of golf the regular *habitués* of the links each had his own recognized caddie. Captain Maitland Dougall, a famous winner of medal competitions at St Andrews, would have been lost without Sandy Pirie to administer encouragement and advice. Nobody ever saw Sandy try a shot himself, but he knew every inch of the course as well as every strong point and every foible of his employer's game. Sandy Herd, grandfather of the later Sandy who was the first to win the Open Championship with the rubber-cored ball, was the henchman of Mr John Whyte-Melville, who for nearly three-quarters of a century played two rounds of golf three days a week all through the year. Whyte-Melville was notorious for his prolonged 'waggle' when addressing the ball, and it is possible that the younger Sandy, another confirmed waggler, was only carrying on a family tradition acquired from imitating his grandfather's patron. Old Bob Kirk always carried for Campbell of Saddell, 'Anera' Strath for old Sutherland, and so on.

In some cases, no doubt, the faithfulness of the henchman was apt to wear a little thin. There is a tale of a famous Scottish law lord who had to rebuke his regular caddie for getting drunk and failing to turn up on the appointed day. 'You know that Wednesday is my day,' he said, 'and I expect you always to keep it for me.' 'Weel, my lord,' was the retort, 'I never heard of but ae lord that has a day of his ain, and I dinna keep it. And I'm daumned if I'm going to keep yours!'

The caddie, nevertheless, was the forerunner of the modern professional, and in the middle of last century he united the duties of club-bearer and coach. A 'professional' meant a professional caddie, and these caddies were the only instructors in the game, with the inevitable result that the caddies were apt to regard the 'side' as a two-man team in which the player was the executant and the caddie the non-playing captain. To this period belong such stories as that of the caddie who handed his employer his cleek for the tee-shot to the short eleventh hole at St Andrews, and then interrupted him at the top of his swing with a frenzied cry of 'Stoap! stoap! I have decided to play the shoat with my iron.'

The modern golfer may describe his caddie as 'something between a hindrance and a help' and complain that he seems to know everything about golf and nothing whatever about caddying, but in the old days he was his patron's guide, philosopher, and friend, his instructor when he was off his game, and co-arbiter with the opposition caddie in all disputes. Who does not recall with pleasure the story of 'Big Crawford's' summing up of the dispute about the mushroom in the great match in which Ben Sayers and David Grant beat Andrew and Hugh Kirkaldy: 'Well, it's the rule o' the game, an''—lifting up a fist like a leg of mutton—'here's the referee!' A very partisan referee it would have been, for in talking of their brave battle afterwards, Crawford used always to ask: 'D'ye ken who really won that match?' and then with a thump of his fist on his great chest: 'Me!'

Except in matches of the very first importance the caddies had usually to be stewards as well as referees, though golf galleries in those days did not attain the numbers that they do to-day. There is a tale of a caddie, a well-known character in Edinburgh, who commenced proceedings at one important match by addressing the crowd on the propriety of 'keepin' weel back off the greens, and giein' the players elby room.' But as hole after hole was played and the contest grew more and more exciting, the gallery on successive greens tended to draw closer and closer in around the pin, until the holing of a ticklish four-yard putt at the ninth found the eager spectators giving vent to a ringing cheer almost in the player's face. The irritated caddie swung round like a flash, and gripping the ear of the nearest offender—a magistrate, no less, of his own town—forced his head down close to the hole. 'D'ye see it now?' he bellowed to the struggling victim. 'There's nae doot the ba's in the hole. But if ye're still jubious, stick yer inqueesitive nose farrer in, an' ye'll feel it.' After such a tableau, it is hardly necessary to add that for the remainder of the round the gallery was on its best behaviour.

It is fairly late in the history of the game before we catch a glimpse of the caddie as a player. Carnegie's famous poem, *Golfiana*, published in 1833, declared that

> ... Davie, oldest of the cads,
> Who gives *half-one* to unsuspicious lads,
> When he might give them *two* or *even more*
> And win, perhaps, three matches out of four,

Is just as politic in his affairs,
As Talleyrand or Metternich in *theirs*,
He has the statesman's elements, 'tis plain,
Cheat, flatter, humbug—*anything* for gain.

This 'Davie' was David Robertson, father of the immortal Allan. A later reference in the same poem makes it clear that the elder Robertson was himself in request both as a player and as a teacher. Yet he was merely a senior caddie, 'the oldest of the cads'; the status of the 'professional' had not yet been invented. It is true that it was not unknown for a Club to have a special 'officer to the Club,' but he was no more than a uniformed caddie, whose duties were to 'carry' for the captain of the Club on important occasions. The date of the transition from the status of senior caddie to professional is fairly clearly defined. David Robertson was the last of the senior caddies, his son Allan the first of the great professionals.

Even up to the time of the Second World War, however, the older caddies at the great golf centres like St Andrews and North Berwick continued to regard themselves as very distinctly the brains of a two-man side. On one occasion when Rex Hartley, the English Walker Cup player, won the Silver Tassie at Gleneagles, he brought his St Andrews caddie over to carry for him. At one hole towards the finish, Hartley asked for his spoon, saying that he thought he could get nicely home with a shot cut up into the wind. But the caddie had no use for any fancy shots that might spoil what looked like a winning score. 'Ye 'll tak' yer iron,' he said, 'and hit it straight! What dae ye think ye 're playing in? A pantomime?' Hartley accepted the rebuke along with the iron, and went on to turn in a winning score.

CHAPTER ELEVEN
(1815–1859)

The First of the Invincibles

PROFESSIONAL golf as we now understand it may be said to have begun with the appearance on the stage of the great Allan Robertson, the first of the great professional *players*. Although his father, the David referred to in the previous chapter, is remembered chiefly as a caddie, the family was of old standing in St Andrews as a firm of ball-makers. In Mathison's well-known poem of *The Goff*, first published in 1743, the rival players are made to tee

> two balls with careful eye,
> That with *Clarinda's* breasts for colour vye,
> The work of *Bobson* who, with matchless art,
> Shapes the firm hide, connecting every part,
> Then in a socket sets the well-stitch'd void
> And thro' the eyelet drives the downy tide;
> Crowds urging crowds the forceful brogue impels,
> The feathers harden and the leather swells;
> He crams and sweats, yet crams and urges more
> Till scarce the turgid globe contains its store . . .
> Soon as *Hyperion* gilds old *Andrea's* spires
> From bed the artist to his cell retires;
> With bended back, there plies his steely awls,
> And shapes and stuffs and finishes the balls.

It cannot be doubted that the poetical Bobson who lived in the shade of Andrea's spires became in everyday prose a Robertson who lived at St Andrews. That balls of his making should be chosen by both the players in a match at Leith shows that he must have been eminently successful in his art. If the lines which follow those we have quoted are to be understood in anything like a literal sense, he had also some skill as a musician.

However that may be, the passage of a century found the Robertsons still established as ball-makers at St Andrews. Peter

Robertson died in 1803, leaving issue David, 'the oldest of the cads' already mentioned in G. F. Carnegie's poem, which apparently refers to a date about 1823. Ten years later in *Another Peep at the Links* the same poet laments the demise of those named in the earlier lay, and among them

> Great Davie Robertson, the eldest cad,
> In whom the good was stronger then the bad;
> He sleeps in death, and with him sleeps a skill,
> Which Davie, statesmanlike, could wield at will!
> Sound be his slumbers! yet if he should wake
> In worlds where golf is played, himself he'd shake,
> And look about, and tell each young beginner,
> 'I'll gie half-ane—nae mair, as I'm a sinner.'
> He leaves a son, and Allan is his name,
> In golfing, far beyond his father's fame;
> Tho' in diplomacy, I shrewdly guess
> His skill's inferior, and his fame is less.

It may be fairly presumed that the poet thought none the less of Allan that he lacked the skill in sharp practice of that artful old diplomat, his father. But even Allan was not without guile. Old Tom Morris described him once as 'an awfu' player, Allan, the cunningest bit body of a player that ever handled club, cleek, or putter. A kindly body, wi' just a wealth o' sly, pawky fun about him.' Kindliness and pawkiness combined to make him an adept at nursing his matches against amateur opponents and just 'snodd'n them at the Burn'—i.e. at the seventeenth. By such a narrow victory he avoided wounding his opponents' pride, and at the same time made it impossible for them to ask for increased odds at the next encounter!

The finest tribute to 'the first of the Champions' is the oft-quoted article which appeared in the *Dundee Advertiser* at the time of his death, in September 1859, and which is still so full of interest that we must reprint a portion of it here:

Allan Robertson, the greatest golf-player that ever lived, of whom alone in the annals of the pastime it can be said that he never was beaten, was born at St Andrews on the 11th September 1815. . . . It is a fact that his very playthings as a child were golf clubs. As he grew up, his natural tendency, joined to a natural desire of his father that his son should continue the business of ball-maker, decided Allan's profession, and in due course of time he likewise took up the awl and the feathers to learn the manufacture of golf-balls. . . .

Who will ever forget Allan, having once seen him? What Sir Hugh Lyon-Playfair has been to the city proper, has Allan been to the Links of St Andrews. They have unwittingly been in close partnership. Sir Hugh renovated a rough ruined street; Allan had an eye the while to the improvement of the Links. Sir Hugh attracted citizens, Allan golfers; ah! it was a magnificent partnership and has done wonders. The analogy holds good between the two in other respects. Who could do the honours of the Links like Allan? He was as perfectly at home with a descendant of William the Conqueror as with one of the caddies. Without the least tinge of servility, Allan could accommodate himself to everybody and arranged everything on the Links with the politeness of a Brummel and the policy of a Talleyrand.

His coolness was unique, and almost miraculous. He was never known to funk or, indeed, change his offhand manner in the least. He was never beaten—proud epitaph! It is something to be the best in anything of all the world, and Allan stood confessed the model player.

All the accounts of him pay tribute to his easy and graceful style, and to his scientific accuracy of, his 'placing' of, his shots, which steered him clear of the gorse and other trouble which beset the narrow fairways in a fashion undreamed of to-day. He was not a long driver; off the tee, as Dr Macpherson assures us, he could not hold a candle to Willie Dunn, but his quarter strokes were deadly and his putting was irreproachable. He was at his best, of course, at St Andrews, for which his style of play was designed. On a rougher links, like Musselburgh, his long and exceptionally light clubs were at something of a disadvantage. The strength of his game lay in the avoidance of mistakes. Below the middle height, thickset and short-necked, he was an example of the perfect golfing temperament, a mixture of imperturbable pluck and good humour. He had above all the same capacity for pulling out the little bit extra in a crisis as you find among modern golfers in such 'bonny fighters' as Walter Hagen and Ben Hogan.

Who can forget the story of Allan's great shot at the dangerous Road Hole, in a foursome for a heavy stake in which he partnered Mr Erskine against Willie Park and Mr Hastie at St Andrews in

1853? At the end of the third and last round of the match the latter pair were one up with two holes to go. Campbell of Saddell offered £15 to £5 on Park and Mr Hastie, and the case of the other pair seemed hopeless when Park got nicely on the green, and Mr Erskine, playing the odd, put Allan on the road. But Allan, playing the two more, studied his path with the same care as I have seen Walter Hagen do in a similar crisis, and pitched his ball on the top footpath within a fraction of an inch of the spot which he had indicated as his mark. Nor were his calculations less exact than his aim, for the ball trickled down the slope and into the hole. If ever there was a shot that turned the tide of battle this was it, for Mr Hastie went bald-headed for the hole and ran a yard and a half past, and Park was unforgivably short with the return, so that Allan and his partner won the hole that seemed irretrievably lost. What was worse, Park, in his vexation, topped the ball off the eighteenth tee into the Burn, with the result that his side lost that hole as well, and with it the match.

Allan's most famous matches were against the brothers Dunn, of Musselburgh and later of Blackheath. In 1843, Allan beat Willie Dunn in a stupendous match of twenty rounds (360 holes) by two rounds and one to play, and six years later Allan and Tom Morris sen. defeated Willie and Jamie Dunn in a great match for £400 over St Andrews and Musselburgh, the home greens of the respective sides, and North Berwick. At Musselburgh the brothers won an easy victory by 13 and 12, Allan and Tom squared the account with a narrow victory at St Andrews, but on the neutral course they were trailing all the way, until they stood four down with eight to go. In this crisis, however, the St Andrews pair displayed the greater steadiness and drew level with the last two holes to play. At the seventeenth a fine drive by Tom Morris found a wretchedly bad lie, and Allan and he were bunkered beside the green in four. But in the meantime the Dunns had hooked their second shot into a still worse lie behind a boulder at the left of the green. An account by a spectator (Mr H. T. Peters) describes the Dunns as having by this time lost all judgment and nerve, and hacking recklessly at the ball, instead of knocking it backwards. Allan and Tom won both that hole and the last—another example of victory snatched out of the fire by tenacity rather than skill.

'THE KOLFER GIRDS
HIS ICE-SPURS ON'

(From a seventeenth-
century print by Romayn
de Hooghe.) Note the
post on the left of the
print and the huge size
of the *kolven* balls,
showing that the game
as played on ice was
much the same as the
courtyard game.

(From an old Dutch
encaustic tile.)

From an etching by Rembrandt dated 1654, and frequently referred to as 'The Golfer'. It depicts the interior of an inn; through the open doorway is visible a figure playing *kolven* in the court outside.

Allan also enjoyed the distinction of being the first player to 'break 80' for St Andrews links, doing a 79 in a round with Mr Bethune, of Blebo, in 1858. In this match Allan was giving heavy odds and went out for everything to give himself a chance.

The claim of never having been beaten put forward in his 'proud epitaph,' is not, I think, to be taken quite to the foot of the letter. He and Tom Morris never met in a big match, but Morris seems to have beaten him in two small encounters, once by 3 and 2 in an eighteen-hole match for a small sum put up in 1853 by Mr William Hamilton, of Cairnhill, and again in a contest for a red coat presented by Mr Wolfe Murray. But these bye-battles between old partners are hardly to be taken seriously, for it must be remembered that the pair were in a sense mentor and pupil. Tom Morris served under Allan four years as an apprentice and five years as a journeyman before starting up as a clubmaker on his own account, and it was during this period that he took part in the big match against the Dunns.

Allan also lost a curious 'freak' match to James Condie, a famous Perth amateur of his day, father of the George Condie who won the Amateur Championship of 1859 at St Andrews. James Condie and Tom Patton, of Glenalmond, had beaten Sir John Muir Mackenzie and Allan in a foursome challenge match, and at dinner afterwards Condie teased Allan by suggesting that the latter had 'a lot of good clubs with a very poor player behind them.' The upshot was that the amateur pitted himself against Allan in a match in which each time a player lost a hole he had to give up one of his clubs to his opponent. Mr Condie, an irrepressible humorist, put Allan completely off his game, with the result that Allan quickly began to forfeit his clubs, and thereby, of course, became the more handicapped for the rest of the match. When they came to the last tee Allan had only his driver and his putter left. He lost the hole and had to give up the driver. And then Condie insisted on playing an extra hole to see what Allan could do with the putter alone! He lost hole and putter, and in spite of all that Allan could say his clubs had to remain, at least for that night, in Perth.

Allan's lasting contribution to the game was his introduction of the use of iron clubs for approach play. Although he had resisted the introduction of the gutta-percha ball, under the impression that it would take away the ball-makers' livelihood, he was quick to realize the difference the less lively ball made in the technique of the game. 'Before Allan's day,' says Dr Macpherson, 'the baffing spoon was the weapon of approach to the hole if a bunker intervened . . . but Allan introduced the deadly "iron" which he wrought with marvellous accuracy.' In the days of the feathery, the iron clubs—cleeks and niblicks—had been designed for hacking the ball out of bad lies. Their greater angle of loft, however, made them specially adapted for use with the 'guttie,' which had to be 'clipped' up to get it into the air. The abandonment of the wooden putter must also be attributed to Allan, who set the example of using the cleek for long green approaches, only reverting to his wooden putter when he had some specially precarious putt to hole.

CHAPTER TWELVE
(1857–1861)

The Start of the Championships

THE golden age of private matches was brought to an end by the inauguration of the first Championships in the middle of the nineteenth century. The whole credit for this development belongs to the Prestwick Club, and the history of championship golf really begins with a letter sent out by that club to seven other leading clubs on 6th April 1857. The letter read as follows:

It is proposed to play a match at golf between the eight undermentioned clubs:

St Andrews, Perth, Musselburgh, Blackheath, Prestwick, Carnoustie, North Berwick, Leven, each Club to send four members to contend. The Game to be played in double Matches, or Foursomes, drawing for opponents by lot before starting, and again after each game by the winners. The remaining winning pair to be considered the champions. The Prize for this competition to be a Medal, or other piece of Plate purchased at the expense of the competing Clubs in proportion to the number of members in each. At the conclusion of the playing by pairs, the winning pair will compete for the prize in a single match, the Winner to become the Possessor.

The game to be played at St Andrews or Prestwick during the Summer Meeting.

If your Club consents to play in this Match will you be kind enough to inform me at your earliest convenience, at the same time naming which of the two links you prefer, as the Majority will decide.

Etc., etc.,

JOHN CUTHBERT.

The response was immediate and enthusiastic. All the clubs named accepted the invitation, and in addition the Honourable Company, Edinburgh Burgess, Bruntsfield, Montrose, and Dirleton Castle expressed a desire to compete, making thirteen entries in all. The total seems small, but a golf manual published in the same year gives what purports to be a complete list of Scottish golf clubs, which at that time apparently numbered only nineteen, so there is no reason to think that the entry was in any way incomplete. The Prestwick club appointed a committee of four to manage the tournament, with power to add to their numbers, the four being Mr Whyte-Melville, Mr O. G. Campbell, Mr (afterwards Sir) Robert Hay, and Mr J. O. Fairlie. It will be seen that the committee was perfectly representative, Whyte-Melville being mainly associated with St Andrews and Robert Hay with North Berwick. Various modifications of the original plan were adopted—for instance, the number of players was reduced to one foursome pair from each club. The wishes of the majority fixed on St Andrews as the scene of the tournament, and it was duly carried through on the last three days of July 1857. The Honourable Company and Carnoustie Panmure failed to find a team, and eleven clubs fought out the tournament. The prize was a silver claret jug, engraved with two golfing subjects, and bears the following inscription:

Won by

GEORGE GLENNIE

and

LIEUT. J. C. STEWART

members of the

ROYAL BLACKHEATH

GOLF CLUB

at the

FIRST GOLF

TOURNAMENT

held at

ST ANDREWS, FIFE

in the year

1857

Twenty-Two Competitors

George Glennie and Lieutenant Stewart, who were both well-known St Andrews players, were made life members of the Royal Blackheath Club in recognition of their success. A card printed by the Club to commemorate their victory records the result of the play as follows:

I

Royal Blackheath beat Royal Perth by eight holes.
Edinburgh Burgess beat Montrose Royal Albert by twelve holes.
Edinburgh Bruntsfield beat Prestwick by three holes.
Royal and Ancient St Andrews beat Dirleton Castle by ten holes.
Innerleven beat Musselburgh by two holes.
North Berwick, a Bye.

II

Royal Blackheath beat Innerleven by twelve holes.
Edinburgh Burgess and Edinburgh Bruntsfield played a Tie.
Royal and Ancient St Andrews beat North Berwick by four holes.

III

Royal Blackheath beat Edinburgh Bruntsfield by six holes.
Royal and Ancient St Andrews beat Edinburgh Burgess by three holes.

IV

The Royal Blackheath Golf Club beat The Royal and Ancient St Andrews Golf Club by seven holes.

Two points about the method of play deserve special attention. In the first place, each match was played out over the full eighteen holes, regardless of the fact that the result, as far as winning or losing was concerned, might be determined several holes from home. Secondly, no workable plan had been arrived at for playing off halved matches, and they adopted the quaint and unscientific system —still amazingly preserved in the knock-out tournaments of the Royal and Ancient Club—of passing both contestants in a halved match into the next round. This plan created no difficulty in this first tournament, in which the only halved match was that between Edinburgh Burgess and Edinburgh Bruntsfield in the second round, but the defects of the system were emphasized by the curious result of the tournament of the following year when the ultimate winner defeated his first-round opponent by 3 and 1, and thereafter reached the final by means of three halved matches and two byes!

For this second Championship Meeting in 1858 the idea of Club Foursomes was abandoned in favour of an individual contest, and the event, which attracted an entry of twenty-eight, followed much the same lines as the present Amateur Championship.   The winner was Robert Chambers, the famous publisher.   At this time he was a youth of twenty and the youngest player in the tournament, for which he had entered from the Bruntsfield Club.   His opponent in the final, D. Wallace, of Leven, was over sixty and the oldest player in the field.   The pair had already met in the fourth and fifth rounds, but each time had finished square—though in the fifth round Chambers had to fight hard to draw level after being four down with five to play.   These, however, were Wallace's only halved matches and he beat four opponents on his way to the final.

Wallace was a notoriously slow player—so that the slow-motion champion was a problem even a hundred years ago.   Dr J. G. Macpherson, in his *Golf and Golfers*, says of him:

Old Wallace would have carried the championship at the final tussle of the first tournament by his wearisome style, had not Robert Chambers's temper been particularly easy-going.   'Give me a novel and a camp-stool, and I'll let the old chap do as he likes,' was his remark when pitted against the slowcoach.

Another famous publisher, Robert Clark, the editor of *Golf: A Royal and Ancient Game*, was one of the favourites in the following year, but in the third round he was beaten by the hope of the Perth golfers, George Condie, in a match which hung long in the balance but eventually ended in Condie's favour by four holes.   Condie's opponent in the final was Robert Hay, who was one of the finest golfers of the day, but Condie was at the top of his form and won the Championship by 6 and 5.   Condie was a long driver.   'Splendidly built, with an irreproachable style,' declares the historian of *Golf in Perth and Perthshire*, 'he had a full swing of great power. He was exceptionally good with the baffy.'

In 1860, the Prestwick Club, with the Amateur Championship apparently well established, turned its thoughts to the inauguration of a similar event for professionals.   The death of the invincible Allan Robertson in the previous year had left the golf world with no recognized leading player and the time seemed appropriate for the suggestion put forward by Major J. O. Fairlie at the Spring Meeting of the Club on 30th May 1860 that 'a private subscription should be opened with a view to procure a Medal for professionals to be competed for under regulations submitted to the meeting.' The sum of five guineas was subscribed right away in the room, but hope of support from other Clubs was not realized and in the end the Prestwick Club took the whole responsibility for the event on its own shoulders. A Challenge Belt, of red morocco, richly ornamented with massive silver plates, and costing what in those days was the handsome sum of thirty guineas, was substituted for the proposed medal. The conditions provided that the trophy was to become the absolute property of any player winning it three years in succession.

The first meeting took place on Wednesday, 17th October 1860, being decided over three rounds of the twelve-hole Prestwick links. Only eight players entered for the event, and the final scores read:

Willie Park (Musselburgh)	174
Tom Morris (Prestwick)	176
Andrew Strath (St Andrews)	180
Bob Andrew (Perth)	191
Daniel Brown (Blackheath)	192
Charlie Hunter (Prestwick St Nicholas)	195
Alex Smith (Bruntsfield)	196
William Steel (Bruntsfield)	232

This first contest for the Challenge Belt is commonly spoken of as the first Open Championship, but it will be realized from the foregoing account that this is not strictly correct. The meeting of 1860 was open to professionals only. This restriction, however, was removed in the following year. Possibly the poor scoring of the 1860 meeting had inspired some of the amateurs with the illusory conviction that they could do every bit as well as the pros. At the Spring Meeting of the Club on 16th May 1861, Major Fairlie proposed 'that the Challenge Belt be opened to be played for by gentlemen players, members of the following Clubs: St Andrews, Honourable Company of Edinburgh Golfers, North Berwick, Prestwick, Blackheath, Carnoustie, Perth, and Leven.' This was unanimously carried, but it is not hard to imagine that such a decision must have evoked all sorts of indignant protests from the Clubs excluded from this arbitrary selection.   At any rate at a committee meeting of the Prestwick Club on 25th September 1861, on the eve of the second contest for the Belt, 'it was unanimously resolved that the Challenge Belt to be played for to-morrow and on all future occasions until it be otherwise resolved, shall be open to all the world.'   That resolution is still the Open Championship charter!   Altered conditions have necessitated altered regulations, but in principle the Open Championship is still open to all the world.

THE FIRST GREEN AT ST. ANDREWS IN 1798
(Reproduced from the well-known etching by Frank Paton, by permission of the publishers, Messrs. Leggatt Bros., of 30 St. James's St., London, S.W.1.

THE PROCESSION OF THE SILVER CLUB

The Edinburgh town crier and his drummers intimating the date of the competition for the Silver Club of the Leith golfers.

(After a drawing by David Allan in 1787.)

This famous portrait by Sir George Chalmers, of William St. Clair of Roslin, captain of the Honourable Company of Edinburgh Golfers, 1761, 1766, 1770, and 1771, is now the property of the Royal Company of Scottish Archers.

CHAPTER THIRTEEN
(1860–1890)

The First Thirty Years of the Open

THE meagre entry of eight professionals for the first contest for the Championship Belt in 1860 was not notably increased during the next few years, and the Open Championship might have faded out just as the earlier Amateur Championship had done, had it not been for the interest excited by the rivalry between 'Old Tom' Morris and the elder Willie Park. Of the first eight Championships Morris won four and Park three, their monopoly of the title being interrupted only by the victory of Andrew Strath in 1865, the sixth year of the event. In these eight years Park was runner-up four times, Morris twice. At the age of eighteen Morris began a four years' apprenticeship with Allan Robertson as a club-maker, and was with him for another five as a journeyman, this being the period of their great matches as a foursome partnership. In 1851 Major J. O. Fairlie, of Coodham, got him to come to Prestwick as custodian of the newly established links, and so when the Championship was established at Prestwick in 1860, Morris was the 'local pro.' representing the West of Scotland, against Willie Park, from Musselburgh, representing the East. Of the two, Park was the more brilliant shot-maker, but he was given to taking unnecessary risks, as in the second championship, which he lost, according to the account in the *Ayrshire Express*, owing to 'a daring attempt to cross the Alps[1] in two, which brought his ball into one of the worst hazards of the green and cost him three strokes, by no means the first occasion on which he has been seriously punished for similar avarice and temerity.' He had neither the steadiness of Morris nor the stamina to stand up to prolonged bouts of play, and though he beat Morris heavily in the first challenge match in which the pair engaged, Morris in the long run had the better of their many encounters, the most notable being the series of 1862 in which he

[1] At the second hole of the round as then laid out, now the seventeenth.

defeated Park on all the four courses of Musselburgh, Prestwick, North Berwick, and St Andrews.   Although 'Old Tom's' fourth championship (in 1867) was gained after his return from Prestwick to St Andrews, he was never again quite so formidable a player as he had been in his Prestwick days, but he continued to play in the Open Championship until 1896, by which time he was seventy-five.   He was head greenkeeper at St Andrews for forty years, and died there at the age of eighty-seven, respected throughout the golfing world for the sterling qualities that had earned him the reputation of the Nestor of the game.

In skill as a player, however, he was completely outshone by his son, universally known as 'Young Tom,' who was unquestionably one of the greatest golfers of all time.   Born at St Andrews in 1851, 'Young Tom' was only thirteen when he won an exhibition match at Perth for a prize of £5 against William Greig, a local boy prodigy. At sixteen he won a big tournament at Carnoustie from a first-class professional field after a play-off with Willie Park and Bob Andrew of Perth.   In the Open Championship of the same year he finished fourth, but in the following summer at the age of seventeen he won the first of four successive victories—a record that has never been equalled before or since.   It is difficult to compare the performances of one generation with those of another, but two points about 'Young Tom's' record are worth noting.   His superiority over his contemporaries is shown by the margin of two of his victories— eleven strokes in 1869, twelve strokes in 1870, a big gap for a thirty-six holes contest.   Then, although scores in the Open Champion-ship have tended gradually to become lower and lower as the years go on, the score of 149 by which 'Young Tom' made the Champion-ship Belt his own property—an average of 74½ per round—*was never equalled*, not even by Vardon, Taylor, or Braid, so long as the Championship continued to be played with the 'guttie' ball—not in fact until Jack White's victory at Sandwich thirty-four years later.   He was only twenty-four, and at the height of his golfing powers, when the death of his young wife in childbirth dealt him a blow from which he never recovered.   He died on Christmas Day of the same year.

His contemporaries all speak of his style as lacking the smooth sweetness that characterized his great friend and rival, David Strath, but probably this means no more than that he did not take the club round with the fullness and freedom of the typical 'St Andrews swing.' It is acknowledged that his broad shoulders gave him tremendous power, that he had an amazing gift of playing full shots from bad lies, which were then more frequent than they are to-day, and that his quarter shots and putting were deadly. His game was marred by no weakness of any kind. He carried Allan Robertson's technique a stage further by introducing the use of the niblick—which became the later 'mashie' or No. 5 iron—for approach shots, which he played with an open stance instead of in the older fashion with the ball nearer the left foot.

In another respect his victories did a great deal of good to golf. By winning the Belt for the third consecutive year at the age of nineteen he made it his own property, and the whole scheme of the running of the Open Championship had to be brought under review. It had at no point been the intention of the Prestwick Club that they should undertake the sole management of the Championship or that it should be played always on their course, but their efforts to secure the support of other Clubs had met with no encouragement. The necessity of providing a new championship trophy, however, presented an opportunity for a fresh effort, and after an interregnum of a year—there being no championship in 1871—the Royal and Ancient Club and the Honourable Company of Edinburgh Golfers joined with the Prestwick Club in subscribing for the Silver Cup which became the permanent trophy of the event, each winner receiving a gold medal, and the three Clubs undertook the management of the Championship, which was to be played in rotation over Prestwick, St Andrews, and Musselburgh. The last-named green was then at the height of its prosperity, for not only the Honourable Company, but also the Bruntsfield Links and Edinburgh Burgess golfers, had removed to it when the Leith and Bruntsfield greens fell into disuse. At Prestwick in 1872 the first contest for the Cup, like the first contest for the Belt, attracted only eight entrants, and gave 'Young Tom' his fourth successive victory. But the introduction of a rota of courses had the immediate result of attracting a larger field, and the first contest at St Andrews in 1873 was contested by the up to that date unprecedented field of twenty-six.

The newcomers to championship management, however, had still to learn that such an event cannot simply be left to run itself. The second St Andrews Championship, in 1876, which produced the first tie for the title and the first serious row over the rules, seems also to have been the worst handled in the history of the event. That was the year in which Prince Leopold of the Belgians played himself in as captain of the Royal and Ancient at the Autumn Meeting of the Club. The Championship was played on the Saturday of the same week, 30th September, but the committee had not realized the necessity for reserving times for the competitors, who had to take their chance on a crowded course, so that couples playing in the Championship found themselves frequently held up by Saturday afternoon players in front of them.

The weather had been bad, the course was unusually heavy, and the scores ran high. Bob Martin and Davie Strath, with 86 for the first round, led the rest of the field at lunch by four strokes. Martin, the earlier of the two to go out in the afternoon, had 90 for his second round, and Strath, partnered with Bob Dow, and taking round with him one of the largest galleries seen up to that date at St Andrews, seemed to have a fair chance of victory when he was two under 5's for the first thirteen holes. At the Long Hole In, however, his drive hit a player—one Mr Hutton, an upholsterer at St Andrews—who was going to the fifth. The ball struck him on the forehead and felled him to the ground, and though the injured man recovered almost immediately and was able to go home under his own steam, the incident upset Strath sufficiently to make him drop a stroke at both this hole and the next. When he came off the sixteenth green he learned how Martin had finished and knew that he wanted two 5's to win—par golf according to the standard of those days. He got his 5 all right at the difficult seventeenth, hitting a beautiful iron shot to the heart of the plateau green for his third, but he slipped a stroke at the last hole and took a 6, to tie with Martin at 176—seven clear strokes ahead of the rest of the field. Willie Park was third with 183; 'Old Tom' Morris, Willie Thomson, of Elie, and Mungo Park tied for fourth place with 185.

Immediately after Strath finished, however, a protest was entered by some of Martin's supporters, asking for Strath's disqualification on the ground that he had played his approach to the seventeenth before the couple in front were off the green. (It appears to be the fact that the ball did touch someone, but it is difficult to see how Strath was supposed to have gained any advantage from this, since the shot is acknowledged to have been a good one, and he did in fact require two putts.) Here was a pretty kettle of fish, for the point was not touched upon by the then existing code. At Prestwick the practice had been to appoint an 'umpire' for each Championship, who would decide on any such point of dispute. For instance, Mr (afterwards Sir) Robert Hay was appointed umpire for the Tournament of 1860, Lord Dalrymple in 1861. But no similar provision had been made by the Royal and Ancient Club for the meeting of 1876. The committee held a meeting but adjourned it until the following Monday without coming to any decision, and in the meantime ordered that the tie for first place should be played off 'under protest' on the Monday forenoon. The triple tie for fourth place was to be played off at the same time.

Strath took up the perfectly logical position that the protest ought to be decided before the tie was played off, since if the decision went against him there was no need for any play off. He did not turn up for the replay and Martin 'walked the course' to take the Championship and the first prize of £10. The protest seems at this point to have been allowed to drop, for Strath was not disqualified and was awarded the second prize of £5. My sympathy in the matter is all with Strath. The incident which gave rise to the protest would now be regarded as a rub of the green. At the worst Strath had been guilty of an inadvertent breach of the etiquette of the game, but such an incident would not now involve any penalty and there was no reason for contending that it ought to do so in 1876.

The outstanding players of the next few years were Jamie Anderson of St Andrews and Bob Ferguson of Musselburgh, who each held the Championship for three years in succession, the St Andrews man from 1877 to 1879, the Musselburgh hero from 1880 to 1882. One of the most exciting finishes the event has ever known saw Anderson gain his second Championship in 1878 at Prestwick. Four holes from home he learned that J. O. F. Morris had finished in 161, which meant that Anderson had to do these last four holes in seventeen to tie. 'I can dae't,' he remarked, 'wi' a five, a fower, a three, and a five.' At the first of the four holes, a weak drive fell short of a bunker, but he had a fine brassie for his second, and followed this up by holing a full iron shot for a 3. He got his 4 all right at the next, but at the 'Short' hole, a fortunate iron shot, a shade too strong, pitched on a small mound at the far edge of the green, hesitated a moment, and then trickled back and into the hole, for the first 'ace' in the Open Championship. With a steady 5 for the home hole Anderson finished in 157—four strokes better than his schedule. Yet he needed every stroke of his luck in the end, for Bob Kirk, coming behind him, had been 'burning up the course' and on the last green had a longish putt for a 4 to tie. He made a tremendous effort to get it down, but was a trifle too strong, the ball hitting the back of the hole and jumping out again. Unfortunately Kirk in his disappointment did not take enough care with the short one and somehow managed to miss that also, so that he actually finished two strokes behind the leader.

Ferguson came nearer than any other champion has ever done to equalling 'Young Tom's' record of four championships in a row, being beaten on the fourth occasion only after a tie. His career was a typical example of the way in which the professionals of that generation rose to fame. Born within sight of Musselburgh links, he was only eight years old when he earned his first wages as a caddie there. And he was still no more than a boy—only eighteen —when he took his courage and a bag of borrowed clubs in his hand and went out to conquer the world in an open professional tournament at Leith. Leith was then a seven-hole course and four rounds were played. Ferguson's score was 131, and deservedly carried off what in those days was regarded as the generous first prize of £10. It is on record that after this victory an enthusiastic patron offered to present him with a set of clubs, and when the set was duly bought in the shop of Douglas McEwan—an ancestor of the well-known Lancashire professionals, now in their sixth generation—the eight clubs were chosen with such care that they lasted him all through his championship career.

Ferguson's greatest strength probably lay in his skill with cleek and iron, which his powerful physique enabled him to use with telling effect. Indeed, in a match in which both players used their cleek only, Ferguson defeated the younger Morris over the latter's home course at Prestwick by four holes. But while science and accuracy were apparent in every point of his game, the greatest factor in his success was undoubtedly the Scots 'dourness' of character that made him rise superior to every ill turn of fortune and every disadvantage of conditions. When the wind was high or the turf slow, Bob Ferguson would be doing as well as ever, while less tenacious rivals were going to bits.

Until an attack of typhoid, soon after the failure to clinch his fourth championship, Ferguson was always to the fore in important events. He and 'Young Tom' for Scotland beat Allen of Westward Ho! and Kirk of Blackheath for England in the professional international which celebrated the opening of Hoylake. It was Ferguson, too, who along with Mr Bloxhom of Aberdeen played sixteen rounds of the nine-hole course at Musselburgh between six in the morning and seven in the evening of a fine summer's day. He averaged 40 for the sixteen rounds, and his fee of £5 for the day's work would strike the modern professional as having been thoroughly well earned.

The Championship of 1883 at Musselburgh, which saw Ferguson lose the title he had held for three years, finished in a blaze of excitement. Popular expectation was all in favour of a fourth win for the local player, but Willie Fernie, then professional at Dumfries, who had been runner-up the year before, fairly startled the natives by finishing with an aggregate of 159, a score which was all the more remarkable for the fact that it included a 10 at one disastrous hole—surely the only time that a winning score in the Open has included a hole in double figures! Ferguson could do no better than equal Fernie's total. Indeed he came to the sixteenth tee with only nine strokes to tie, but got 3's at each of the last three holes, which was itself a sufficiently remarkable performance. The play off was very close all through, and the pair came to the last tee with Ferguson a stroke to the good and his fourth Championship almost within his grasp. He got the hole in 4, the par figure, but this was not good enough, for Fernie not only drove the green but holed a long 'steal' for a 2 and the Championship.

Strangely enough, Fernie seemed to have exhausted his Championship luck in that glorious effort, for, great golfer though he undoubtedly was, he never won the title again, but continually just missed it, being runner-up on five different occasions. In match play his biggest success was in a challenge match against Andrew Kirkaldy over Troon, Prestwick, and St Andrews, Fernie winning by 4 and 3.

Fernie belonged by birth to St Andrews, but his name is always associated with the west of Scotland, for he was professional at Troon for nearly thirty-seven years, from 1887 till a few months before his death in 1924.

At least two of the Championship winners of this period were what would now be called 'artisan golfers' rather than golf professionals.   David Brown, the Open Champion of 1886, was a slater by trade, and only competed in golf events when they came to his native Musselburgh, or when trade was slack.   Jack Burns, the champion of 1888, was a plasterer at St Andrews, one of three Open Champions—Willie Fernie, Jack Burns, and Sandy Herd—who, as Herd points out, all served their apprenticeship in Andrew Scott's plasterer's yard.   After his victory Burns went as professional and greenkeeper to the then recently formed Warwick Club, and for a time did well.   But it is evidence of the smallness of the rewards which the game in those days held out for Open Champions, that within a few years Burns was back at St Andrews working as a platelayer on the railway, because he preferred a steady job!   In later days when asked about his golf, his favourite joke was to reply: 'Never better!   I haven't been off the line for years.'

The successes of the Royal Liverpool amateurs, John Ball and Harold Hilton, in 1890 and 1892 presaged the end of this early period of the Scottish monopoly of professional golf.   In 1894 the Championship was held on an English links for the first time, and that year saw the first victory for an English professional and the dawn of a new era in the development of the game.

'IN TYME OF SERMONIS'

(After J. C. Dolman's picture 'The Sabbath Breakers'. Reproduced by permission of the Fine Art Society, 148 New Bond Street, London, the publishers of the coloured print.)

CHAPTER FOURTEEN
(1658-1873)

How Golf came to England

WHEN James VI and I brought golf with him to London in 1603, it may be conjectured that the golf of the royal princes was played in private in the royal parks. That their example did not lack imitators in more public places of amusement is indicated by a petition presented in 1658 by one Thomas Harbottle, the keeper of Vincent Square, or 'Up-Fields,' Westminster, to 'the Honoble Ye Governors of the College and Free Schools of Westminster' complaining of certain 'partyes' whose actions tended to the defacing of the fields and the 'hindrance of the meeting of the gentry for their recreation of bowles, *goffe*, and stowball.'

Exactly a century later we have evidence of the existence of some sort of course on Molesey Hurst. David Garrick, the actor, had a house at Hampton, where he gave a dinner in 1758 to John Home—the author of *Douglas*—and a party of the latter's Scottish friends. The party included the Rev. Dr Carlyle, of Inveresk, to whose *Autobiography* the game is indebted for the only record of the existence of the course at this time. That it was no merely temporary affair is indicated by the fact that Garrick had told his visitors to bring their clubs with them. As a matter of fact only three of the party, 'John Home and myself and Parson Black from Aberdeen,' were golfers, but immediately after their arrival they 'crossed the river to the golfing ground, which was very good.' Dr Carlyle after dinner astonished his friends by the dexterity with which he pitched a ball into the mouth of the archway between the upper and lower garden of Garrick's house, so that it rolled through the opening and down the slope into the Thames. Garrick was quite surprised 'and begged the club of me by which such a feat had been performed.'

Curiously enough there is a putter of Home's in the possession of the Royal Blackheath Club, presented to them along with 'the detail of an original feat of golfing by the Rev. Dr Carlysle [sic] of Inveresk.'   Is it possible, I wonder, that this is the club and that Home begged it or bagged it from Garrick in order to insure for it a permanent resting place along with the record of the 'feat of dexterity' which it had helped to perform?   It is a putter, to be sure, but a putter would in those days be quite a natural club to take for a pitch and run shot through an archway, and if it were not Carlyle's own club the accompanying 'detail' of Carlyle's unusual shot would seem to be quite irrelevant.

For more than half a century the Blackheath Club was the only Golf Club in England, and goodness only knows for how much longer than that the course on Blackheath Common was England's only established course.   This splendid isolation came to an end in 1818 when the Manchester golfers laid out a course on Kersal Moor. There is a tendency to ignore this activity on the part of what is now the Old Manchester Golf Club, and undoubtedly there was at least one serious gap in the continuity of the Club's existence.   But two world wars have accustomed us to gaps in the history of even the most successful organisations, and I am prepared to support Old Manchester's claim to be the second of the English Clubs.

The first English seaside Golf Club, and third in order of seniority among English Golf Clubs, is the Royal North Devon Club at Westward Ho!   Play on burrows at Northam would appear to have begun in 1863 and the Royal North Devon Club—of which more hereafter—was formed in the following year.   It is thus exactly one year ahead of the London Scottish Golf Club at Wimbledon, which came into being in 1865.   Most, if not all, of the sixteen gentlemen who inaugurated the London Scottish Golf Club were members of the London Scottish Rifle Volunteers, and in 1866 the Golf Club was adopted into the regiment, as appears from a regimental order to that effect dated 2nd May of that year.   The colonel of the regiment, Lord Elcho, became president, and all rules and regulations of the Club had to be submitted for the approval of the Commanding Officer.   This was also the case with the other sports sections of the regiment, such as the Football Club and the Curling Club, but this typically military regulation was to be the cause of trouble in the future.

Even from the beginning the Club was not absolutely confined to members of the regiment. As in the case of later Services Clubs at Gosport and Plymouth, a small number of civilian local residents appear to have been admitted as 'honorary' members. But in 1871 a motion was carried that the Club should be open to out-siders, and as a result of this the membership of the Club grew so rapidly that even by 1875 the fifty or so playing members belonging to the corps were outnumbered four to one by the honorary members. The corps members, however, continued to pay only a ten-shilling subscription, while successive increases had raised the entrance fee for honorary, i.e. civilian, members to four guineas, and their subscription to a guinea.

Another source of dissatisfaction was the lack of a proper club-house. The original headquarters of the Club had been in Mrs Doggett's cottage, under the shadow of the historic Windmill, but in 1871 the growing numbers of the Club had necessitated a removal to 'the Iron House' which was in fact part of the canteen of the regiment. By 1878 this had become inadequate for the increased membership of the Club, and an agitation for better accommodation proved hopeless in face of the opposition of the corps members and their Commanding Officer, for the honorary members, though in the vast majority, had no vote in the government of the Club's affairs.

In such a state of matters a split was inevitable. In 1880 the civilians formed themselves into the Wimbledon Golf Club with a clubhouse of their own at the Wimbledon end of the Common. For many years after that, the Wimbledon Club—which became Royal Wimbledon in 1882—and the London Scottish Club both continued to play over the Common, each starting from its own end of the course. In 1908 the Royal Wimbledon Club opened its own course at Caesar's Camp, and since 1909 its place on the Common has been taken by the Wimbledon Common Golf Club.

The details I have given of this curious dispute are confirmed by the interesting *History of the Royal Wimbledon Golf Club*, for a copy of which I am indebted to the present secretary of that Club, Captain G. N. Openshaw. My sympathies in the matter are all with the civilian members who formed the Royal Wimbledon Club, but I cannot accept the contention sometimes put forward that the facts quoted justify the Royal Wimbledon Club in claiming to have existed from 1865.

The point is of purely academic interest, because the facts are not in dispute, but it is right to observe that Royal Wimbledon's claim has never been accepted by the London Scottish Golf Club. In a letter to me in November 1924, Mr Hugh Royle, for many years the honorary secretary of the latter Club, wrote:

My Committee hope that you will assist the London Scottish Golf Club in correcting a misapprehension which has arisen. It has been stated that the Royal Wimbledon Golf Club was founded in 1865, and therefore claimed to be 'the oldest truly English Golf Club in the London district.' Facts are absolutely at variance with that claim. There was no Wimbledon Golf Club in existence before 1880. In that year it was started by some seceders—principally Scotsmen—from the London Scottish Golf Club. With the exception of the Royal Blackheath and possibly Westward Ho! the London Scottish is the oldest Golf Club in England. It is still connected with the London Scottish Regiment whose tenant it is, and has been without a break since the Club was originally founded in 1865, in which year Earl Spencer gave Lord Elcho permission for the Regiment to play on Wimbledon Common.

From a purely legal point of view there seems to me to be no doubt about the matter. The power of veto of the London Scottish Regiment's Commanding Officer was an integral part of the constitution of the original Club, a part which the civilian members were powerless to alter. Their only remedy was to leave and form a new Club, but although they were in fact a majority of the old Club, that does not entitle them to consider that in forming the new Club they took the old one with them. It is a well established rule of law, accepted in both hemispheres and more than once confirmed in our own House of Lords, that when the constitution of any body or association does not provide for its own amendment, the rights and assets of the body or association remain the property of the members—however small a minority they may be— who adhere to the original constitution. In my opinion what is now the Royal Wimbledon Club only came into being in 1880 and is only the fourth in order of seniority among London's Golf Clubs, being junior to the Clapham Common Golf Club, which was formed in 1873.

The course of the Royal North Devon Club at Westward Ho! has a good claim to recognition as the cradle of English golf. It was the first seaside links outside of Scotland, and at the present time can fairly be described as the oldest course in England, because although the Royal North Devon Club is actually junior to the Royal Black-heath Club, and also to the Old Manchester Club, the old course on Blackheath Common has been out of existence for many years, and I do not think there is any evidence that the present course of the Old Manchester Club occupies the original site on Kersal Edge.

The Royal North Devon Club, moreover, enjoys the distinction of being the first Golf Club to be founded by English golfers. At Blackheath, at Manchester, and later at Wimbledon, the courses were laid out by Scottish exiles, but the genesis of Westward Ho! was purely local. The golfing possibilities of this little corner of Devon were pointed out by a visitor from St Andrews, General Moncrieff, who came for a short stay with the vicar of Northam, the Rev. J. H. Gossett, and it was the vicar who was the moving spirit in the formation of the Club.

One of the earliest and most enthusiastic of his converts was Captain Molesworth, in whose house at Bideford Charles Kingsley lived while writing the novel from which the golf links and the village took their name. A house at Northam known as Borough House—I believe it is still in existence but has been entirely recon-structed—was adopted by Kingsley as the fictitious home of Mrs Leigh and of her sons Frank and Amyas, the heroes of his story. A mile or so to the west of Northam lay the famous Pebble Ridge and the sand-hills, with a single farmhouse representing what is now the village of Westward Ho! Captain Molesworth and his three sons were among the early giants of the game on the Royal North Devon course. Mr Horace Hutchinson, in his reminiscences, recalls how the gallant captain was wont to drive his horse and trap over to the links from Bideford, 'manipulating the reins in strictly professional style, as a sailor fingers the yoke lines, the carriage going at the full speed of the horse and making very heavy weather of it over the ruts and bumps, and only the sailor's special Providence bringing them safe to port before the Iron Hut.'

The Iron Hut, a round structure of wood covered with corrugated iron, set close up against the Pebble Ridge, was the first permanent clubhouse. When the Club began its existence, in 1864, its headquarters had been a bathing-machine dragged out by the local coastguards to the first tee. Later a tent took the place of the bathing-machine, until the tent in its turn was superseded by the Iron Hut. The Hut, in spite of the protection of the Pebble Ridge, which rises to a height of forty feet, was invaded by a tidal wave later on and had to be moved to a safer position among the sand-hills. It was no more than big enough to hold a rough table, some forms for seats, and a primitive sort of bar, but under the roof there were all sorts of corners available in the rafters for storing clubs and gear, and it served the simple needs of these pioneers for a good many years until the present clubhouse began to take shape some time in the seventies.

Curiously enough, Captain Molesworth, already mentioned, provides a literary link with Kipling as well as Kingsley, for he is the original of the 'Colonel Dabney' immortalized in *Stalky & Co.* His eldest son, Arthur Molesworth, became one of the best amateurs of his time.

Horace Hutchinson was only a schoolboy of sixteen when he won the Scratch Medal of the Club Autumn Meeting. A few years later he played at the head of the Oxford team in the first University match, and a few years after that when the Amateur Championship was inaugurated, he reached the final in each of the first three years, and won two of them.

In the days when young Master Hutchinson was only able to play golf at Westward Ho! when he came home on vacation from Oxford, he had as his caddie a little flaxen-haired laddie from Northam village who was employed as house-boy in the Hutchinson home. The boy was destined to become the most famous of all the golfing sons of Westward Ho! His name was John Henry Taylor, the first English professional to beat the Scots at their own game and win the Open Championship, which he has held five times in all. So you see that the first English amateur to win the Amateur Championship and the first English professional to win the Open Championship both came from this little corner of Devon.

CHAPTER FIFTEEN
(1868–1908)

The Start of the University Match

ONE thing that did almost more than anything else to set the game going on the English side of the Border was the inauguration of the annual match between Oxford and Cambridge in 1878. At that date the only first-class fixture in the golfing calendar was the Open Championship. The first attempt to establish an Amateur Championship had faded out in 1860. The earlier open meetings for the Silver Club of the City of Edinburgh and similar trophies had degenerated into Club competitions. The University Match is actually the oldest first-class amateur event in the world—older than the Amateur Championship by seven years, older by a couple of years than the oldest of the surviving open meetings, the Glasgow Club's annual competition for the Tennant Cup.

The credit for starting the Oxford *v.* Cambridge Match belongs to the late W. T. Linskill, who introduced golf to Cambridge when he came up from St Andrews in 1873, and in 1875 founded the Cambridge University Golf Club, playing in those days over Coldham Common. The Oxford University Golf Club was founded in the same year, but it was not until three years later that the two Universities were sufficiently organized to arrange their first match. Even prior to 1873, however, various attempts had been made at both Universities to get golf going, usually with some temporary success, giving rise in after days to competing claims to the honour of being the pioneer of University golf.

Actually the earliest attempt to introduce the game at Cambridge would appear to have been the work of Andrew Graham Murray, afterwards Lord Dunedin, the famous Scottish advocate and judge. When he came up to Trinity in 1868, he was determined to get some sort of golf going there, despite the unsuitable nature of the Fen Country and the unconcealed derision of the local 'sports.' In his first term he and Cecil George Kellner, who had come up to King's in the same year, proceeded to Midsummer Common with a few clubs and a hole-cutter under their arms, and laid out a course of eight holes, starting near the end of Park Street, skirting the River Cam for half a mile or so, and returning to the starting point.

Other kindred spirits with some pretensions to be golfers began to be attracted by the idea of a University Golf Club, notably George Gosset, who had come up to King's a couple of years earlier, James Charles Miller, from Jesus College, and Claud Cathcart Carnegie, who came up to Trinity at the same time as Murray. But by May 1869, when the proposal began to take shape, it was clear that some better course must be found. Murray and Gosset were deputed to go out to Royston to spy out the land, and there they laid out an eighteen-hole course, on which the first Inter-College Match was played in the Michaelmas Term of that year between Trinity and King's. At the last moment Carnegie, who was to have been the Trinity second string, had to call off, and Murray played alone, but he was in first-class form and defeated Gosset and Kellner by 4 and 2.

Unfortunately the Club faded out again at the end of that winter, and with it the course at Royston, which did not come into being again until the formation of the Royston Club in 1892. Lord Dunedin died in the autumn of 1942 in his ninety-fourth year, having continued to play quite a good game till he was in the eighties. He was elected a member of the Honourable Company of Edinburgh Golfers in the same year as he came into residence at Cambridge, and of the Royal and Ancient Club two years later. His seventy-four years' membership of the former body is itself a remarkable record.

At Oxford the prime mover in the formation of the Golf Club would seem to have been R. W. Sealy Vidal, afterwards principal of Hertford, who hailed from Westward Ho! and was an enthusiastic golfer. As early as 1874 he marked out a course on Cowley Marsh, 'cutting the holes himself with a long knife,' and so far succeeded in attracting other enthusiasts that the Oxford University Golf Club was formally founded on 10th February 1875, with seventeen members, Sealy Vidal becoming its first president, secretary, and treasurer. The annual subscription was 10s. and the Club finished their first season with a surplus of £4.

In the following winter Oxford golf was put on something like a firm footing by the enthusiasm of three players, all from the north of the Tweed: C. K. Mackenzie, of University College (afterwards Lord Mackenzie), who played in the first University Match, A. H. Baynes, of Oriel, and A. Pearson, of Balliol, who was a member of the Oxford Cricket XI in 1876 and 1877. The University and College grounds were in those days situated at Cowley Marsh, a long walk or a moderate drive in a hansom beyond Magdalen Bridge. The Balliol College cricket ground was one of several in the meadows well out on this road, and as there were a greater number of would-be golfers in Balliol than in any other college, their cricket pavilion became also the first headquarters of the Golf Club. Around the cricket fields the pioneers laid out a nine-hole course, and Rogers, the ancient Balliol cricket professional, was entrusted with the upkeep of the greens. The hazards consisted of the ditches which separated one cricket field from another, with here and there a hedge or a pond to negotiate, and occasional patches of long grass and thistles supplying the place of the 'rough.' Of necessity the 'course' was out of play in summer when the ground was wanted for cricket, but in the autumn and spring terms golf rapidly gained popularity and the number of players steadily grew.

The first University Match was played on the course of the London Scottish Golf Club at Wimbledon on 6th March 1878, and resulted in a decisive victory for Oxford. Here is the bald account which appeared in *The Times* two mornings later:

> On Wednesday a match was played between the Oxford and Cambridge Golf Clubs on the Wimbledon-links. The game consisted of four single matches over one round of 18-holes. Oxford was represented by Messrs H. G. Hutchinson, C.C.C.; A. Stuart and W. S. Wilson, Exeter; C. Mackenzie, University. Cambridge by Messrs W. Adams, Caius; C. H. Spence, Trinity; W. T. Linskill, Jesus; P. R. Don, Trinity. In each game Oxford were victorious, as will be seen from the following table.

	Oxford	Cambridge			Oxford. Holes up
(1)	Hutchinson	Adams	..	..	3
(2)	Stuart	Spence	..	..	5
(3)	Wilson	Linskill	..	..	12
(4)	Mackenzie	Don	..	..	4

Oxford won by 24 holes.

Mr Adams played an uphill game with much pluck, but it was plain from the first that Cambridge were overmatched. The weather was very unfavourable for golf, as a boisterous wind was blowing all day.

Horace Hutchinson as a student was probably the finest amateur golfer of his day. Alexander Stuart, from Edinburgh, in after years became the first winner of the Irish Open Amateur title. With two such players at the head of their team Oxford in the following year were confidently expected to repeat their initial success. That they failed to do so must be attributed in part to the primitive arrangements of the time. It was the custom in those early days for the teams to leave their Universities in the cold grey dawn on the morning of the match, and return the same night, play being over a single round of the Wimbledon course in the afternoon. The Cambridge team drove from King's Cross to Wimbledon in an old-fashioned four-in-hand coach complete with guard and posthorn, all in red coats and with the occasional accompaniment of the bagpipes!—to the admiration of all beholders. The Oxford men travelled in more prosaic fashion across London from Paddington to Waterloo, thence by train to Putney and thence by cab to the London Scottish 'Iron Hut.' Some years ago the tragedy of that second match was unfolded to me by one of the Oxford players who took part in it. Their train broke down on the way to Putney, they arrived at Wimbledon hungry and dispirited, had, I imagine, to be content with bolting a sandwich before going out to play, and were handsomely defeated, Horace Hutchinson losing the top match to F. G. H. Pattison after being three up with five to play, and Andy Stuart only halving the second match in which he was opposed to Linskill, to whom he could normally have allowed a third! So largely did this unexpected set-back bulk in Horace Hutchinson's mind that it seems to have wiped out all recollection of his own and Oxford's triumph in the first match of all, and in his reminiscences Hutchinson actually describes his defeat as having taken place in the inaugural match, to the complete confusion of his whole account of the start of University golf!

For the first fifteen years the University Match was played at Wimbledon. It is difficult, in fact, to see where else it could be played so long as the teams were to get back to their Colleges the same night. Thereafter for ten years or so Royal St George's became the venue, but from 1904 onwards the Universities adopted the plan of playing over a different course each year, the right of choice alternating between the captains of the two sides.[1]

In 1908 an important change was made in the method of scoring. Up to that time the result had been decided by the aggregate of holes up, but in 1907 a tragic thing happened. With one match still to come in, the Dark Blues held what seemed like a secure lead of 12 holes over their opponents, but in the encounter between the two captains, the Hon. C. N. Bruce, now Lord Aberdare, who was suffering from a strained heart, and in order to be able to go slowly had arranged with his opponent that they should go out as the last couple in the afternoon, was so completely overwhelmed by M. T. Allen that he finished no less than 13 holes down, thus wiping out at one fell swoop all the modest gains of the rest of his side and leaving Cambridge victorious by a single hole. This was a somewhat unhappy exposition of the obvious defect of the method of scoring by holes, that a single member of the side who is ill or out of form may let his team down completely. And so, for better or for worse, the system of scoring one point for each match was adopted, and the change thus made has ever since set the fashion for team matches all over the globe.

It is a strange coincidence that the alteration in the method of scoring was accompanied by a change in the record of results. Up to 1907, the tendency had been for victories to go in runs. From 1899 to 1904, for instance, Oxford had won for six years in succession, including a famous victory by 69 holes to nil in 1900. The match of 1907, which saw M. T. Allen win the day for Cambridge, brought the records level at 14 victories each with one match halved. And then with the change to the system of scoring by one point for each match, the event seemed to pass into the guardianship of the double-faced God of Alternate Victory and for nearly twenty years neither side could claim two victories in succession. At first it was the Light Blues who kept getting one ahead, always to be pegged back again in the following year. Then came two halved matches in 1912 and 1913. And from that point it was Oxford

---

[1] In the 1950's there has been a reversion to the earlier practice and the match is played at Rye each year.

who were steadily gaining the lead and losing it again. They won in 1914; and Cambridge squared in the first match after the war, in 1920. Each odd-numbered year after that Oxford went ahead; each even year saw Cambridge draw up again. It was not the least curious thing about this 'swing of the pendulum' that more often than not the results were in most flagrant contradiction to paper form—the most astonishing instance being in 1920, when a Dark Blue 'team of all the talents,' led by Roger Wethered and Cyril Tolley, who was to win the Amateur Championship a couple of months later, was unexpectedly beaten by six matches to three.

This period of the 'swing of the pendulum' came to an end when Cambridge brought off a string of four successive victories from 1926 to 1929, but it was Oxford's turn in the next three years and when Oxford won at Formby in 1934 the record was 'all even,' with 24 victories to each side and three matches halved. From 1935 onwards, however, the Light Blues have drawn gradually ahead. Their success is the more commendable because it has always been the role of Oxford to produce the preponderance of golfing genius while Cambridge has had to get along as best it could on solid merit. The list of Oxford stars begins with the name of H. G. Hutchinson, twice Amateur Champion. It includes Sir Ernest Holderness, Cyril Tolley, and Roger Wethered, who have won five Amateur Championships among them, and Robert Sweeny, the American, who carried off the title in 1937. To these must be added such 'names to conjure with' as R. H. de Montmorency, H. C. Ellis, J. A. T. Bramston, J. A. Robertson-Durham, C. V. L. Hooman, J. J. F. Pennink, and the list could easily be made longer. Cambridge by contrast can claim only one winner of the Amateur Championship, Eric Martin Smith, who won at Westward Ho! in 1931, and though their list of minor lights includes John L. Low, H. W. de Zoete, Bernard Darwin, E. F. Storey, W. L. Hope, and L. G. Crawley, it does not compare at all with the Oxford galaxy of stars. The moral would seem to be that it is not the stars who make the team!

CHAPTER SIXTEEN
(1885–1914)

The Amateurs make a Fresh Start

THE history of the Amateur Championship resumes in 1885, with the issue by the Royal Liverpool Club of invitations for a great Open Amateur Tournament to be held on their course at Hoylake in the week of their Spring Meeting. The Royal Liverpool Club was eminently qualified to launch such a tournament by the central situation of its links, midway between the famous Scottish golf centres and those of London and the south, and the success of the venture was so immediate and complete that it led to the establishment of the Amateur Championship as an annual affair, starting at St Andrews in the following year, and played in England and Scotland in alternate years. The tournament of 1885, however, was the actual start of the Championship, though it was not until many years later that it occurred to the governing body to give it official recognition as such. Incidentally, it is interesting to note how big a part the Royal Liverpool Club has played in inaugurating the chief amateur events. The Amateur Championship and the English Close Amateur Championship were both initiated at Hoylake, and in each case the first winner was a member of the home Club. It was the Royal Liverpool Club that in 1902 arranged the first amateur international match between England and Scotland, and by a happy coincidence it was also on their links that the first amateur international between Great Britain and the United States was played in 1921.

Royal Liverpool was the second of the great English seaside Clubs, being formed in 1869, but Hoylake was not without claims to historical notice long before the golfers came along to turn the Cheshire village into one of the dormitories of Liverpool. The Hoyle Lake silted up owing to reclamation work higher up the River Dee in the eighteenth century, and now the golfer looking seaward from the holes immediately after the turn sees only a vast

stretch of level sand, barely covered at high tide.   But in 1690 the
sea lake was deep enough to shelter nearly a hundred vessels when
Dutch William, with an army of 10,000 men, embarked there for
Ireland to defeat the forces of James II at the Battle of the Boyne.

Hoylake at that time must, I suppose, have been of some standing
as a port, but with the silting up of the lake it dwindled into an
insignificant fishing village, amid a waste of sand dunes so apparently
valueless that the price of £10 was at one time refused for the whole
of the links, which the Royal Liverpool Club purchased from Lord
Sheffield a hundred years later for £30,000.   The story goes that
in 1809, Samuel Baxter, of Hinderton, who a few years before had
acquired the Manor House of Hoylake together with the township,
determined to sell a portion of the estate in order to provide a
marriage portion for his daughter, and a price of £90 was agreed
between him and a fisherman named Eccles.   This, however, was
somewhat less than Baxter wanted to realize, and he offered for a
further £10 to throw in the rest of the township.   Eccles was
willing enough, but asked time to consult his wife, and that thrifty
lady, seeing no possible source of profit in a barren waste of sand,
advised against the bargain.

Although Mr Guy B. Farrar, the historian and present secretary
of the Club, starts off his account with the founding of the Club in
1869, it would appear that some of the Liverpool Scots who had
come to reside in West Kirby had begun to play golf on the fields
that form the slope leading down from the parish church to the
Dee as early as 1852, and in 1865 a nine-hole course of sorts appears
to have been laid out on Hoylake Warren itself.   At this period
Hoylake was a small fishing village with a racecourse on the Warren
and the Royal Hotel, built in 1792 by Sir John Stanley, for the
benefit of visitors coming to the place for the bathing.   'The
Liverpool Hunt Club,' Mr Farrar tells us, 'had held meetings from
1849, both for flat racing and steeplechasing, and before golf was
started these were the great events of the year. . . .   The last race
took place on the 8th April 1876.   Two posts in the middle of the
eighteenth fairway and the old saddling bell, are now the only
remaining relics of the Hoylake racecourse.   Races and golf did
not combine well, and I have been told that after the race meetings
there were always grumbles from those golfers unfortunate enough

to find their ball lying in hoof marks left by the horses; posts and rails made poor hazards, and there were few regrets when the meetings came to an end.' Conceivably the racing men might have a different version of it, but it is evident that golf quickly ousted racing from Hoylake, which became so famous for the condition of its turf that it used to be said that 'the man who can't putt at Hoylake, can't putt!'

The conditions under which this inaugural tournament of 1885 was played differed in several respects from those adopted when the Championship was formally launched in the following year. For instance, in the 1885 tournament halved matches were not played off hole by hole, but were simply replayed. Byes were not eliminated in the first round, and as there were forty-eight entrants, three players reached the semi-final. The man who drew the bye at this stage was A. F. Macfie, a Scottish member of the home Club and the ultimate winner; but if he was lucky under this rule, he was not so under the other, for in the fourth round he and H. W. de Zoete played two halved matches before Macfie, at the third attempt, won by two holes, getting a 'one' at the Rushes (the present thirteenth) to help him to do it.

Horace Hutchinson was the runner-up in that inaugural Championship, and he was the winner in each of the next two years. Then for five years piquancy was lent to the event by the fact that 'the two Johnnies,' John Ball and John E. Laidlay, won the title alternately. For nine years in succession—from 1887 to 1895—one or other of them appeared in every final and twice they contested it between them. During these nine years John Ball won the Championship four times, John Laidlay twice; Ball was twice runner-up, Laidlay thrice. They were much of an age and died within a few months of one another in 1940, Laidlay being eighty at the time of his death and Ball seventy-nine when he followed his rival to the grave. But although those nine years represent the Golden Age of the Amateur Championship, they cover only a fraction of the career of the greatest of British amateur golfers. To the men of Hoylake, of course, John Ball was always the invincible champion, but outside critics will find more to marvel at in the immense period of time during which he maintained his position in the front rank of players.

As a boy of fourteen he finished fifth in the Open Championship
of 1878, and he made his last appearance in the Amateur Championship at Hoylake in 1927, when he was sixty-five.   Between 1888
and 1913 he won the Amateur Championship on eight occasions,
the Open Championship once, the Irish Open Amateur Championship thrice, and the Royal St George's Cup four times, to say
nothing of his long list of triumphs in the scratch events of the
Royal Liverpool Club.   His biggest season was undoubtedly 1890.
In that year he won the Amateur and the Open Championship, being
the first Englishman and the first amateur to win the Open.

The years of rivalry between the two Johnnies were succeeded by
those of rivalry between the second of the Royal Liverpool champions, Harold Hilton, and the idol of Scottish crowds, the incom-
parable Lieutenant 'Freddie' Tait.   For a time there was only
one man in it, for if Hilton was the greater artist, the soldier was the
bonnier fighter, almost as dangerous an opponent when he was
playing badly as when he was playing well.   He was at his triumphant best in the Championship of 1896 at Sandwich, when the
draw brought him up in successive rounds against Charles Hutchings, J. E. Laidlay, John Ball, Horace Hutchinson, and H. H. Hilton,
and he mowed them down like grass, beating Hilton in the final by
8 and 7.   But at Hoylake two years later he was sadly out of form,
saving himself in round after round by incredible recovery shots
and only getting home after extra holes.   He struck his true form,
however, for the final, which he won from S. Mure-Ferguson by
7 and 6.   At Prestwick in the following summer, when Freddie
reached the final for the third time in four years, John Ball beat the
Scot at the thirty-seventh hole in one of the finest finals on record.
It was the soldier's last championship; in February of the following
year he was killed while leading his company of the Black Watch
in an attack on the Boer position at Koodoosberg.

That final of 1899 gave John Ball his fifth Amateur Championship.   Then came a lean period in which he was more interested in
his garden and his motor-cycle than in adding to his golfing laurels.
But in 1907 at St Andrews he won again and just before the war
of 1914–18 the Hoylake school entered upon an Indian summer of
success, Ball and Hilton winning in alternate years from 1910
to 1913.   Ball's victories of 1910 and 1912 brought his total of

'The Stymie'

The picture represents a foursome at North Berwick in the eighteen-forties. The Bass Rock is visible in the distance. Note that in those days caddie-bags were unknown, the caddies carrying the clubs loose under one arm. (After the painting by J. C. Dolman, R.I. *Reproduced by permission of The Fine Art Society, 148 New Bond Street, London, the publishers of the coloured prints.*)

Amateur Championships up to eight, an achievement which no player has ever come near to equalling nor is ever likely to equal.

The only players who could claim that they had the best of their contests with Ball were the hard-hitting Douglas Rolland and Robert Maxwell. The former, shortly before he became a professional, accepted a challenge issued by Hoylake backing John Ball to beat any amateur in the world. The match was home-and-home, and Rolland won by 11 and 10, being 9 holes up at Elie and 4 holes up over the complete round at Hoylake. The matches between Ball and Maxwell were a 'standing dish' in the first ten years of the Amateur International Match, when they almost invariably figured at the head of the English and Scottish teams. They met seven times in all, but of the seven Maxwell won five to Ball's two. Ball's greatest international triumph was in 1899, when he and Harry Vardon represented England against Freddie Tait and Willie Park for Scotland, in an amateur-professional foursome over thirty-six holes at Ganton, and won very handsomely by 5 and 4.

There never was a victor who bore his laurels more quietly or modestly. His famous explanation of his victory in the Open Championship, that he had happened to be 'hitting his drives the right height for the day,' has become a classic, but this masterpiece of understatement was characteristic of the man. No pushful pressman ever succeeded in getting an interview with John Ball; no American visitors arriving red hot with enthusiasm at Hoylake could lure him to more than the most casual of friendly games, played with real reluctance and rather as an act of courtesy to the stranger than out of any feeling of complacency to the admirer. His style was in some respects unorthodox, for he stuck to the old-fashioned palm grip with both hands well under the shaft, and the exaggeratedly open stance of his early days represented too strong a reaction from the older style with the left foot forward. But he had a smooth and easy swing and his temperament was the absolute ideal for the game.

Harold Hilton, at any rate in his early days, seemed to be temperamentally better suited to medal play than to match play. Prior to the coming of Bobby Jones the Open Championship was only thrice won by an amateur and two of these three victories stand to the credit of Hilton. The first of them was at Muirfield in 1892. This was not only the first Championship to be played at Muirfield, but it was also the first time the Open Championship was played over seventy-two holes instead of thirty-six, and Hilton's victory, with an aggregate of 305, was a sad surprise for the Scots professionals, who up to that time had enjoyed an almost complete monopoly of the title—a monopoly broken only by John Ball's victory at Prestwick a couple of years before.   Hilton repeated his Open Championship success at Hoylake in 1897, but the Amateur Championship crown did not come his way until three years later at Sandwich.   He successfully defended his title at St Andrews in 1901, beating John L. Low by a single hole in a famous final.   Then followed a period of comparative eclipse, but in 1911 he staged a tremendous comeback.   At Prestwick he won the Amateur Championship for the third time; he tied for third place in the Open Championship at Sandwich; and he went over to the United States to win the National Championship at Apawamis, being the only British amateur who has ever managed to do so.   That meeting was a great triumph for the English player, for not only did he win the Championship itself, but he finished at the top of the list in the stroke play qualifying stage which preceded it and followed it up by winning the great amateur tournament which celebrated the opening of the National Links at Long Island.   In the final of the Championship he built up a long lead in the morning against his opponent, Fred Herreshoff, a member of the famous family of yacht designers, but in the heat of the afternoon this lead melted away like butter in the sun, and the match was only decided at the thirty-seventh hole. Another attempt on the U.S. title in the following year was unsuccessful, but in 1913 at St Andrews he won the British amateur title for the fourth time, beating Robert Harris in the final by 6 and 5.

It is inevitable that this chapter on the first thirty years of the Amateur Championship should be very much of a Hoylake chapter. The Scots in this period could claim a greater number of first-class golfers and were almost invariably successful over England in the international match.   But after the death of Freddie Tait, they had no one to match the brilliance of the two Royal Liverpool stars. It is a fact worth recording that these two, John Ball and Harold Hilton, were the only English players to win the Open Championship until John Henry Taylor came along to set the ball rolling for the English professionals in 1894.

CHAPTER SEVENTEEN
(1886–1900)

The Father of English Golf

A NOTABLE landmark in the development of golf was the appointment of Mr A. J. Balfour as Chief Secretary for Ireland in 1886. In that year the Amateur Championship, which the greatest of English Clubs had inaugurated the year before, was established on a permanent basis. The University Golf Match had been in existence for eight years. The game, in short, had taken firm root in England, and as is the way of such things, its first success had produced something of a reaction. Upholders of other sports, especially of the good old English sport of looking on at other people playing, poured scorn on 'the old man's game.' A weekly paper put forward the curious contention that only stupid people played golf, and that in fact stupidity was one of the essential qualifications for success at it. At this critical juncture a fresh impetus was given to the interest in golf by the example of Britain's most popular young statesman, already marked out for the future leadership of the Conservative party.

Several factors contributed to make Mr Balfour the most prominent figure in England at this time. The recent Phoenix Park murders had made the task of the new Irish Secretary one of singular difficulty and even of some personal danger, and his visits to the Phoenix Park links, under the inadequate protection of a couple of plain-clothes detectives, were popularly considered as a sort of challenge to any would-be assassin, while the fact of the young statesman insisting on his weekly game under such conditions was a tribute to the fascination of golf that no one could mistake. Unfortunately Mr Balfour's visits spelt the death knell of the little course in Phoenix Park, because when the Land Leaguers realized that the Irish Secretary was one of the regular players they dug up the course, and for the moment that was the end of the game in Dublin. The following summer, however, saw the Royal Dublin

Golf Club firmly established on its present delightful links at Dollymount.

Add to all this that Arthur Balfour already enjoyed a considerable reputation as a sportsman. He had been a successful tennis player at Cambridge; among the deer-stalkers of Strathconan he had a remarkable record as a shot. His attainments as a scholar and a philosopher were beyond dispute and of a sort which had attracted an unusual amount of public notice. To all the scoffs at golf, therefore, he seemed in his single person to provide a complete and perfect answer, and with him as its acknowledged exponent the game leapt into popularity with the speed of a new religion.

His keenness for golf was all the more noticeable owing to the fact that he had only recently taken it up. Although he came of a golfing family, his father and his uncle both being members of the old North Berwick Club, it was not until 1884, at the age of thirty-six, that he turned serious attention to the game, undergoing a fortnight of intensive instruction from Tom Dunn before venturing on his first efforts in a match. In after years he was wont to explain that he belonged 'to that unhappy class of beings, for ever pursued by remorse, who are conscious that they threw away in their youth the opportunity of beginning golf at a time when the muscles can be attuned to the full perfection for that most difficult game.' He therefore never reached the top class as a player. His driving and brassie shots were his strong points, but with the irons he was apt to fail in the half and quarter shots. When he won the Parliamentary Tournament in 1894, his handicap was 13, promptly pulled down to 8, but I do not think it was ever lower than that. At Sandwich in 1910, when he won the tournament for the third time, his allowance was 11. The press, however, naturally threw a very roseate limelight on his golfing performances; around London, where the majority of would-be golfers were new to the game, no one was disposed to be critical, and he was in constant demand to play in exhibition games at the opening of new courses, a request to which he acceded whenever possible with inexhaustible good nature.

So immense was the effect of Mr Balfour's influence that in after years he was frequently described as 'the Father of English golf.' His appearance on the golfing scene was perhaps a trifle too late for this title to be entirely appropriate, but he was assuredly golf's first and best publicity agent. Inevitably no opening ceremony at which he was present could be complete without him being called upon for a speech, and his entertaining and witty propaganda in favour of the game had all the effectiveness of a political campaign. What, for instance, could be better than his claim that 'Black Care may ride behind the horseman; he never presumes to walk with the caddie,' or as an expression of personal preference, 'Give me my books, my golf clubs, and leisure, and I would ask for nothing more. My ideal in life is to read a lot, write a little, play plenty of golf, and have nothing to worry about.'

Mr Balfour's example had another result of deeper and more permanent significance; it set the seal on golf as the sport of busy men! At St Andrews in the early days, local wits divided golfers into two classes, the idle and the busy. The busy were those who played two rounds a day; the idle were content with a single round. The new discovery was that here was the ideal pastime for people who had to snatch their opportunities of relaxation in such odd intervals as they could find, or in the more common case for those who could count on brief intervals of relaxation at the week-ends, but had no leisure to learn to play well! It was left for another golfing premier, Mr Lloyd George, at a later day, to lay his finger with characteristic acuteness on the reason that lies behind all the other reasons for golf's popularity. 'Golf,' he said, 'is the only game in which the worst player gets the best of it. He obtains more out of it as regards both exercise and enjoyment!'

From the point of view of prince or president, prime minister or politician, golf has the advantage over all other outdoor games of being simple to arrange. A round of golf can be fixed up at the shortest notice; there is only one other person to consider, only one to disappoint if a game has to be cancelled at the last moment; a four-ball or a foursome can still carry on even if one of the quartet has to be called away in the middle of the game. But more than its mere convenience is the consideration that it is the one sport in which lack of skill does not detract from the pleasure of the game. At games such as billiards the weak performer has to watch with such patience as he can muster while his more skilful adversary monopolizes the play. At golf it is the bad player who has the fun of playing the greater number of strokes! And there are few golfers so poor that they are not rewarded by the occasional brilliant shot, and even the occasional run of holes played in perfect figures, to lure them on to hopes of improving their play. In golf, more than in any other sport, to travel hopefully is better than to arrive.

The golf boom in England put an end to the Scottish monopoly of the Open Championship. In 1894 the Championship was held for the first time on an English course, the links of the Royal St George's Club at Sandwich, and by a happy coincidence that year saw the first victory for an English-born professional, a young man of twenty-three named John Henry Taylor, who had learned his golf as a caddie at Westward Ho! and was at this time professional at Winchester. Curiously enough this first English success ushered in a period of eclipse for the Scottish professionals. At St Andrews in the following year Taylor repeated his success. In 1896 at Muirfield a new star floated into the golfing firmament in the person of another young man named Harry Vardon, who came from the village of Grouville in Jersey, the first of a notable list of great players who were to come from the Channel Islands.

Vardon won again in 1898 and 1899 and Taylor in 1900, and sandwiched in among these victories Harold Hilton on his home course at Hoylake scored an English amateur victory in 1897. So for seven successive years the Championship came to England, but just when Scottish golf seemed to be fading out of the picture yet another young man, a joiner from Earlsferry named James Braid, who had come to London to take up a job as a club-maker, started a Scottish counter-attack that fairly restored the balance of power. In the twenty-one years from 1894 to 1914 these three players, Taylor, Vardon, and Braid—'the Great Triumvirate' as they came to be called—won the Championship sixteen times among them. The existence of three such outstanding players contemporaneously with one another was a piece of unexampled good fortune, and the rivalry between them as representatives of England, Scotland, and the Channel Isles focused the attention of the whole world on the game. With the three must always be associated Sandy Herd, who only won the Open Championship once but came in to make the 'Great Triumvirate' a 'Great Quartet' as Braid's partner for Scotland in numberless international matches against Vardon and Taylor for

England.   Of him as of Benaiah, the son of Jehoida, it might fitly be said that 'he was more honourable than the thirty, but he attained not to the first three.'

If this were a History of Golfers rather than a History of Golf, each of the four would require to have a long chapter to himself. J. H. Taylor, though a year junior to Vardon and Braid, was, as we have seen, the first of the three to write his name in the scroll of golfing fame: his successes were also more evenly distributed than those of his two great friends and rivals, for after his two early wins already mentioned he won the Open again in 1900, 1909, and 1913, and even as late as 1922, the year which saw the first triumph of an American-born player, he finished in the first half-dozen.   He also won the Professional Match Play Championship in 1904 and 1908.

James Braid's championship career was the briefest of the three but the most brilliant.   In the first ten years of the present century he won the Open Championship five times; between the inauguration of the Match Play Championship in 1903 and 1911 he won that event four times, and it may fairly be said that during those eleven years he outshone both his rivals.

Harry Vardon's best golf was divided between two periods. During Braid's perihelion he won the Open Championship only once, but between 1896 and 1899 he won it thrice in four years and also carried off the U.S. Open Championship in 1900.   The change to the rubber-cored ball seemed for a time to upset his putting, but he staged a come-back to win the supreme crown again in 1911, and by winning for the sixth time in 1914 he set up a record that seems likely to stand for ever.

It is not, however, by his wonderful achievements as a player that Vardon earned a special place of his own in golf, so much as by the service he did the game in providing a model of style.   Prior to Vardon's day there was no standard style; each man hit the ball in the way that seemed best to himself.   The majority still stuck to the exaggerated swing and closed stance which had come down to them from the days of the feathery ball and which was very ill suited to play with the 'guttie' that had superceded it, but individual players were distinguished by all sorts of idiosyncrasies of grip and swing. Vardon's coming changed all that.   His style was so 'easy' that it seemed easy to imitate, and so effortless that it seemed suited to any physique.   It had certain peculiarities of its own, but they were not such as to attract attention, and the general impression of his swing was one of grace and simplicity.   The effect of his example was to discourage all strained attitudes and exaggerated movements, which pretty well passed out of first-class golf.

It is commonly supposed that Vardon was practically 'nurtured on the links' of his native Jersey, but this is not strictly the case, for up to the time he was twenty his opportunities for golf had been few and far between.   He was only seven when the coming of golf to Grouville Common excited the indignation of the local tenant farmers, and no doubt as golf became established there he had occasional opportunities of caddying for visitors and of swiping balls about the links with crude home-made clubs.   But at the age of twelve he went to work on a dairy farm and a year or two later became page-boy in the service of a doctor, and it was not until he entered the employment of Major Spofforth—a brother of the famous Australian cricketer—as an assistant gardener, that he got an opportunity to join a working men's golf club and took to the game in earnest.   Previous to that he had engaged in all sorts of sports, his biggest successes being as a sprinter.   In the meantime his younger brother Tom had gone to St Anne's as assistant to George Lowe, and the news that Tom had won a £12 10s. second prize in a tournament inspired Harry with the idea of taking to golf as a profession.   Lowe, who was laying out a nine-hole course for Lord Ripon at Studeley Royal, obtained for Harry Vardon the post of greenkeeper and professional there, and at the age of twenty the future champion was fairly embarked on his golfing career.

There was not much doing at Ripon, however, and at that time Vardon was playing more cricket than golf.   A shift to Bury a year later gave him more opportunity of improving his play.   It was from Bury he entered for his first attempt on the Open Championship at the age of twenty-three.   Three years later he went to Ganton and celebrated his first summer there by winning the Championship at the fourth attempt.   His American tour of 1900 had a momentous effect upon the development of the game in the United States and provided a basis for the more scientific American approach to the analysis of style.

1780
**THE GOLDEN AGE OF
GOLF UNIFORMS**
Mr. Henry Callendar, captain
of the Royal Blackheath Club
in 1790, 1801, and 1807.
(After the painting by Lemuel
Abbott.)

1630
A Young Golfer of Friesland.
(After Gerbrand de Geest.)

GOLF AT NORTH BERWICK (1835)

After the picture by Sir Francis Grant, P.R.A., H.R.S.A.

CHAPTER EIGHTEEN
(1657–1894)

The Beginning of the Game in the States

WHAT has often been described as the earliest reference to golf in the American continent is contained in a Dutch ordinance of the magistrates of Fort Orange—the old name of Albany, N.Y.—dated 10th December 1659. The late Mr John Campbell, the first curator of the Golf Museum of the James River County Club, was good enough to obtain for me a photostat of this ordinance, with a translation by Mr Arnold J. van Laer, the archivist of the University of the State of New York, which reads as follows:

THE HONOURABLE COMMISSARY and Magistrates of Fort Orange and the village of Beverwyck, having heard divers complaints from the burghers of this place against the practice of playing golf along the streets, which causes great damage to the windows of the houses, and also exposes people to the danger of being injured and is contrary to the freedom of the public streets;

THEREFORE their honours, wishing to prevent the same, hereby forbid all persons to play golf in the streets, under the penalty of forfeiture of Fl. 25 for each person who shall be found doing so.

THUS DONE in Fort Orange, at the meeting of the honourable court of the said place, on the tenth of December, Anno 1659.

I was able, however, from my own records, to refer Mr Campbell to a still earlier reference in the minutes of the same Court of Fort Orange and Beverwyck, which Mr van Laer translates as follows:

Ordinary Session held in Fort Orange, March 20 Anno 1657. The officer plaintiff, against

Claes Hendericksen	⎫	
Meeuwes Hoogenboom	⎬	defendants.
Gysbert van Loenen	⎭	

The plaintiff says that Jan Daniel, the under-sheriff, reported to him that on the 7th of March, being the day of prayer ordered by the honourable director general of New Netherland and proclaimed here, the defendants played hockey on the ice, demanding therefore, that the said defendants be condemned to pay the fine indicated in the ordinance.

The defendants, appearing, maintain that they did not play hockey and promise to prove it.

The parties having been heard, the court orders the defendants to produce their evidence on the next court day.

As far as I can make out the crabbed writing, the word used in both passages for the game referred to is *kolven*, which Mr van Laer in one case translates as 'golf' and in the other as 'hockey.' He explained, however, that in the second instance he had translated '*kolven op het ijs*' as 'hockey on the ice' as being the best equivalent of the actual game. There is no reason to suppose that *kolven* as played in the Dutch colony in 1659 differed in any respect from the Dutch *kolven* already described in Chapter III.

To Mr Campbell I am further indebted for a photostat of a famous advertisement in Rivington's *Royal Gazette* of 21st April 1779, which confirms the tradition of golf being played by Scottish officers in New York during the period of the Revolutionary War. James Rivington, it should be explained, as well as being the King's Printer in New York, was an importer and shopkeeper who frequently advertised sporting goods; the reference to the *Caledonian* balls leaves no doubt that the advertisement relates to the Scottish game. It reads as follows:

To the GOLF PLAYERS

The Season for this pleasant and healthy Exercise now advancing, Gentlemen may be furnished with excellent CLUBS and the veritable Caledonian BALLS, by enquiring at the Printer's.

Some of the history of what may be termed the Middle Ages of American golf is preserved in the advertisements in the Charleston and Savannah papers of the last years of the eighteenth century. An interesting collection of these notices is contributed by 'Chick' Evans to the symposium of golf humour and philosophy which he and Barrie Payne published under the quaint title of *Ida Broke* ('I 'd 'a broke ninety but . . .'). 'Chick' mentions that his father had come across these advertisements some time before while making researches for a work on American bibliography. The earliest advertisement in this collection, however, is dated 1795, but further researches on the same ground have produced evidence of the South Carolina Golf Club playing the royal and ancient game on Harleston Green, Charleston, as early as 1786, and of the inauguration of the Dutch version of the game a couple of years later.

The earlier notice appears in a bound pamphlet copy of the *South Carolina and Georgia Almanac* for the year of our Lord 1793, by William Waring, Charleston, printed by Markland and McKiver, No. 47 Bay. Under the general heading of 'Societies Established in Charleston' occurs this item:

Golf Club Formed 1786.

Dr Purcell—President. Edward Penman—Vice-President. James Gardner—Treasurer and Secretary.

The Charleston City Gazette and Daily Advertiser of 18th September 1788 contains the announcement that

There is lately erected that pleasing and genteel amusement, the KOLF BAAN. Any person wishing to treat for the same at private sale, will please apply to Mr David Denoon, in Charleston, or to the subscribed on the spot.

HENRY WELSH.

Typical advertisements of the South Carolina Golf Club in the same journal are these:

Anniversary of the South Carolina
GOLF CLUB

Will be held at Williams Coffie House on Thursday, the 29th instant, where the members are requested to attend at two o'clock precisely, that the business of the Club may be transacted before dinner.

(20th September 1791).

South Carolina Golf Club.

The anniversary of this Society will be held on Harleston's Green THIS DAY, the 15th instant, where the members are requested to attend at one o'clock to transact business before dinner, which will be on the table at three o'clock. By order of the President.

EDWIN GAIRDNER, Secretary.

(15th November 1794).

Golf in Georgia is almost as old. The earliest reference to the game in Savannah that has been discovered appears in the issue of 22nd September 1796 of the *Georgia Gazette* published in that city:

Saturday, the 1st of October, being the anniversary of the Savannah Golf Club, the members are requested to attend at the Merchants and Planters Coffee House on that evening at 6 o'clock for the purpose of electing officers for the ensuing 12 months, and to transact other necessary business.

The Savannah Club was still in a flourishing condition in 1811, as we know from an invitation card to a ball given by the Club in that year. One of the cards which is still in the cherished possession of the Johnston family, and a photostat of which is included in the American Golf Museum, reads as follows:

GOLF CLUB BALL

The honour of, Miss Eliza Johnston's Company is requested to a Ball, to be given by the Members of the GOLF CLUB, of this City, at the EXCHANGE, on Tuesday evening, the 31st instant, at 7 o'clock.

George Woodruff ⎫
Robert Mackay ⎪
John Caig   ⎬ Managers.
James Dickson ⎭
George Hogarth, Treasurer.
Savannah, 20th December 1811.

A reference to golf in Georgia appears as late as 1818, but the declaration of war by the United States against Great Britain in 1812 may have had something to do with the fading out of the popularity of the game.

For the next seventy years or so golf in the United States would appear to have fallen into desuetude, and it is not until the early eighties that we find the game beginning to attract attention again. A shadowy Colonel Gillespie seems to have made an attempt to introduce golf into Florida about this time, but the researches of the James River Country Club seem to have established that the oldest of the modern Clubs is the Oakhurst Golf Club, formed at White Sulphur Springs, Western Virginia, in 1884. The five founder members were Alexander E. McLeod, George Grant, Russell W. Montagu, Lionel Torrin, and Roderick McIntosh McLeod. Golf continued to be played on the Oakhurst course until its place was taken by the formation of the Greenbrier Golf Club ten years later.

For some reason, however, the Oakhurst Club has not attracted anything like the same amount of interest as some of the others. It was not, for instance, one of the five charter members of the United States Golf Association, and the Club which did most to set the ball rolling was the St Andrews Golf Club at Yonkers. The founder of the Club would appear to have been one Robert Lockhart, a linen-merchant in Yonkers, who had learned his golf at Musselburgh. In 1887 Mr Lockhart returned from a visit to his native Dunfermline, bringing with him a supply of clubs and balls, and was in the same year arrested for hitting a golf ball about on the sheep pasture in Central Park!

Other Scots rallied round the pioneer, and through the summer and autumn of 1888 golf so monopolized the available pasture land that 'any cow who craved a little meadow-grass had to do her lunching at night.' The next step forward occurred when five of these players got together to form 'the St Andrews Golf Club of Yonkers,' with Mr John Reid, another Dunfermline native, as its first president, on 14th November 1888. A six-hole course was laid out on the Yonkers meadows, and the first regular meeting took place on 22nd March 1890.

Here the chief difficulties were the numerous apple-trees, which brought out the players' skill in quick-rising approach shots designed to sail clear over the trees.   From this unusual type of hazard the Yonkers pioneers derived the honoured title of 'the Apple-Tree Gang.'   So famous did the apple-trees become that when the Shinnecock Hills Golf Club laid out its course on Long Island in 1891, one distinguished visitor who was familiar with the Yonkers course advised the new Club that in spite of its delightful turf and charming ocean views it was not suited to be a test of golf at all, since it lacked the apple-trees that were the essential feature of the game!

A few years before the Second World War Mr Robert H. Davis, one of the members of the Yonkers Club who had been active in recording its history, sent over a piece of the famous apple-tree, mounted in silver, to be presented to the Prince of Wales as captain of the Royal and Ancient Club, together with an album containing a history of the Club, and illustrated by several photographs among which is the earliest photograph in existence of American golf, taken at Yonkers in 1888.   The players shown in the photograph are Messrs Harry Holbrook, Alexander P. W. Kinnan, John Upham, and John Reid, the two caddies being the sons of Mr Holbrook. From one of these caddies, himself become a full-fledged member of the Club, Mr Davis obtained an interesting account of the conditions of those pioneer days.

I remember that each player had an equipment of six clubs.   Three wooden, a driver, a brassie and spoon, three irons, a cleek, a sand iron and a putter, all with long heads and heavy shafts. . . .   No bags were used, and but one gutta ball was carried by each player.   I think the name of the ball was the 'Eclipse.'   They cost thirty-five cents each, and when one was lost St Andrews Golf Club declared a moratorium until it was found.   The clubs cost from $2.00 to $2.50 each.   When one was broken, it was necessary to send to Scotland for the head, or shaft, as the case might be.   The caddie fee was twenty-five cents per round.

The originator of the Shinnecock Hills Club was Mr Samuel L. Parrish.   Mr Parrish first heard of golf, while he was on holiday in Italy, from a friend of his who was passing the winter at Biarritz, and invited Mr Parrish to a game there.   This proved impossible to fix up, but it was arranged that Mr Parrish should be initiated into the sacred mysteries by another Biarritz American, the late Mr

Edward S. Mead, on the return of both to Southampton, N.Y., in the early summer of 1891. Mr Mead so successfully communicated his enthusiasm for the game to Mr Parrish and another of his friends, that they requested the Royal Montreal Club to allow their professional to come over and examine the ground. As a result Willie Dunn came to Southampton in July 1891 and laid out a twelve-hole course. It is interesting to note that the original course and the original clubhouse of 1891 still form integral parts of the course and clubhouse of the Shinnecock Hills Club as it is to-day.

The Tuxedo Club, formed in 1894, invited the Shinnecock Hills Club to a seven-a-side match in that year at Tuxedo, and this appears to have been the first inter-club match played in the United States.

CHAPTER NINETEEN
(1567–1810)

Women's Golf before Waterloo

IN women's golf as in men's, the first player whose name has come down to us is a monarch of the royal house of Scotland.

One of the charges brought against Mary Queen of Scots was that in 1567 after the death of Darnley she was seen playing golf and pall-mall in the fields beside Seton. The accusation was put forward by the queen's political enemies as evidence of her lack of decent feeling, but it is to be noted that it amounts only to the assertion—probably quite true—that she amused herself by knocking a ball about 'in the fields beside Seton,' i.e. in the grounds of Seton Castle, where she was staying as the guest of Lord Seton, the half-brother of one of the queen's 'Four Maries.' To expand this charge, as some modern writers have done, into an allegation that she was playing golf along with Bothwell on Dunbar links immediately after her husband's murder, is to paint a totally false picture in a few ill-chosen words. There is nothing to support the suggestion that Bothwell was with her at this juncture; he appears to have remained at Holyrood with Huntly in charge of the young prince. The very idea of a woman of rank playing golf in public 'on Dunbar links' would be entirely at variance with the spirit of the times. And in any case I do not think there was any course at Dunbar prior to 1854, when some officers of a militia regiment which was quartered in the town laid out a few holes and induced the inhabitants to take up the game.

There is a gap of more than two centuries before we come to any other reference to women's golf, and then it is at the other end of the social scale. Yet women golfers there certainly were. Musselburgh would seem to have played the same sort of part as the metropolis of women's golf as Leith did in the old days of men's, if

A GROUP OF OLD MASTERS AT ST. ANDREWS

Left to right the players are: Tom Morris, Mr. Robert Cathcart of Piccairlie, D. Anderson (Daw); then close together on the extreme right, Allan Robertson, Mr. Wallace of Balgrummo, and (addressing the ball) Mr. Hay Wemyss.

(*Right*)
THE OLDEST
CHAMPIONSHIP TROPHY
The Silver Claret Jug won by
the Royal Blackheath Club
in the Amateur Foursomes
Championship of 1858, and
still in the possession of the
Club.

Mr. George Glennie (*above*)
and Lieut. J. C. Stewart were
the winning Blackheath pair.

we may judge from a curious passage in the *Statistical Account of Scotland* (*Inveresk*):

The golf, so long a favourite and peculiar exercise of the Scots, is much in use here [i.e. at Musselburgh]. Children are trained to it in their early days, being enticed by the beauty of the links, which lie on each side of the river between the two towns [i.e. Musselburgh and Inveresk] and the sea, and excited by the example of their parents. To preserve the taste for this ancient diversion, a company of gentlemen about eighteen years ago purchased a silver cup, which is played for annually in the month of April, and is for a year in the possession of the victor, who is obliged to append a medal to it when he restores it to the company. . . .

After a few words of advice to the burgesses of Musselburgh to keep their links secure from the encroachments of building, the worthy chronicler goes on:

When speaking of a young woman, reported to be on the point of marriage, 'Hoot,' say they [i.e. the burgesses], 'how can she keep a man, who can hardly maintain herself?' As the women do the work of men, their manners are masculine, and their strength and activity is equal to their work. Their amusements are of the masculine kind. On holidays they frequently play at golf, and on Shrove Tuesday there is a standing match at football between the married and unmarried women, in which the former are always victors.

This account is confirmed by a curious entry in the minutes of the Royal Musselburgh Golf Club, whose Silver Cup is obviously the trophy referred to in the passage quoted above. We know from the early entries in the minute book that it was annually played for in April. The Cup, however, was not subscribed for, as above suggested, but was presented to the Club, as we have already seen, by Thomas McMillan, Esq., of Shorthope, in 1774. (This, by the way, supplies us with the date of the account we are quoting, since the eighteen years would take us to 1792.) Twenty years later the athletic ladies of Musselburgh were still keen on golf. Mussel-burgh, of course, was a fishing town, and it would appear that the majority of the lady golfers there were fisher lassies. At least so I judge from a minute of the Club dated December 1810, in which is recorded a resolution to present a prize of a creel and 'skull,' with consolation prizes of two of the best Barcelona silk handkerchiefs, to the best female golfer who played on the annual occasion on the following 9th January, 'to be intimated to the fish ladies by the officer of the Club.' I should explain that the 'skull' was the name given to the small fish basket attached to one end of the larger 'creel.' By an understandable error the learned editor of *Golf: a Royal and Ancient Game*, misread the writing of the old minute and substituted for 'skull' the more plausible sounding 'shawl'—a blunder which has been blindly followed by quite a number of famous writers who have not taken the trouble to verify the reference.

It is clear, therefore, that in certain districts women's golf was already going strongly in the days before Waterloo. It is a pity that no record of their scores or their successes is available for comparison with the men's performances of the same era. But before abandoning a subject so fascinating I must make mention of one famous lady whose connection with golf was the most extraordinary ever known. This was Dame Margaret Ross, of Balneil, the wife of the Earl of Stair, and the original of that formidable character, Lady Ashton, in *The Bride of Lammermoor*. This great dame had the reputation of being a witch. According to Colonel Fergusson, it was seriously believed of her that she carried political animosity to the length of interfering with her opponents' games of golf. She used her unholy powers to convert herself into the golf ball they were playing, and spoiled their game by deliberately rolling out of line on the putting green, or hopping of malice aforethought into the deepest depths of a hazard! However, we have all had experience of golf balls affected by this sort of witchcraft, and it appears a little unnecessary to attribute the ill fortune of these particular players to the interference of Dame Margaret.

Another form of the tradition concerning this remarkable lady is rather more specific. Sir Patrick Murray, the representative of Stranraer in Parliament, owed his seat to the influence of her witchful ladyship. 'She promised him Old Nick's assistance, if he voted her way in Parliament, and accordingly she ordered his ball while at golfe,' in this case, of course, favourably. That such a story should find credence, even among the vulgar, seems scarcely possible to modern minds, but as a matter of fact the Lady of Stair was not the only golfer to be credited with such a knowledge of the black art. William St Clair, of Roslyn, who won the Silver Club of the Honourable Company four times between 1761 and 1771, was commonly reputed to have attained his exceptional skill at golf and archery by the same dangerous means.

It was not until well past the middle of last century that golf began to be generally recognized as a game for ladies and the first ladies' Clubs came into being. The earliest of all would appear to be the St Andrews Ladies' Golf Club, which was formed in September 1867. It was not very far in front of the Westward Ho! and North Devon Ladies' Golf Club, which dates from the following year. Next came Musselburgh and Wimbledon in 1872, Carnoustie in 1873, and Pau in 1874.

Even at this stage, however, as Lord Wellwood points out in the Badminton *Golf*, women were relegated to links of their own— a kind of Jews' quarter—generously provided for them by many of the bigger Clubs. He lays it down that ladies' links 'should be laid out on the model, though on a small scale, of the "long round"; containing some short putting holes, some longer holes admitting of a drive or two of seventy or eighty yards, and a few suitable hazards,' explaining that he restricts the estimated length of a lady's drive to seventy or eighty yards because 'the posture and gestures requisite for a full swing are not particularly graceful when the player is clad in female dress.' It apparently did not occur to the simple-minded old Victorians that it might be possible to devise a ladies' golfing garb to suit the swing. They could not foresee the day when a Lady Champion like Miss Joyce Wethered (Lady Heathcoat-Amery) could reach a standard differing from that of her Amateur Champion brother Roger by 'from two to seven strokes *according to the course*.' That was the family estimate, and they would know what they were talking about. Still less could the Victorians fore-see the day when women golf professionals in the United States, headed by such stars as Mrs 'Babe' Zaharias, Miss Patty Berg, and Miss Louise Suggs, would in their own big money tournaments be giving displays of golf that differed from the men's only in being on a slightly smaller scale of distance, and hardly at all on a lower scale of skill.

CHAPTER TWENTY
(1893–1914)

The Rising of the Amazons

THE modern history of women's golf begins with the formation of the Ladies' Golf Union and the inauguration of the Ladies' Championship in 1893. There was an awkward fortnight at the beginning of that year in which it appeared that two sets of people had thought of the same idea at the same time. The Lytham and St Anne's Golf Club advertised its intention to hold a Golf Championship for Ladies, and this announcement came as a bit of a bombshell to the founders of the Ladies' Golf Union, who had arranged their inaugural meeting in London for exactly sixteen days after the announcement appeared, and who had naturally planned to hold a Championship of their own. However, after both parties had got over the first shock of dismay, a happy solution was found in the amalgamation of the two schemes. The newly formed Union took over the management of the Championship, but agreed to hold it at St Anne's.

It is difficult at this time of day for anyone to realize how important a contribution the founding of the L.G.U. was to the cause of the emancipation of women. This side of the matter is well put by Mrs Blanche Hulton in an article which she contributed to the first issue of *Ladies' Golf*:

The whole-hearted adoption by women of the Royal and Ancient Game marks an epoch in the history of the sex, and, without unduly straining a point, it may be said that golf has been a factor of no small importance in the mental, as well as the physical, development of the modern girl. Before the era of golf the recreations of girlhood were practically restricted to croquet, and later to lawn tennis; only a fortunate minority were permitted to go in for horse-riding, clad in dangerous, flowing garments, and seated on sleek and ambling steeds discarded by their fathers.

Married women were even less happy. The store-room, the kitchen, and the nursery supplied not only their serious occupation, but also their relaxation.   This 'daily round,' lasting all day and every day, produced a dullness of spirits that, while it shortened life, made it also less pleasant. The comings and goings of these ladies' more or less attached husbands, who golfed, fished, and shot, were veiled in mystery.   When men and women met there was no common ground for companionship and sympathy.   Almost invariably at a party the sexes separated, the men to talk politics or sport, the women to discuss domestic worries.

None of the pre-golf pastimes led their devotees far afield or brought them together in such numbers as golf has done.

A significant feature of the movement is that so many of the ladies' Golf Clubs formed at this period were entirely independent of the men's Clubs, usually possessing their own clubhouse and in many cases their own course.   In modern golf the normal practice is for the ladies' Club to be a section of the men's Club, but even yet you find ladies' Clubs like Wirral and Formby which possess their own eighteen-hole course entirely free from masculine over-lordship, and it was not until after the Second World War that the Royal Ashdown Forest Ladies' Club gave up the eighteen-hole course, over which it had played since its institution in 1889, and amalgamated with the men's Club.

The pioneers of the Ladies' Championship had to put up with a good many gibes from self-sufficient males who were sure that the women would prove quite incompetent to run a championship or anything else.   The event was to prove these critics entirely wrong.   The business-like way in which the L.G.U. has managed its ever-extending empire has from the very beginning compelled the admiration of the golfing world.   Indeed, if there is any com-plaint to be made it is in the opposite direction.   The only criticism of the L.G.U. that you ever hear nowadays is that they are inclined to take themselves too seriously, and have thereby contrived to take some of the pleasure out of the game for the rank and file of players.

Their biggest achievement was the gradual establishment of a national system of handicapping.   Handicapping had always been a pet subject of Mr W. Laidlaw Purvis, whose assistance in the founding of the L.G.U. had been invaluable, and he had communi-cated his zeal to Miss Issette Pearson, as she then was, under whose dictatorship the Union moved from success to success. The L.G.U. handicapping system was not perhaps quite so fool-proof as some of its authors imagined, and it has more than once been seriously modified since, but it was a sound, workable system. What was more important was the efficiency with which it was enforced. No doubt it was uphill work at the start, but within eight or ten years the L.G.U. had done what the men had signally failed to do—had established a system of handicapping that was reasonably reliable from Club to Club.

Prior to this time handicaps, both in men's and in women's golf, were in a state of absolute chaos. Within each individual Club, no doubt, the handicaps of the members were adjusted with a fair degree of accuracy. But standards varied to an amazing degree from Club to Club. In a large proportion of Clubs some outstanding player was rated at scratch, and the others handicapped from him. It can be imagined how impossible it was to convince some of these Clubs that their best player, thus rated at scratch, would be no better than 10 or 12 at Prestwick or Hoylake. Other Clubs adjusted their handicaps by comparison with a bogey figure so generously calculated that—to quote a notorious instance— Gordon Simpson, the Scottish internationalist, had a handicap of plus 8 at Tayport! The L.G.U. showed the world that this muddle could be straightened out, and the men have been forced, somewhat reluctantly, to follow suit.

The weak point of the L.G.U. in these early days, as it is possible to see looking back on them, was that the competitors in these first Championships had scarcely one first-class golfer among them. The links on which the first meeting began on 13th June 1893 was the original nine-hole course of the Lytham and St Anne's Club, now long given over to the builders. Even in those gutta days it could not be considered a severe test, for the total length of the eighteen-hole round was no more than 4,264 yards, the longest hole measuring 337 yards! The card gave the lengths of the nine holes as 244 yards, 221, 328, 182, 207, 337, 120, 272, and 221, and the hazards were in no sense formidable. Miss A. M. M. Starkie-Bence, who was perhaps the longest driver in the field for that first championship (she figures as 'Miss Starkie-Bence, with drive immense' in the immortal Littlestone ballad of the following year), thus described the course in a delightful article which she contributed to one of the first issues of *Ladies' Golf* in 1912:

> I recall the grief and terror of the first hole and the last, of that turf banked-up erection called a 'cop,' bordered on each side with a ditch of sand. In the middle of the Cop there were steps with a handrail against which we invariably drove and cannoned back to be dead in that abominable trap, the ditch. The other bunkers on the course were mild; at least in these days we should call them so. But in those first days they seemed impossible to get out of.

That probably sums up the position fairly enough. I imagine that a respectable score for a scratch man amateur (remember that those were the days of the gutta ball) would have worked out at something like 70 for the double round, but with the single exception of the winner, Lady Margaret Scott, none of the competitors came within measurable distance of this standard. There is no room for doubt that Lady Margaret, who won the first three Championships with effortless ease, was a great golfer, but with that one bright exception the standard of play in the first two Championships was surprisingly low. In the final at St Anne's Lady Margaret took 41 strokes to complete the first nine holes, which in view of the table of lengths given above cannot be regarded as more than moderately good, but it sufficed to enable her to defeat Miss Issette Pearson by 7 and 5. In the semi-final Miss Effie Terry, the youngest player competing, 'provided the eventual champion with the best fight she had in the competition,' but was nevertheless beaten by 6 and 4. It does not seem to have occurred to any of the pioneers that if Lady Margaret was to be rated at scratch, the handicaps of the best of her opponents ought to be something like 10 or 12!

It was unfortunate that the entry of 44 for that first Ladies' Championship (38 actually took part) did not include a single player from Scotland, although both Ireland and France were represented. It was perhaps even more unfortunate that when, in its fifth year, the Championship was held for the first time on a Scottish course, at Gullane, Lady Margaret Scott was no longer competing. The result was a massacre. The Scots took the first three places in the medal competition, and carried off the driving competition and other minor events; they supplied all but two of the players in the last sixteen, and the final was fought out between two very fine local players, the sisters Orr, Miss E. C. Orr defeating her older sister by 4 and 2. Time, however, was to set this matter right with a vengeance, when Miss Cecil Leitch and Miss Joyce Wethered in turn showed the Scots what the standard of English golf could be like.

There is much the same sort of story to tell of the start of women's golf in the United States. Two years after the British ladies had set the ball rolling at St Anne's, the U.S. ladies held their first Championship on the Meadowbrook course at Hempstead, Long Island. Subsequent Championships have been decided by match play in the usual form, but this first Championship was a stroke competition, and the winner was Mrs Charles S. Brown, of Shinnecock Hills, with an aggregate of 132. This seems a remarkably fine performance, until you discover that it was for two rounds of a nine-hole course, a total of eighteen holes. A contemporary account of the play states that 'Mrs Brown was hard pushed by Miss N. C. Sargent, of the Essex Golf Club, there being only two strokes difference in Mrs Brown's favour, she doing the first round of nine holes in 69 strokes to Miss Sargent's 70 and the second round in 63 to Miss Sargent's 64 . . . Mrs Brown did not start off with very good prospects as she took 11 strokes to make the first hole. The second she made in 4 and the third in 9.' Her scores for the last six holes of the first nine appear to have been 4, 5, 7, 9, 14, 6. Total 69!

It is easy to appreciate how the low standard of play in the first championships of both sides of the Atlantic created future difficulties in the handicapping problem. The pioneers of the L.G.U., in fact, fell into the very error that they had seen so clearly in the handicapping of the Clubs. They set up their own best players as the 'scratch' standard without seriously considering the possibility of other players coming along who could give these same 'scratch' players half a stroke a hole! It was many a long day before all the snags could be ironed out, but in a sense these readjustments were of very minor account, once the real spade-work had been done. The whole credit of showing that a universal system of golf handicapping could be successfully established belongs to the pioneers of the L.G.U.

CHAPTER TWENTY-ONE
(1900–1914)

America steals the Picture

THE first tremendous fillip to the progress of golf in the United States was given by the tour of American courses undertaken by Harry Vardon in 1900. During that tour he won the U.S. Open Championship at Wheaton, Illinois, and it is a startling example of the vagaries of golf that his score of 313 included one stroke that missed the ball altogether—a short putt in which the head of the club caught the ground and jumped over the ball! Vardon's amazing accuracy with his long game, combined with his graceful and easy style, brought converts to the game wherever he went and started a new golf boom in the States. Three years later the Oxford and Cambridge Golfing Society arranged the first American tour by a British golf team—the beginning of an international rivalry which has been of incalculable benefit to the game.

The Society itself was then only in its infancy, having come into being in 1898. At first its activities were in the main confined to matches against the Universities and South of England Clubs, varied with an Easter tour in Lancashire in which matches were played against Royal Liverpool, Royal Lytham and St Anne's, and Formby. But in its sixth year the vaulting ambition of the Society led to a proposal for a tour of the States. The Society got together a strong team and did reasonably well against American sides, winning eight and halving one out of the ten matches played. Their one defeat was sustained at the hands of an 'All America' side at Nassau Country Club, and the result of that contest depended on the odd match of nine, which went to the 38th hole!

Golf in America was at that time only entering on its teens, so that the Society's tour was a little in the nature of a missionary visit. But the British golfers brought back with them a new respect for the possibilities of American golf. It was the experience of that tour that led John L. Low to utter his famous warning that he already heard the whistles of the boats of the invaders in the Mersey! How right he was!

British golfers received their first lesson in the need for tightening up their short game when Walter J. Travis carried off the British Amateur Championship at Sandwich in 1904, and I have always regarded it as a singular stroke of ill fortune that the peculiar circumstances of that victory caused the warning to pass unheeded. Travis, as a matter of fact, was by birth an Australian, but he had been for many years in the States when the Niantic Club, of Flushing, Long Island, of which he was a member, decided to add golf to its other interests, and it was in 1896 that W. J. Travis, a 'late beginner' of thirty-four, played his first game on the nine-hole Oakland course at Long Island. It is curious to record that he learned his golf almost entirely from books, but he practised unceasingly until he had acquired a remarkable precision with all his shots. He was the holder of the American Amateur Championship for the third time in four years when he came over to Sandwich and took the Amateur Championship trophy for its first trip overseas.

It must always remain a matter of controversy whether Travis's game was really up to first-class standard. To American golfers he was, of course, the Grand Old Man of the game, but his three American Amateur Championships were won when golf in the States was more or less in its infancy, and after his victory at Sandwich he did not win another national title. But who shall say whether the explanation lies in the possibility that he could no longer maintain his old form—remember that he was a man of forty-two when he carried off the British Championship—or that he had not the strokes to enable him to maintain the fight with the stars of the second generation? His putting, of course, was superlatively fine, but his shots from the tee and through the green were sadly lacking in length, and even in spite of his wonderful putting the scores with which he won his matches at Sandwich were not particularly good. He was a most courageous fighter, but it is a significant fact that none of his British opponents put up a very good fight against him, and there is some reason for thinking that he won his championship chiefly because the British players allowed themselves to be put off their game by the consciousness that against this particular opponent the hole was never won until the putts were down.

It was a singularly unfortunate accident that the American's victory should have been specially associated with a freak putter. What actually happened was this. Travis, on his arrival in this country, had gone to St Andrews, and from there to North Berwick. I imagine that the change to the British seaside courses troubled him in just the same way as it has done other invaders since; at any rate, on the Scottish courses his form was very poor indeed. He has himself put it on record that for that reason he postponed his arrival at Sandwich until as late a date as possible, but that almost with his first practice shot on the Royal St George's links he felt that his game had come back to him. I have been told that the conditions at Sandwich that year were exceptionally favourable to the inland golfer, but whether that is true or not, the course undoubtedly suited Travis. He had always been a wonderful putter, playing with an ordinary putting-cleek, but at St Andrews his putting had suffered along with the rest of his play, and at Sandwich he was induced to try a Schenectady putter belonging to one of his compatriots.

This famous weapon is most easily described as a square slab of metal with the shaft set into the centre of it. But in Travis's hands the thing became a magician's wand. Even he himself has probably never holed so many twenty-yard putts in one week as he did in that Championship. I fancy that this was merely because his newly recovered confidence found expression in the department of the game in which he had always been superlatively good; I don't suppose the Schenectady putter had anything to do with it. But at the time everyone was more ready to give the credit to the putter than to the player, and St Andrews itself took alarm at the possibility of the game being ruined by new inventions which would enable the player to buy his shots in a shop!

Centre-shafted clubs of any kind were officially barred in Great Britain and it is only in recent times that saner councils have prevailed.

The next great shock to British self-complaisance came with the triumph of Francis Ouimet in the U.S. Open Championship of 1913. At that time American professional golf was just beginning to wake up, and in fact the victories of J. J. McDermott in the same event in 1911 and 1912 were the first successes of a home-bred player. So the presence of Harry Vardon, who had won the American title during his former visit to the States thirteen years before, and of Ted Ray, the British Open Champion of the previous season, converted the American Open of 1913 into an international trial of strength of a kind that was at that time comparatively new.

In that Championship, played on the course of the Brookline Country Club, near Boston, fortune fluctuated in an amazing way. At the end of the second round the two British champions seemed to have established themselves in an impregnable position, but they both contrived to drop a lot of strokes on the outward half of the fourth round, and when they both finished with an aggregate of 304 the general opinion was that this figure would certainly not be good enough to win. However McDermott and the other American professionals who had a chance to beat it all failed in their turn, and at last it became known that the only player who had a chance even to equal the British score was a young amateur who was playing in the event for the first time.

This was Francis Ouimet, who at the age of nine had begun to play golf with an old iron club on the meadows around his home, which was near the Brookline course. At a sufficiently early age he took up caddying and would no doubt seize an occasional chance to play a few holes over the course himself. In 1913 he was a tall lank youth of twenty and a member of the Woodland Club.

His chance at the best was a thin one, and with four holes to go he had only fourteen strokes left to tie with Vardon and Ray. Listen to the epic of these last four holes, as it was told to me a few months after by Ted Ray himself:

The par of these four holes is 4, 3, 4, 4, so that Ouimet had to get one under the par figures at one of them and par figures for the other three, if America was to remain in the picture. At the fifteenth it was difficult to pitch over the bunker and stay on the green, and Ouimet's shot was pushed out to the right, but he got his 4 by laying a chip shot dead. He did not get on to the green at the short sixteenth either, but again he put his chip near enough and got his 3.

Still, that was two of his chances to beat the par figure gone, and he could hardly hope to do better than a 4 at the last, which was over 400 yards long with the track of the race-course and the bank beyond it to carry with the second shot. As a matter of fact when Ouimet came to this hole he did not quite carry the bank. His ball stuck at the top of it and he had to play another good chip and hole a seven-foot putt to get his 4.

When he came to the seventeenth, therefore, he knew that if he was to get his 3 anywhere it must be here, and a 3 at the seventeenth at Brookline is a man's-size job. The hole was 360 yards long and the approach had to be played on to a sloping green, with the hole cut so close to a bunker that it was impossible to pitch for the pin. Ouimet's ball finished twelve feet or so from the tin, leaving him with the most difficult kind of putt in the world, with a down-slope and a side-slope to negotiate at the same time.

Only perfect judgment of both line and strength would get the ball in the cup, but Ouimet stepped up to it without batting an eyelid. His putter swung smoothly and evenly, and the ball took the slope down in a gentle curve, and hit the very centre of the cup. I have never seen such a putt more confidently played. Coming at such a crisis, with so much depending upon it, I count that that putt was one of the master-strokes of golf.

After that the play off of the triangular tie on the following day over eighteen holes was something of an anticlimax. By all the canons the boy ought to have cracked up. Instead he played good, steady stuff and allowed the two famous professionals to beat themselves. He won by five strokes from Vardon and by six from Ray.

In the following spring, when Ouimet came over to compete in the British Amateur Championship at Sandwich, certain points of his style attracted a good deal more attention than they would to-day. He used the interlocking grip, which the Whitcombes and Gene Sarazen have since made familiar to everyone. In those days it was almost unknown among first-class players, although it was by no means new. If my recollection serves me, Ouimet declared that he had copied it from Willie Anderson, the Scottish professional who had captured the American Open in the three successive years from 1903 to 1905. On the green also he used the 'soldier stance' with both heels together, his elbows sticking out fore and aft, and the club swinging like a pendulum from the shoulders, a style which was then considered the typically American one. Ouimet has stuck to it all his life, and it has served him well, for his putting is perhaps the strongest feature of a game that is sound and solid in every department.

Ouimet's chances in that championship were so strongly fancied that an enthusiastic American fan wagered £10,000 to £30,000 that the title would fall either to him or to Jerome D. Travers, the holder of the American Amateur Championship, who was also competing. Ouimet, however, like many another invader, found the British seaside courses a difficult problem at the first attempt, and neither he nor Travers got beyond the second round. Later in the year, however, the pair were the finalists in the American Amateur Championship at Vermont, when Ouimet proved that his Brookline victory was no fluke by beating his fellow voyager by 6 and 5.

It is a strange thing that a golfer who found himself world famous in the space of a single day should from that time onwards have been distinguished for solid consistency rather than for brilliance. After the First World War Ouimet was runner-up to Chick Evans in the American Amateur of 1920, but thereafter year after year he was the victim of a 'semi-final hoodoo.' In 1923 he won the Royal St George's Challenge Cup at Sandwich, and was a semi-finalist in both the British and American Amateur Championships, and he again reached the semi-final of the American event in 1924, 1926, 1927, and 1929. And then just when everyone was beginning to take it for granted that any further championship success would for ever elude him, he staged a come-back by winning the American Amateur title at the Beverley Country Club in 1931. It has fallen to few champions to score a repeat after an interval of seventeen years!

Francis Ouimet is one of the great figures of the game. In 1951 he was elected captain of the Royal and Ancient Golf Club—the first American golfer to be so honoured—and duly played himself in at St Andrews. But he never did greater service to golf than when he changed the course of history at Brookline.

CHAPTER TWENTY-TWO
(1618–1902)

From Feathery to Rubber Core

AMERICA'S first and most important contribution to the development of golf was the invention of the rubber-cored ball. And as in the case of so many other great inventions, it was only after its advent that the world was able to realize how badly it had been needed.

It is generally assumed that the earliest golf balls were the leather balls stuffed with feathers which were still in use up to the middle of the nineteenth century, but it is much more probable that in the early days of golf the balls were of turned boxwood similar to those used in the kindred games of *chole* and pall-mall. It is said that a skilful player at pall-mall could drive these boxwood balls 400 yards with his light, supple, long-handled mallet, but as Mr Andrew Lang has acutely suggested, that was no doubt on a smooth, hard, prepared surface, like that of the Mall in London, where Pepys saw the Duke of York play. The same authority found support for the wooden ball theory in a dispatch of the reign of James VI and I, in which the writer, describing the siege of a castle belonging to the Earl of Orkney, speaks of the cannon balls bursting into fragments 'like golf balls' against the walls. It need not be pointed out that the leather ball stuffed with feathers, which was familiar to later times, would not break into pieces in this fashion, however fierce the impact, but would simply split open.

One of the odd bits of evidence sometimes put forward as indicating a Dutch origin for the game is contained in the grant made by James I in favour of James Melvill, giving him a monopoly of the golf ball trade for a period of twenty-one years. The 'Letter' authorizing this is dated 5th August 1618, from the Court at Salisbury. The preamble of this much-quoted document sets forth that our 'Soverane Lord the King understands that thair is no small quantitie of gold and silver transported zeirlie out of his Hienes

kingdome of Scotland for bying of golf ballis, usit in that kingdome
for recreatioun of his Majesties subjectis.' There is nothing,
however, in the letter to bear out the suggestion that the balls were
imported *from Holland*; that appears to be an addition on the part
of Robert Clark, and like some of his other *obiter dicta* has been
echoed by all sorts of later writers without critical examination.

I do not believe that in 1618 Scotland was importing golf balls
either from Holland or from anywhere else. The mere nature of
the document is itself sufficient ground for suspecting the honesty
of the king's statement. It is a grant of a monopoly, and the sale
of monopolies was among the chief of the grievances which by 1618
had set the king at loggerheads with the English Parliament. The
greatest objection to these monopolies, as historians have not failed
to point out, was not that they were constitutionally illegal, but
that the damage they did to trade was out of all proportion to the
revenue the Crown derived from them. It is true that most of
the monopolies were made at the expense of his English subjects,
but there is no reason to suppose that this grant of a Scottish monopoly in golf balls differed in any essential respect from the rest.
The reason for these grants of monopolies is not in doubt; they
were simply a means of raising cash for the royal treasury. But
naturally that could not be allowed to appear on the face of the
document. Some specious and fair-seeming phrases about pro-
tecting the trade of 'his Majesties subjectis' would need in each case
to be introduced into the preamble, if only for the sake of saving
the royal face. And I think that the statement about the import
of balls falls into this category.

Incidentally, it is commonly assumed from this document that
James Melvill was a ball manufacturer, but it is clear from the
wording of it that he was not. He was merely the purchaser of the
monopoly. He had already fixed up an arrangement with a firm
of ball-makers named William Berwick & Co. Any other firms
who wanted to carry on the manufacture of golf balls had to do so
under licence from Melvill. In fact, the usual ramp!

I would venture a guess that Melvill's monopoly did not bring
in the return he expected. In 1642 we find the town council of
Aberdeen granting 'licence and tolerance to John Dickson to use
and exercise his trade of making gowff ballis within this burgh in

GOLF AT BLACKHEATH IN 1863

A humorous sketch by C. A. Doyle in *London Society* of that year.

The first Inter-Club Match at Blackheath: Royal Blackheath *v.* London Scotish. From the *Illustrated London News* of 1870.

respect ther is not sich ane tradisman in this burgh.' That, to be sure, is three years outside the period covered by the grant to Melvill, but it reads as if other burghs had their recognized ball-makers. Of all the monopolies granted by James in England, the most generally unpopular were the monopolies for the granting of licences for ale-houses. The local justices everywhere considered that they were the best judges of suitable licensees, and I fancy that the magistrates of the Scottish golf centres would be of the same opinion regarding the appointment of golf-ball makers.

To my mind the most interesting point about the whole thing is that in 1618 the trade in golf balls was sufficiently important to make a monopoly worth securing. The grant to Melvill fixed a 'maximum price' for golf balls at fourpence each ('four schillingis money of this realme,' i.e. Scotland—being equivalent to one-twelfth of that amount in English money). A hundred years earlier, King James IV had bought his golf balls at fourpence a dozen. So the price in 1618 represents a big jump. By 1672, as we learn from the Note Book of Sir John Foulis of Ravelstoun the price of golf balls had risen to fivepence each (five shillings Scots).

Of course the value of money was different in those days. The learned author of *The Golf Book of East Lothian* estimates that the purchasing power of the money of 1672 was four times that of 1896, so that the fivepence seems reasonable enough. But we can apply a different kind of check by comparing the prices of clubs and balls. In 1506 two new clubs cost King James IV a penny each—as compared with balls at fourpence a dozen. In 1672 a ball at fivepence cost almost as much as a club. I think it is a reasonable deduction that between the balls of 1503 at fourpence a dozen, and the balls of 1618 at twelve times that price, the 'form and make' of the ball had changed. And it is tempting to conjecture that the rise represents the difference in cost of production between wooden balls turned on a lathe and leather balls elaborately stuffed with feathers in imitation of the balls then used in games like tennis.

When did the change-over take place? Some time, I think, in the reign of James VI and I. The dispatch cited by Andrew Lang belongs to the earlier part of that reign, the grant to Melvill to the latter part. It is even possible that the change to the feathery ball, with its increased price, was the factor that made it worth Melvill's while to try to grab a monopoly of the trade in the new ball.   That, to be sure, is not much more than a guess on my part, but it would suggest a meaning for a curious phrase in the grant, which describes William Berwick and his partner as the 'inbringeris off the said trade,' and the sole manufacturers.   This of course may only be more 'build-up' to justify the grant of the monopoly.   Berwick & Co. cannot possibly have been the only golf-ball manufacturers, for if they were there would be no point in paying down good money to secure a monopoly.   But if they were the first people to start manufacturing the new type of ball and wanted to keep the others out, the reference to the 'inbringeris off the said trade' has a sort of sense.

With the coming of the 'featheries,' ball-making became one of the fine arts.   The leather cover was stitched first, leaving only a small hole open, and through this hole the feathers were thrust in by means of an iron spike fixed in a wooden framework upon which the ball-maker leant all his weight for the better compression of the stuffing.

Mr Peter Baxter, in his *Golf in Perth and Perthshire*, thus describes the initial part of the operation: 'The leather was of untanned bull's-hide.   Two round pieces for the ends and a strip for the middle were cut to suit the weight wanted.   These were properly shaped, after having been sufficiently softened, and firmly sewed together, a small hole being of course left through which the feathers might be afterwards inserted.   But before stuffing it was through this little hole that the leather itself had to be turned outside in, so that the seams should be inside—an operation not without difficulty.'

With regard to the distance to which the feathery balls could be driven we have fairly exact information.   Undue importance has been given to a passage in the chronicles of the Blackheath golfers, which records that in 1813 'Mr Laing bets that in the course of the season he will drive a ball 500 feet [167 yards], he having the chance of ten strokes to accomplish it.'   It appears that five years later Mr Laing won both the scratch medal of the Knuckle Club and the scratch competition for the Silver Club of the Blackheath golfers, and it has been assumed from this that he was above the average of players and—what does not necessarily follow—at least an average long driver, but in 1813 Mr Laing may have been a mere beginner and the bet may only be to the effect that he wouldn't hit a decent drive in ten attempts.

We have more illuminating information in the records of the Glasgow Club, which show that in 1786 a player named John Gibson made a series of measured drives with a feather ball, the distances ranging from 182 yards to 222 yards. It need not be pointed out that the rugged turf of Glasgow Green afforded hardly the most favourable of surfaces for an attempt at a record drive. Yet the figures quoted compare favourably with the winning shot of 175 yards in a long driving competition with the gutta ball at Cupar in 1859.

What was undoubtedly the record drive with the feathery ball was set up in 1836 by Monsieur Samuel Messieux, a French master in the Madras College. His name appears as that of the winner of the Royal and Ancient Gold Medal in 1827, and of the Silver Cross in 1840, and in the well-known poem *Golfiana*, published in 1833, he is thus referred to:

> Here's Monsieur Messieux, he's a noble player,
> But somewhat nervous—that's a bad affair,
> It sadly spoils his putting when he's pressed,
> But let him win, and he will beat the best.

Professor James Stuart, who was one of his pupils, says in his reminiscences: 'He was a golfer of some repute, and lived for long in history as having made the longest drive that ever was made; but whether this record has since been beaten I cannot say. It was on a slightly frosty day, with a gentle wind with him, and he was playing over what were then called the Elysian fields.' This longest drive was measured as 361 yards, and it is notable that it was not regarded as having been beaten by Lieutenant Freddie Tait's famous drive of 341 yards 9 inches, made many years later at the same place with a gutta ball.

At their best, therefore, the featheries flew further than the gutties, but they were seldom perfectly spherical, were apt to become waterlogged in wet weather, were ruined as soon as one hack with an iron club broke the surface of the distended leather, and cost what then seemed the extravagant sum of half a crown apiece. Small wonder, therefore, that William Graham, LL.D., could say

in the song he wrote for the meeting of the Innerleven Club in
1848:

> Though Gouf be of our games most rare,
> Yet, truth to speak, the tear and wear
> O' balls was felt to be severe,
>   And source o' great vexation.
> When Gourlay balls cost half-a-croun,
> And Allan's no' a farthing doun,
> The feck o 's wad been harried soon
>   In this era of taxation.
>
> Right fain we were to be content
> Wi' used-up balls new-lickt wi' paint
> That ill concealed baith scar and rent—
>   Balls scarcely fit for younkers.
> And though our best wi' them we tried,
> And nicely every club applied,
> They whirred and fuffed and dooked and shied
>   And sklentit into bunkers.

The poem fixes the date of the coming into use of the gutta
balls at 1848. They did not at once drive the older balls out of
the field, however, for we find that as late as 1851 Gourlay received
a medal for the manufacture of feathery balls.

Who first conceived the idea of making golf balls of gutta-percha
it is impossible to say, but it seems probable that it was someone on
the staff of W. T. Henley's Telegraph Works Co., who were particularly well placed for manufacturing golf balls of this new construction, since the firm had acquired an unrivalled experience in the
handling of gutta-percha in the production of cables insulated with
this material, which had been found particularly suitable for long-
distance submarine cable work. It seems certain that the new balls
were first tried out at Blackheath. Mr James Balfour, father of Mr
Leslie Balfour-Melville, the Amateur Champion of 1895, in his
Reminiscences of Golf on St Andrews Links, records that at the
beginning of the year 1848 'my brother-in-law, Admiral Maitland-
Dougall, played a double match at Blackheath with the late Sir Ralph
Anstruther and William Adam of Blairadam and another friend, with
gutta-percha balls on a very wet day. . . . Sir Ralph said after

dinner, "A most curious thing—here is a ball of gutta-percha; Maitland and I have played with it all day in the rain, and it flies better at the end of the day than it did at the beginning." Maitland came to Edinburgh immediately after and told me of this. We at once wrote to London for some of these balls and went to Mussel-burgh to try them. Gourlay, the ball-maker, had heard of them and followed us around. He was astonished to see how they flew; and, being round, how they rolled straight to the hole on the putting green. He was alarmed for his craft, and having an order from Sir David Baird to send him some balls whenever he had a supply by him, he forwarded to him that evening six dozen!'

Gourlay was not the only member of his craft to take alarm. Allan Robertson's hostility to the new balls led to a breach between him and Tom Morris. But in a few years the club- and ball-makers, who had imagined their occupation gone, found the loss of revenue from ball-making far more than made up by the vast increase in the number of players taking up the game, whose chief drawback up to then had been the short life of the expensive feathery balls. At first the gutta balls proved unsatisfactory because they flew badly when new, but it was soon noticed that the ball flew beautifully after its smooth surface had been hacked about a bit with the iron clubs. The obvious answer was to give the ball an artificial marking by hammering it with a chisel-headed hammer, and these 'hand-hammered' balls remained in use until about 1880, when the use of moulds superseded the hammering process. The gutties had the added merit of being practically indestructible. In my boyhood, when balls became too badly hacked about to be fit for play, we simply laid them aside, and took them down to the professional's shop in batches of a dozen to be remoulded and repainted!

The gutta ball, by making golf so much cheaper, created some-thing of a boom in the game in Scotland, but the hard ball was not without defects of its own. It made the game distinctly hard work, for the player had to do the whole work of getting it up in the air; and its unyielding solidity frequently gave an unpleasant jar to the player's arm if he mishit a shot with an iron club.

All this was changed by the advent of the rubber-cored ball at the beginning of the present century. The new ball was the inven-tion of a Cleveland golfer, named Coburn Haskell, and was brought into production by the Goodrich Rubber Company. Its general form was much the same as it is to-day, a gutta-percha cover enclosing a ball of rubber thread wound under tension round a solid rubber core. The first Haskell ball, as I can personally testify, did not outdrive the gutta ball by any exaggerated extent; that was to come later. Its greater elasticity at first made it seem more difficult to control on the green, but for ladies, for young players and for old ones, it made golf a different game, and if its liveliness occasionally made it bound into places the gutta ball would never have reached, this was more than balanced by its readier response to the player's efforts from these and other awkward lies. The first great success for the new ball was Walter Travis's victory in the U.S. Amateur Championship in the autumn of 1901. In the following spring the new ball invaded England. Sandy Herd, who prior to the Open Championship at Hoylake had been one of the many players vociferously hostile to the new idea, was persuaded to try it in practice, decided to play it in the Championship, and came home the winner by a single stroke from Harry Vardon, who was sticking to the old ball.

There was not much in point of distance between the old ball and the new at this stage, for the Haskell was both lighter and larger than the present-day standard. It was perhaps a pity that it was not allowed to remain so, for as time went on the ingenuity of manufacturers reduced the thickness of the cover, increased the tension of the winding, and substituted a liquid centre for the solid core (I am told that a central sac filled with tapioca proved one of the most effective materials for this purpose), and by reducing the size and increasing the weight, produced a missile capable of being propelled over ever-increasing distances with the trajectory of a bullet. The only result was to give golfers more and more walking for fewer shots, and in mere self-defence the rulers of the game found themselves forced to impose a minimum limit of size and a maximum limit of weight in a not altogether successful effort to restrict the distance to which the ball can be hit.

CHAPTER TWENTY-THREE
(1741–1947)

From Baffing Spoon to Sand Wedge

In the days when archery was still of the first importance in war and the chase, the bow-maker was also the source of supply for other sports. When James IV began playing golf at Perth after the treaty of peace with England it was to the local bow-maker that he sent for clubs and balls. Exactly a hundred years later, we find James VI appointing William Mayne, 'bower burges of Edinburgh,' to be the royal fledger, bower, club-maker and speir-maker for life. The appointment is dated from Holyrood, 4th April 1603.

Unfortunately no specimens of the art of these worthy bow-makers have come down to us. What are believed to be the oldest clubs in existence are preserved in the clubhouse at Troon. They are a set of eight, discovered a good many years ago in a boarded-up cupboard in a house in Hull, along with a newspaper bearing the date 1741. The house, which during the greater part of the eighteenth century had been the residence of a family named Maisters, had been rebuilt, and the probability is that the clubs were already old when they were stowed away in the disused cupboard. The late Lord Balfour expressed the opinion that they belonged to the period of the Stuart kings. This set of clubs was on view in the Historical Section of the Glasgow Exhibition in 1911, and there I was even more interested in another of the items included in that collection, which appeared to me to belong to a period not much later. It is a driver bearing the initials 'A. D.,' which are almost certainly those of Andrew Dickson, who, as we learn from Mathison's poem, had a notable reputation as a club-maker in Leith in the first part of the eighteenth century. If I am correct in believing him to be the Andrew Dickson already referred to as caddying for James II in 1682, he would be over seventy at the date of the poem, but this is not improbable if we suppose him the head of a family business.

143

The amazing thing about these old clubs is not their uncouthness, crude and unfinished though they are; it is their size. Horace Hutchinson's logic tutor, who produced the famous definition of golf as a game of 'putting little balls into little holes with instruments singularly ill-adapted for the purpose,' would have found his opinion doubly justified by these gargantuan weapons. They are so long in the shaft that it is difficult to see how the old heroes of the game contrived to hit the ball at all. Even after the clubs became the beautiful and well-balanced weapons which reached their highest perfection in the workshops of the great Hugh Philp, this incredible length of shaft still persisted. I once essayed a few shots with a 'play-club' which was made in the year of Waterloo. It came from the collection of the late Charles Neaves, for many years professional to the Moray Golf Club at Lossiemouth, and had been given to him more than half a century earlier by an old St Andrews golfer. Its age was self-evident, if only from the fact that the head had not been varnished, but had been protected from the weather by being covered with keel, varnish first coming into use for this purpose about 1810.

This club was certainly a magnificent specimen, far more elaborately made and ornately bound than any modern driver, though less graceful in its lines than the clubs of Philp and his successors. But it was, as I say, of a quite incredible length, and I found the greatest difficulty in wielding it with any effect. Apparently our great-grandfathers favoured what would now be considered an excessively flat swing, and stood very far from the ball, as the lie of the heads of these clubs would pretty well compel them to do. Only by such a flat, sweeping swing could they avoid disaster from the long thin heads of the drivers, or rather of the 'play-clubs,' for in those days, as we have already seen, the word 'drive' had not yet come into familiar use in the game. Even the approach shots were then played with wooden clubs of varying degrees of loft, and the names of long spoon, mid spoon, short spoon, and baffing spoon indicated a graduated range of shots, just as definitely as the modern 2, 3, 4, or 5, etc., irons. With the baffing spoon—'employed only for skying a ball over a hazard on to the putting green when the stroke is too short for any of the other spoons'—the player obtained something of the effect of the modern pitch with 'stop' by 'baffing' or striking the ground with the flat sole of the club a fraction of a second before impact with the ball, which was caught up by the club as it rebounded off the turf! It seems to me to be a stroke which must have called for a considerable degree of delicacy in execution.

The earliest iron clubs, starting with the coarse, clumsy-looking 'Carrick' irons which figure in so many collections of old clubs, were excessively deep in the blade, and seem to have been introduced mainly for the purpose of hacking the ball out of the cart-ruts which were to be found at Musselburgh and other primitive courses. The determining factor, as a moment's reflection will enable anyone to see for himself, was the old 'feathery' ball, whose distended leather hide was far too easily cut by the edge of any misapplied iron club. Even the niblicks were originally wooden clubs: the first iron-headed niblicks were excessively short in the blade—again with the idea of being able to use them in cart-ruts and similar awkward lies.

When Allan Robertson once realized that the advent of the guttie did not after all spell ruin to his craft, he was the first to appreciate that the new ball was admirably adapted to the use of iron clubs in the approach shots. He also introduced the use of the putting cleek on the green, because the guttie, being perfectly round, made possible a rolling shot in place of the jumping shot with which the old feathery sprang off the face of the wooden putter. 'Young Tom' Morris carried the development of the iron clubs a step further by the use of the niblick for the shorter pitch shots. In a famous series of matches in which he gave 'a third' (i.e. six strokes per round) to Arthur Molesworth, the famous Westward Ho! amateur, and easily defeated him, one or two of the rounds were played on a frostbound course, with only a small area of each green swept clear of snow. But time and again Young Tommie pitched the ball right up to the pin with enough back-spin to make it stop there as if it had a string tied to it.

This use of the niblick led to the invention of the mashie, the equivalent of the No. 5 iron, and at the end of last century this was the most lofted club in the normal set. The wizard with the mashie was the great John Henry Taylor, who had an amazing mastery of the 'cut' shot with this club. In the cut shot the stance was more than usually open and the club brought on to the ball 'from the outside in,' so that the blade was drawn across the back of the ball from right to left at the moment of striking.   The spin thus imparted made the ball draw up sharply on landing, but also made it 'break from the off,' and the player had to allow for this by aiming slightly to the left of the flag.

It is characteristic of the unscientific British approach to the game that it does not seem to have occurred to anyone that the mathematical principle underlying the use of this right to left skidding blow was merely to increase the effective loft of the club, because viewed in relation to the line of movement of the club head, the blade was more open than normal.   Still less did it occur to them that the same result could be attained by making a blade with still greater loft and hitting the ball straight—and this without the unnecessary complication of the off break!   On this side of the Atlantic clubs with increased loft were originally designed to facilitate the recovery shots from sand, and only gradually brought into use for approach play.   It was left to the Americans to develop the use of lofted clubs for the shorter pitch shots, using the loft of the club not to toss the ball higher in the air, but to hit down on the ball with the hands in advance of the club head and so produce a low flying ball with a tremendous amount of back spin—the much discussed 'wedge shot.'

Another development that helped to simplify the mechanics of the golf swing was the substitution of steel shafts for hickory.   The shortage of hickory made such a change inevitable, but though many old timers will tell you that the best hickory was better than steel, it was not without the defects of its qualities.   The chief difference was in the 'torsion' of the hickory shaft, which tended to make the toe of the club twist outwards as the club was taken back and twist back again as the club came down.   It is true that a skilful player could use this torsion to get some slight addition to the length of the shot.   It is equally true that a bad player who got his timing wrong would sometimes bring the toe of the club forward so quickly that it caught the ground before it ever got to the ball.   The modern steel shaft allows no more torsion than is necessary to prevent a sensation of deadness in the swing, but it has increased the power of the drive in two distinct ways.   It can be constructed to the optimum degree of 'whippiness' to suit the individual player. And by the elimination of torsion it makes it possible for the player to hit harder without risk of getting his timing wrong.

The steel shaft, moreover, has the great advantage of uniformity. I mean that one steel shaft can be constructed to match another of a given specification.   With hickory shafts there was no guarantee that one shaft of a given weight and length and diameter and apparent degree of whippiness would behave the same as another. So the steel shaft made possible the idea of 'matched sets' in which the whole range of clubs, Nos. 1 to 4 woods, Nos. 1 to 9 irons, and even the putter, would be expertly graduated in length and weight and loft and degree of whippiness to fit with one another.

Even forty years ago the majority of golfers were content to build up their armoury of weapons haphazard, buying a brassie here and a new mashie there, and allowing their choice to be dictated rather by fancy than by science.   The result, in many cases, was the assembly of a bagful of implements which were eternally at odds one with another.   Stiff shafts and whippy shafts, heavy clubs and light clubs, heads with flat lies and heads with upright lies, were unequally yoked together, and their bewildered owners were constantly lamenting the inexplicable fact that when they were 'on' with one club they always seemed to be 'off' with another!

The coming of 'matched' sets has changed all that.   If a player has a favourite club which never lets him down, club-makers can use this as a model, and give him a whole set to suit his individual swing.   Yet the improvement in their game did not completely reconcile the golfers of the old school to the abandonment of their early fancies.   The late Lord Birkenhead, for instance, was persuaded by Archie Compston to substitute a matched set for the very heterogeneous collection he had been trying to use, and his play was undoubtedly the gainer thereby.   But once he told Compston: 'I never go out for a round without a feeling of regret that I am leaving that old set in the locker.   They were clubs *of a rare vintage.*'

The trouble that most of us find with the modern matched sets of clubs is that they don't really seem to know any more about the game than the old ones did!   'Did you take the wrong club, old man?' our opponent asks, in the familiar tone of false sympathy, when our approach shot finishes thirty yards short of the green. How rarely do we have the candour to reply: 'No! I took the right club, but it had the wrong sort of golfer swinging it!'

Yet the coming of matched sets and the vast improvement in the standard of club-making has had a noticeable effect on the outlook of the general run of players. 'You must learn to let the *club* do the work!' the instructors of the old school were wont to tell their pupils when they tried to scoop the ball up with their approach shots, instead of trusting to the loft of the club face to get the ball in the air. Golfing error now goes to the opposite extreme. Players are not merely willing to let the club do the work; they expect the club to do *all* the work. And players of the old school, who can remember Harold Hilton's ability to match an opponent's best iron shots with a half-shot of his spoon, are apt to grow a trifle impatient when they hear the modern golfer asking for his No. 6 iron, as if it were beyond his powers to play a three-quarter shot with his No. 5 or hit a trifle more firmly with his No. 7. The modern player has grown so accustomed to having a special club for every conceivable stroke that he fails to realize how much of his vaunted skill is due to the science of the club-makers, who have introduced limber shafts to give him greater length, spade-faced lofted clubs to put stop on his approach shots, and blasters and sand-wedges of amazing design to dig him out of the bunkers that a better man would never have got into.

It is one of the inevitable penalties of this scientific standardization that individuality in clubs has been almost entirely destroyed. A century ago Allan Robertson had a name for every club in his bag. Let him come within reach of the green with any of his favourites, 'Sir David Baird,' 'the Doctor,' 'Sir Robert Peel,' 'Thraw-cruik,' or 'the Frying Pan' (his iron), he was invincible. Captain Moles-worth, R.N., one of the pioneers of the game at Westward Ho! never carried more than three clubs: play-club (i.e. driver), lofting iron, and putter, which were known respectively as 'Faith,' 'Hope,' and 'Charity.' However, I have an idea that in this case the names were not of the owner's choosing, but were bestowed by the same ribald adversaries who shortened the name of the veteran himself to 'Old Mole,' because, as they insinuated, he kept to the ground all the way from tee to tin! A famous legal luminary also possessed a club called 'Faith'—his niblick—because, as he delighted to explain to his friends, faith can move mountains.

Nowadays the only club whose choice allows scope for individual fancy is the putter, and few even of the putters have names. One of the few is 'Old Pawky,' the putter of the greatest exponent of the short game of his day, Willie Park, junior, which hangs in the club-house at Woking. But probably the most famous weapon the game has ever known was Bobby Jones's putter, 'Calamity Jane.' It seems an ideal name for a putter. What greater calamity can befall a golfer than a short putt missed? What greater averter of calamity could there be than a long putt holed? Whether from the point of view of the optimist or the pessimist nothing could be more suitable. It appears, however, that the name has a deeper significance than I in my innocence imagined. The original 'Calamity Jane' was an historical personage, a notorious female 'cattle-rustler' of the bad old days in the Far West. In a film of her life-story, when one of her admirers is represented as inquiring why she was given the name, she replies: 'Oh! I guess it's because of what happens to my enemies!' However, I have witnessed too many examples of the good nature with which Emperor Jones treats his opponents to imagine for a moment that the name was chosen as a hint of what was going to happen to his opponents. As a matter of fact it was not he who gave the putter its name. What happened was that Bobby had putted badly in the match in which he was rather heavily beaten by Francis Ouimet in the U.S. Amateur Championship of 1921, and on the following day he went over to Nassau, Long Island, to visit Jimmy Maiden, the brother of Stewart Maiden, the pro-fessional of Bobby's home club at East Lake. Jimmy presented his visitor with a rusty old putter to which he had given the name of 'Calamity Jane,' and with this Bobby holed so many long putts in the course of the day that the thing became a joke. No one at that stage could foresee that 'Calamity Jane' was to become one of the most famous clubs of all time.

CHAPTER TWENTY-FOUR
(1857–1922)

A Science Instead of an Art

AMERICA'S greatest contribution to the development of golf, more important even than her improvements in the weapons of the game, has been the building up of a scientific conception of the principles of good style. A Baconian epigram of the links declares that there are three ways of learning golf: by study, which is the most wearisome; by imitation, which is the most fallacious; and by experience, which is the most bitter. In the early days of golf, players were content to learn by imitation, which meant that in a large proportion of cases they copied the mannerisms of good players without examining their methods. In 1857, when 'A Keen Hand' (H. B. Farnie) compiled the first manual of golf instruction ever published, his division of players into two classes, 'agile' and 'non-agile,' was regarded as the quintessence of golfing wit, but apart from his chapters on the uses of the different clubs (now, of course, wholly out of date), he does not take us very far on the road to a perfect swing. Dr J. G. Macpherson's comments on the style of his contemporaries at St Andrews at a slightly later date are full of insight, but he too is more concerned with the peculiarities of individuals than with general principles.

In the portrait of St Clair of Roslin which appears on another page the hero is depicted standing to his ball for the drive with the left foot far advanced and the right drawn well back. Indeed, the right foot is drawn so far back as to leave the left about midway between it and the ball. All the old-time golfers seem to have adopted this stance. They were pretty well forced to do so, because the excessively long clubs which were then in vogue could not have been swung in any other way. And this old-fashioned stance, which had come down from the days of the feather ball, still continued in use long after golfers had changed over to the guttie. As late as 1891, when the Badminton *Golf* was published, Horace

Hutchinson could lay it down that the correct stance for the drive was with the left foot two or three inches further forward than the right and the ball opposite a point behind the left heel.

This was the method of the North Berwick golfers whose hero was John E. Laidlay, but already at Hoylake there was springing up a school of imitators of John Ball, who drove with the right foot advanced instead of the left and with the ball teed considerably further back. The rivalry between the two Johnnies in the Amateur Championship served to accentuate the contrast between closed stance and open stance, and the defects of the habit of learning by imitation made itself visible in a tendency to exaggerate the difference. There is no doubt, however, that the open stance was more suited to the guttie ball. The closed stance of Willie Park or J. E. Laidlay produced a low ball with a shade of draw and made up for the shorter carry by an excess of run. It suited the feathery ball, which sprang off the face of the club with the same sort of liveliness as the modern rubber-core. (I can vouch for this myself, for I once experimented in playing one of the old featheries with modern clubs. As I had paid five guineas for the ball I did not dare to go in for any wild swiping with it, but even after eighty years the packed feathers still seemed to retain their original elasticity and the ball flew off the face of the club as no guttie would ever do.) With the less lively guttie the difficulty was to get the ball up in the air, and the open stance and the upright swing of John Ball and Harry Vardon made this part of the task considerably easier, producing a maximum of carry with some sacrifice of run. The controversy was decided by the success of Vardon and for a while an exaggeratedly open stance became the rule, and tended to linger on after the change to the rubber-cored ball had robbed it of much of its usefulness.

Harry Vardon's swing was so smooth and unforced that it seemed easy to imitate and within a few years of his first championship victories he became the model of style for the whole world to copy, with the happy result of discouraging all forced and exaggerated mannerisms. His greatest contribution to golfing style, however, was his adoption of what is universally known as 'the Vardon grip,' though he was not in fact the inventor of it, and it seems to have been used by Mr Laidlay, among others, long before Vardon

came on the scene.   It was Vardon's use of it, however, that brought
it into general acceptance, and with minor variations it is the grip
used by the vast majority of golfers to this day.

The feature of it is the 'overlapping' of the little finger of the
right hand over the forefinger of the left.   The hands are brought
as close together as possible, with the two V's formed by the forefinger and thumb of each hand on top of the shaft, and the little
finger of the right hand riding in the hollow between the forefinger
and second finger of the left.   The effect is to cut out the natural
gripping fingers of the right hand, the third and little finger, so
that the club is really grasped by these fingers of the left hand and
the thumb and forefinger of the right.   This gives the maximum
distance between the two points at which the grip is exerted and
consequently the maximum of leverage when the right forearm
comes into play at the moment of striking.

As regards the actual stroke, however, British teachers had not
got much beyond the idea of the swing as a winding-up movement
round the fixed axis of the backbone, and it was left to the Americans
to develop the scientific conception of the stroke as an effort of
mechanical power exerted by a human machine.   They simplified
the game by the adoption of the same style of swing for all strokes
with the exception of the putt; they led the way in the shortening
of the swing made possible by the coming of the rubber-cored ball
and the steel shaft, and they gave golfers a new picture of the stroke
in the theories of the 'grooved swing' and 'the straight left arm.'
The idea of the grooved swing, which was borrowed, I believe, from
baseball, is that the club should as far as possible be kept travelling
up and down in one plane of movement throughout the stroke.
The purpose of the straight left arm is to keep the club head travelling in as wide an arc as possible, which allows the player time and
space in which to work up to the maximum speed at the moment
of striking.

These and other 'mental pictures' of the swing were not laid
down as absolute rules.   Indeed there are no absolute rules of
golfing style.   The Amateur Championship of India has thrice
been won by a player, J. D. Gatheral, who holds his clubs the wrong
way round, with the left hand below the right, and there have been
several other first-class golfers with the same peculiarity.   The

St. Andrews Old Course in 1898: 'Old Tom' Morris driving from the First Tee

Photo: G. B. Farrar

THE TWO 'JOHNNIES'

John Ball (left) and John E. Laidlay, the great rivals of the early years of the Amateur Championship, photographed at the start of the final of the Championship of 1890 at Hoylake.

U.S. Open Championship of 1954 was won by Ed Furgol, who plays under the handicap of a stiff left elbow and a left arm several inches shorter than the right as the result of a boyhood fall from a crossbar in a Utica playground.   But by the presentation of scientific principles on which the beginner can try to work, American instructors have raised the standard of play to a notable degree.

In all departments of the game American science modified the *conception* of good style, but in the matter of holing out they brought about a complete revolution of *method*.   The man who taught the world how to putt was Walter Hagen.   He raised the standard of the short game to such a degree that, as Archie Compston once said to me, 'the rest of us had to do the same or quit!'   At first the accepted explanation was that British inferiority near the pin was due simply to the fact that our players did not practise enough. But that was by no means true of all of them.   Professionals of the old Scots school, like the two Willie Parks, father and son, and Jack White, were assiduous in practice on the green.   It is related of Willie Park, the elder, four times winner of the Open Championship, that he owed his skill on the green to the practice obtained as a boy over 'the baker's holes' at Musselburgh.   It seems that close to the home green on that once-famous course there was a practice putting-green of four holes arranged in the form of a rough square, twenty-five to thirty yards apart.   They were known as 'the baker's holes' from the circumstance of an enterprising local baker coming there on most days with a stock of pies to offer to hungry golfers.   In the intervals of trade the baker was not unwilling to engage in a putting match with any opponent who offered, no doubt losing one or two of his pies to the most skilful of the caddies. Night after night Willie Park as a boy was to be seen engaging in this putting game.   It is said that his record for the four-hole round was 5!

His son, the younger Willie Park, who won the Open Championship in 1887 and 1889, was the author of the claim that 'the man who can putt is a match for anyone.'   When he came to Ganton for the second half of his great challenge match against Harry Vardon, Vardon had built new tees at some of the holes so as to give a longer carry over the bunkers—quite a legitimate bit of tactics, since the match was in some sense a test of driver *v.* putter.   But in after years, when I once chaffed Harry about arranging the course to suit his own play, he told me very seriously that he thought he had been perfectly fair about it. When Park came to Ganton for a couple of day's practice before the match, Harry took him round and pointed out the longer carries, which his rival could quite easily have accomplished if he had tackled them with a high-flying shot instead of his usual low hooking drive. But Park was so obsessed with his 'man who can putt' idea that he would not even trouble to test the carries, but spent all his time practising on the glorious Ganton greens.

So it was not from any lack of understanding of the value of practice that these old heroes failed to pass the torch to the generation that succeeded them. The trouble was that they had no scientific method to teach. The old axiom that 'driving is an art, approach play a science, and putting an inspiration' fairly summed up their game. Holing out was just another golf stroke, dependent upon accuracy of striking and sensitiveness of touch. It was left to the Americans to evolve a method that is to a limited extent foolproof, the idea of straight-line putting. The feature of this method is that the head of the club is kept travelling along the prolongation of the straight line from hole to ball throughout the stroke. The left hand pushes the club back, the right brings it forward with the left hand acting as a hinge; and the blade of the club is kept at right angles to the line throughout the stroke. Hagen used to play it with the ball more or less opposite his left foot and his weight piled on the left leg, but the method can equally well be used with any stance, and nowadays most players prefer an upright stance with the feet close together in the manner of Bobby Jones.

How little the old Scots professionals understood the new idea is shown by Jack White's criticism that if the blade of the putter is to be kept at right angles to the line of the putt throughout the back-swing, the impact, and the follow-through, it can only be done by crooking the right elbow outwards on the back-swing and also crooking the left elbow out on the forward swing. As he said in his book *Easier Golf*, this is simply the application of the principle of the 'shut face' on a small scale, and he went on to argue that 'it introduces a complication in muscular control which is quite fatal to the consistent success of the shot.'

The golfers of the old school like Park and White loved to talk of the putting stroke as being played with the action of a pendulum, only the hands and wrists being used in the swing and the club head moving in a short but wide arc struck from a centre somewhere behind the heels.   White observes that when you putt naturally and easily with this swing 'you will infallibly find that . . . when the face makes contact with the ball, it is dead at right angles to the line.'

The naïveté of this argument is almost incredible.   It only amounts to saying that if you have a perfect swing you will make a perfect stroke.   It would be just as fair to apply White's own line of argument and say that the swing he advocates involves the club moving in something of an arc, and that the necessity of hitting the ball at the precise moment when the club is at right angles to the line 'introduces a complication which is quite fatal to the consistent success of the shot.'

There were good putters before Walter Hagen, but the old school had no means of imparting their skill to others.   Straight-line putting, by contrast, is practically foolproof.   Admittedly it is not a natural movement.   But the player's muscles will have no difficulty in accomplishing it if he will leave it to them and refrain from interfering!   It is still quite easy to go wrong, but the straight-line theory provides a guide which the eye can follow, whereas the arc-like swing allows no test of its own accuracy—except the result.

Along with these improved methods of execution, American keenness introduced new standards of achievement.   The Scots had been too long inured to rough courses and old-fashioned weapons, and were content to accept the new standards of greenkeeping and new standards of distance as making the game easier, without troubling to consider that easier conditions ought to be reflected in better scores.   When the Americans began to talk of 'knocking three shots into two' from distances of ten, twenty, thirty yards off the green, the old-timers required time to adjust themselves to the new idea.   I remember Charlie Whitcombe telling me once that it took him a couple of seasons to get used to the idea of saving himself with a pitch and a putt when he failed to hit the green with his second shot.   He had been brought up to the idea that if he missed the green with his approach, he *didn't deserve* to get down in two more, and it took him quite a time to get rid of the feeling that there was something not quite fair in trying to snatch a 4 after the failure of his second shot.   The American attitude might be summed up in the slogan 'Figures talk.'   For the golfer the score is the thing that counts; for him Horace's classic advice,

Rem facias, rem
Si possis recte, si non quocunque modo rem,

may be freely translated: 'The figures are the thing; get them in the orthodox way if you can; if not, by any means at all, get the figures.'

Add to this that the intense competition of the U.S. tournament season—the Gold Dust Circuit—has made their professionals 'tournament tough' to a degree unequalled in any other country. The late Lord Castelrosse used to tell a story of the coolness of Walter Hagen in this respect.   On one occasion when he was studying the line of a more than missable putt to secure first prize in a big tournament, a stray dog dashed up, seized the ball in its teeth, and made off with it.   The spot was immediately marked, the dog pursued, the ball recovered and replaced, and Hagen duly holed the putt.   A friend who came forward to congratulate him expressed his relief, saying: 'I was afraid you'd be upset by that dashed cur making off with your ball.'   'Why should I be upset?' retorted Walter.   'It was still the same putt, wasn't it?'   That is a philosophy to which British golfers find it difficult to rise.   If you are left with a simple six-footer to hole on a keen green, what difference does it make that the result of a whole Walker Cup or Ryder Cup Match depends upon it?   It is still the same putt, isn't it?

CHAPTER TWENTY-FIVE
(1829–1914)

Putting a Girdle Round the Globe

ALTHOUGH Ireland's somewhat shadowy claim in support of the Celtic origin of golf is nowadays commemorated by an annual five-mile cross-country competition from the first tee at Kildare to one of the holes on the Curragh course, there was little golf in Ireland prior to the golf boom of the nineties. It is true that there was at least one attempt to bring the game into the Green Isle in the reign of James I, for we find Hugh Montgomery, afterwards Viscount Montgomery of the Ards (in County Down), one of the Scottish settlers who received grants of land in Ireland at the time of the Plantation of Ulster, making a gift of land for the establishment of a grammar-school, with ground on which the scholars might 'play at golf.' The school, however, disappeared in the troublous times of the Civil War, and the links no doubt with it.

There is also a tradition of golf being played early in the nineteenth century at Laytown in County Meath, but modern golf in Ireland is generally accepted as beginning with the founding of the Royal Belfast Golf Club by a Scottish golfer, Mr George Baillie, in 1881. Its first home was 'the Kinnegar' at Holywood, since used as a rifle range, and there it remained until 1892, in which year a move was made to the famous course at Carnalea, which became a municipal course in 1926 when the Club moved on to its present home at Craigavad. Even before the establishment of the Royal Belfast Club, however, the game had been played at the Curragh, chiefly by the officers of Scottish regiments quartered there, and the Royal Curragh Club has a vague sort of claim to an existence dating from immediately after the Crimean War.

The man who introduced the game to Dublin was a young subaltern in the Grenadier Guards, who later became Brigadier-General Sir David Kinloch of Gilmerton. He had learned his golf as a boy at St Andrews, and he had been one of the pioneers of the game at

Oxford. In the autumn of 1884, when he was quartered with his regiment in Richmond Barracks, Dublin, he and Mr John Oswald, of Dunnikier, who was at that time one of the viceroy's staff, laid out a few holes in the Phoenix Park. The idea caught on, and a small Club was formed, the members later including Mr A. J. Balfour. It was the destruction of the Phoenix Park course by the Land Leaguers that led to the formation of the Royal Dublin Golf Club at Dollymount, as I have already narrated.

In the early part of the present century Ireland's championship honours all stood to the credit of her girls. In the nine seasons from 1899 to 1907 Miss May Hezlet and Miss Rhona Adair brought the Ladies' Championship to Ireland five times. Miss Hezlet (Mrs Adrian Ross) made her first attempt on the title when she was thirteen, and she had just turned seventeen when in 1899 she won the Irish Ladies' Championship and the British Ladies' Championship within a fortnight of one another at Newcastle, Co. Down. Her brother, now Lt-Col. C. O. Hezlet, D.S.O., was runner-up in the Amateur Championship in 1914, but that was as near as any of the men from the Green Isle got to winning a British Championship until after the Second World War. Then just at the time when amateur golf in England and Scotland seemed to be entering on a period of eclipse, the Irishmen stepped into the breach. In the first eight years after the war, the only breaks in a run of U.S. successes were the victories of James Bruen at Birkdale in 1946, of Max McCready at Portmarnock three years later, and of Joe Carr at Hoylake in 1953, in all three cases with an American as runner-up. In 1947 Fred Daly won both the British Open Championship and the Professional Match Championship—the first Irishman to hold either title and the first player to hold both in the same year since James Braid did so forty-two years before him. In the following year Daly won the match play title again and was runner-up to Henry Cotton in the Open, and in the great Ryder Cup Match of 1952 he and Harry Bradshaw from Eire were responsible for 3 points out of Great Britain's total of 5½. Lucky! Well, when anyone talks of the luck of the Irish, it seems to me only another way of saying that 'fortune favours the brave.'

The story of golf on the Continent of Europe begins in romantic fashion with the Peninsular War. It is said that after Wellington's victory at Orthez in 1814, two officers of Scottish regiments who were billeted at Pau and who had optimistically included their golf clubs in their kit, played a rough and ready game or two on the plain of Billere. They were so taken with the attractions of Pau that twenty years later they both returned on holiday to Pau and again brought their clubs for a round or two of golf. It was not until 1856, however, that the Pau Golf Club came into being with a nine-hole course and a clubhouse in a room in a wayside inn. The names of three officers of field rank figure along with that of the Duke of Hamilton in the list of five founders, so presumably the Orthez tradition still survived.

Pau was the first of many continental resorts in which golf was introduced for the benefit of British holiday makers. Elsewhere on the Continent interest in the game developed slowly, but a tremendous fillip was given to it by the victory of the French professional Arnaud Massy in the British Open Championship at Hoylake in 1907. That was the year that saw the introduction of the qualifying rounds into the British event, and Massy's superiority was emphasized by the fact that he had headed the list in the qualifying stage as well as in the Championship itself, and that his aggregate over the six rounds was several strokes better than that of anybody else. Accordingly the flower of the British professionals went over to La Boulie to try to reverse the decision in the French Championship, which had been instituted the year before, and of which Massy was the holder. The result was to redouble the French triumph, for though James Braid, who had held the British Open for the two previous years, finished at the top of the British contingent, he was only third, with two Frenchmen in front of him, Arnaud Massy and Jean Gassiat. After that it became the fashion for the winner of the British Championship to go over to France for a sort of retrial in the French event, and for a year or two James Braid and J. H. Taylor divided the honours. In 1908 Braid won the British and Taylor the French event; in 1909 Taylor won both, and in 1910 Braid won both.

These events brought the continental players very definitely into the limelight, and the new continental keenness for the game was reflected in the triumph of Mlle Simone Thion de la Chaume (Mme

René Lacoste) and Mlle Manette le Blan (Mme Robert de la Chaume), who in 1927 and 1928 took the Ladies' Championship to France for two successive years.   Since the Second World War we have had another French winner of the Ladies' Championship in the Comtesse de Saint Sauveur, who as Mlle Lally Vagliano had already won the British Girls' Championship of 1937.   Arnaud Massy never again quite succeeded in recapturing the form of his championship year, but in later years Flory van Donck, of Belgium, and a growing host of first-class professional players from Italy and the Western European countries have maintained the continental challenge.

The oldest Golf Clubs outside of Scotland and England are the Royal Calcutta Golf Club, founded in 1829, and the Royal Bombay Golfing Society, which dates from 1842.   In the middle of the nineteenth century, therefore, there were as many Golf Clubs in India as in England.   The jute trade, of course, had brought about a close association between Calcutta and Dundee, and as a natural result of this many of the original members—and in later years a stout proportion of the winners of the Amateur Championship of India—came from Tayside.   The Amateur Championship of India, in the same way, is the oldest national championship outside of the British Isles.   In 1892 the Calcutta Golf Club—it became Royal Calcutta in 1912—sent out a letter to all the Golf Clubs in India, Burma, Ceylon, and the Straits Settlements, proposing the institution of an 'Amateur Golf Championship of India and the East,' to be held at Calcutta, and this met with so favourable a response that the first Championship was carried through in December of the same year, the first winner being J. F. Macnair.

For the first seven years the Championship was decided by stroke play, and scores ranging from J. F. Macnair's 288 to the 265 with which J. Stuart Smith won the title in 1898 seem to indicate an impossibly high standard of play.   As a matter of fact they are not remarkable, because the totals are for 54 holes, the result of a curious arrangement such as has never been adopted in any other event of like importance.   In those days the Calcutta Club were the possessors of a nine-hole course at Dum Dum and two nine-hole courses on the Maidan, and the Championship was decided over four rounds at Dum Dum plus one round on each of the Maidan nines.

In 1896 the nine-hole course of the Tollygunge Club took the place of Dum Dum. In 1899 play on the Maidan was discontinued and from that date until the First World War the Championship was decided on the course of the Tollygunge Club, which by 1906 had been extended to the full eighteen holes. In 1913 the first of the Royal Club's present two eighteen-hole courses—also located at Tollygunge—was opened for play, and after the war the Championship was played in alternate years on the Old Course of the Royal Calcutta Club and the course of the Tollygunge Club. Since 1930 the Championship has always been held on the former course.

The pioneers at Calcutta and Bombay were the forerunners of a great number of Clubs in the Far East. The Bangalore Club dates back to 1870, the Colombo Club to 1881, the Royal Hong Kong Club to 1889. Outside of the British Commonwealth Batavia, in Java, had a nine-hole course in 1872, twenty years before there was any course in Holland. The Rangoon Club was instituted in 1887. Golf in Siam is almost as old as in the United States, for the Royal Bangkok Club was founded in 1890, and had as its first clubhouse and ancient and exceedingly picturesque temple. At Singapore the original nine-hole course was situated around the grounds of the gaol and the hospital, and the names of the holes were a veritable *memento mori*, including the Cholera green, the Smallpox green, the Mortuary, the Gallows, and the Gaol.

The humorists may affect to find evidence for a Chinese origin of golf in ancient references to 'the torture of the thousand slices,' but apart from the Royal Hong Kong Club's courses, there appears to have been no golf in China prior to the formation of the Shanghai Club in 1896. Golf in Japan dates from the construction of a course of four holes by a pioneer named A. H. Groome, on the summit of Mount Rokko, Kobe, in 1903. The course soon became a flourishing full-size affair, in spite of the fact that in pre-motor days the journey to it involved a ride by rickshaw to the foot of the Cascade Valley, from which the visitor was carried up the mountain side by coolies—a journey that took the best part of an hour and a half. The formation of the Tokyo Club at Komazawa by Japanese enthusiasts in 1914 marked the beginning of a golf

boom in Japan, and between the two world wars Japanese professionals competed in both the British and U.S. Championships.

The earliest of the Canadian Golf Clubs anticipated the renais-
sance of the game in the United States by fifteen years or so.
Ignoring the claims to pioneer honours of a young Glasgow sailor
named William Dibman, who, finding himself in the Port of Quebec
in 1854, 'carried his clubs to the heights of Abraham and there
entertained himself in solitary contentment,' we can say that the
history of golf on the American continent began with the founding
in November 1873 of the Royal Montreal Club, which originally
played over Fletcher's Fields in Mount Royal Park.   The expansion
of the city, however, soon forced them to change their local habitation to Dixie—so named by a colony of Southern refugees who
gathered there at the time of the American Civil War.   Dixie,
where the Club has now two famous eighteen-hole courses, is nine
miles out of the city, but the view up the river from the course is
alone worth the journey.   There is good reason to suppose that it
was the Royal Montreal Club who brought out the first of the great
army of professionals who have gone over to the States and Canada
from Carnoustie and Musselburgh and other centres of the game in
Scotland and England.   Curious to relate, this pioneer was not a
Scot, but a Hoylake player named W. F. Davis.   He came to
Montreal in 1881 at a salary of just under 5 dollars a week in addition
to the profits of his shop, which were regulated, however, by a
contract which provided that he should not charge more than 60
cents for a club head and 50 cents for a shaft.   His teaching fee for
a round of nine holes was to be 25 cents, of which one-third had to
be handed over to the Club!   Davis, nevertheless, seems to have
been able to thrive on these terms, for he remained at Montreal for
thirteen years.

In 1875, rather more than a year after the foundation of the
Montreal Club, a Club was started in Quebec.   The Club owed its
inception to Mrs Hunter, a daughter of old Tom Morris, who came
to Quebec with her husband, and its course was established on the
'Cove Fields,' which lie between the citadel and the historic Heights
of Abraham.   I have been told that many an ancient bullet was dug
up by enthusiastic players taking too much turf with their mashie.

But alas! the modern bullets wrought more harm to the game than the ancient ones, for first the building of the Ross Rifle Factory shore off nine of the holes, and soon the remainder were threatened, so that in 1917 the Club was forced to move to its present location at Montmorency Falls. On the old course on the Heights of Abraham the first inter-Club match played in America took place in 1876, the Quebec Club entertaining the senior organization from Montreal and defeating their visitors by 12 holes. It is recorded that in those early matches flannels and red coats were the proper wear, and that the two captains, who were expected to oppose one another in the top match and drive off first, always wore white gloves on the first tee, though the gloves were always discarded before the second shots were played.

Toronto followed the lead of the other two in 1876, and those three clubs, formed within a space of less than as many years, must rank as the advance guard of the immense army of American golf. None of the three clubs in those early days possessed anything in the nature of a clubhouse, and the Toronto historian records that 'members frequently took picnic baskets with them and had their lunch under the trees.' *O fortunati nimium!* Toronto Club, like Montreal and Quebec, found itself forced by the growth of the city to betake itself to 'fresh greens and bunkers new,' and the Club migrated in 1912 to Long Branch.

In the early eighties golf had got going in every part of the British Commonwealth. The first of the Australian Clubs, the Royal Adelaide Golf Club, was formed in 1870. In New Zealand the Christchurch Golf Club dates back to 1873. The Royal Cape Golf Club, at Wynberg, formed in 1885 by some officers of Scottish regiments quartered at the Cape, is frequently spoken of as the senior Golf Club of South Africa, but I believe that the Maritzburg Golf Club, the first Club in Natal, came into being in the previous year.

Both in Australia and in South Africa the progress of the game was retarded by problems of turf maintenance, but since these were solved both countries have won a big place in the golfing sun. Arthur D'Arcy (universally known as 'Bobby') Locke capped several seasons of notable performance in the U.S. tournament circuit by winning the British Open Championship thrice in four years. Australia's banner year was 1954. Peter Thomson, still only twenty-four and no more than at the outset of his professional career, carried off both the Open Championship and the Professional Match Play Championship. Douglas Bachli won the Amateur Championship at Muirfield, and followed up his victory with an unexampled run of success at the head of the Australian team in its matches on tour. Another member of the team, Harry Berwick, won the St George's Challenge Cup at Sandwich, and Peter Toogood replaced American Frank Stranahan in the position of 'first amateur' in the Open. The Australian amateur team won the Commonwealth Tournament held at St Andrews to celebrate the bicentenary of the Royal and Ancient Club. In the wider field of world events, the Canada Cup, open to teams of two professionals nominated by countries from every part of the globe, was won for Australia by Peter Thomson and Kel Nagle, who beat the holders, Roberto de Vicenzo and Antonio Cerda, of Argentina, by four strokes. By a happy coincidence Lord Bruce of Melbourne had early in the year been nominated as the new captain of the Royal and Ancient Club, and duly played himself into office at the Autumn Meeting of the Club in September. There is no question but that the future will hold its share of Australian triumphs, but such an amazing sweeping of the board may not be repeated in a lifetime.

CHAPTER TWENTY-SIX
(1774–1953)
The Development of Golf Architecture

IF one of the crack golfers of a hundred years ago could return to the links, it is safe to say he would be absolutely astounded to witness the degree of skill expected of his opposite number of the present day. From a distance of a quarter of a mile a first-class player normally counts on being able to propel his ball into a hole four and a quarter inches wide in four strokes; a player of championship class is expected to do better than that, and has no hope of a leading place unless he can manage to mingle a proportion of 3's among the 4's. But this standard of skill is only made possible by the fact that the modern golfer is playing on a course specially prepared to suit his play; the heroes of George Glennie's day were playing a cross-country game and had to take the links as they found it.

Dr J. G. Macpherson, who played his best golf as a student at St Andrews in the middle of the last century, estimated that the Old Course had become six strokes easier during the ensuing thirty years. The coming of the guttie ball, which reduced the expense of the game by two-thirds, brought an immense influx of new players on to the course, and at the same time the use of iron clubs through the green gradually cut down the gorse and bents along either edge of the fairway, which in consequence became appreciably widened. Yawning bunkers that had to be carried when the fairways were narrower could now be avoided by steering down the side. Most serious change of all was in the *uniformity* of the greens. In earlier days, says Dr Macpherson, 'there was a variety of surface which brought out the greater skill; now all are nicely turfed over and artificially dressed like billiard tables. Then, at the Heather Hole one had to dodge about and watch the lie of the green.... Now, a dead straight putt suffices. The Sandy Hole puzzled the uninitiated with its heavy putting surface; now it is a stroke easier.'

A point that must not be lost sight of is that at this early stage the links received no attention; the only greenkeepers were the rabbits.   As early as 1774 the Edinburgh Burgess Society decided that a boy should be appointed to undertake the duty of calling on each member every Saturday morning, taking the names of those proposing to dine at the Golf Tavern, acting as caddie to the Preses on the Saturday and as waiter at the dinner.   'In consideration of his trouble' the Society with princely generosity 'resolved to pay him six shillings per quarter out of their funds.'   You will observe that in the true spirit of that age his duties were more concerned with the arrangements for dining than with the arrangements for golf, but it is probable that his minor duties included the cutting of new holes.   A century later affairs were still in much the same state. In 1866 a joint council, made up of two members each from the Burgess, Bruntsfield, and Warrender Clubs and of one member each from the Merchiston and Allied Clubs, was appointed to take charge of the Bruntsfield links and to be jointly responsible for paying a person 'to make the holes, look after the flags, and mend the turf.' A similar arrangement for the upkeep of Musselburgh links was later entered into between the Honourable Company, Royal Mussel-burgh, Burgess, and Bruntsfield Clubs.   But the 'mending of the turf' probably involved no more than the repair of divot marks in the immediate vicinity of the hole, which was still the teeing ground as well as the putting green.   Nobody had yet conceived the fantastic notion that the putting greens should be mown and rolled! In other places even more primitive arrangements prevailed.   When the Notts. Golf Club first came into being in 1887, there was no Sunday play on their course on Bulwell Common.   The last match to go out on the Saturday were expected to gather the flags and bring them in with them, and the first match to go out on the Monday carried them back again.

Alterations in the links were no doubt occasionally made by energetic committees.   Dr Macpherson draws a picture of the veteran George Glennie, 'the best golfer of his day,' watching the filling in of 'Tam's Coo' bunker, like a knight of old regarding the dead body of an honoured and valiant adversary.   But in the main things were left much as nature made them.   When a new course came to be laid out anywhere, the sites of the greens were determined by the existence of attractive hollows of smooth turf, or of equally natural plateaux, and by the proximity of suitable hazards. It had not yet occurred to anyone that turf and hazards, hollows and plateaux, could all be artificially created.

In Scotland as well as England the earliest inland courses were laid out on public commons, where there were usually plenty of natural hazards in the shape of ditches and gorse to take the place of the bunkers and dunes of the seaside links. It is surprising to find that the oldest private course in the environs of Edinburgh is Mortonhall, which only came into existence in 1892. As late as 1927 the Worcestershire Club was still playing over the old nine-hole round on Malvern Common, under much the same conditions as prevailed in 1880, when Colonel R. Prescott-Decie brought Matthew Allen over from Westward Ho! to help him with the lay-out of the course. I even yet entertain sentimental recollections of golf on the Common, with its ducks and hens, its cyclists and grazing horses and donkeys, its lamp-posts and rows of washing fluttering on the line to add to more conventional obstacles. The courses on the commons as a rule did not call for the creation of any artificial hazards, because they offered an ample variety of natural difficulties of their own.

It was a different story when the golf boom led to the construction of innumerable courses in private parks. On both sides of the Atlantic lawn-like putting greens called for new standards of construction and upkeep, and artificial cross-bunkers at appropriate intervals made the course a steeplechase rather than a point-to-point affair. For the time being courses were laid out to suit stereotyped shots instead of the player being expected to choose his shots to suit the course. This penal school of golf architecture, however, was soon superseded by the strategic school, which treated golf as a contest of risks, laid it down that weak shots punished themselves, and sited the hazards to interest the stronger player, rewarding the longer carry or the more accurately placed drive by the prospect of the possible saving of a stroke.

A tremendous step forward was the discovery that the roughest of heathland could by suitable treatment be converted into turf within the space of a few months. Sunningdale, sown with seed in September 1900, took exactly twelve months to be fit for play. Four years later Walton Heath was got ready in eight months.

The heath soil at Sunningdale was exceptionally poor and when it was sown there was no lack of knowing people who jeered at the folly of imagining that grass could be got to grow there. Eight months later the same critics were saying that anyone could lay out a good course in such a bit of natural golf country. But it took a bit of imagination on the part of the pioneers to discover that sour heath was natural golf country.

Promoters of Golf Clubs all over Europe and America began to discover that first-class courses could be carved out of primeval forests and built up on sandy wastes wherever people were willing to spend the money to do it. In 1909 Charles B. Macdonald, the first winner of the United States Golf Association Amateur Championship, designed the National Links at Long Island with eighteen holes copied from eighteen of the most famous holes on the classic courses of Scotland and England, a successful demonstration of what could be done in the way of reproducing the strategy, if not always the appearance, of the great tests of play. Golf architecture became one of the fine arts, and except as regards the difficulties arising from a sea breeze, the best inland courses became as stiff a test of the game as the most famous of the seaside links.

Yet even the architects of the strategic school have failed to cope with the development of longer drives and quick-stopping iron shots to well-watered greens, and modern golf, especially in the States, tends to become a game of target shots. I saw a good example of this in the Ryder Cup Match of 1953 at Wentworth in the foursome in which Jack Burke and Ted Kroll went round in 66 to build up a big morning lead against Jamie Adams and Bernard Hunt. In the afternoon the thirteenth hole was halved in 4, but the two sides adopted two entirely different methods of attack.

The hole is 429 yards long and dog-legged to the left, with the ground rising at the finish to a tightly guarded green on a bit of a plateau. Trees and bushes on the left come unpleasantly close in to the line of the approach if you get over to that side, and the green itself is orientated to suit a second shot from the right. The British pair played the hole perfectly, in the way the golf architect who designed it intended them to do. Hunt placed his drive with admirable accuracy on the extreme right of the fairway so as to open up the hole. Adams played a beautiful pitch and run shot up the

Photo: G. B. Farrar

The start of the Amateur Championship final of 1901 at St. Andrews in which Harold Hilton (driving) defeated John L. Low (right) by one hole. Hilton was twice victorious in the British Open Championship, four times in the British Amateur Championship. In 1911 he won both the British and U.S. Amateur titles.

(*Right*)
Horace G. Hutchinson, who reached the final of the first three Amateur Championships and won two of them.

The great Harry Vardon at the
time of his first Championship
victories at the end of last century
and (above right) in 1910.

Golf's Ablest Publicist: the Rt. Hon. Ar
James Balfour (afterwards Lord Balfou

slope leading to the front of the green. The ball ran, I dare say, eight yards past the hole and Hunt put the first putt a couple of inches from the edge of the tin.

The Americans also played the hole perfectly, but according to an entirely different school of tactics. They took no heed of how the golf architect meant the hole to be played, but were content to put their drive down the middle of the fairway, with plenty of margin for error on either side. Actually Kroll got a shade further to the left than I imagine he intended, and if Burke had been planning to play the same type of approach as Adams he would have been distinctly awkwardly placed.

In fact, it made no difference whatever. Burke's iron shot dropped about four yards short of the tin, gave one little bounce of six inches, and lay still. The ball was just near enough the tin to encourage Kroll to go for the 3. He didn't get it down, but Burke and he made the 4 very easy for themselves.

Here then was another example of the difference in the two mentalities. The British pair played that hole with the perfection of artists, the Americans with the precision of machines. And in the long run the artists will always be beaten by the machines.

Yet even while I admire the marvellous co-ordination between eye and muscle called for by this modern target golf, I cannot but regret that it has taken us so far from the original conception of the old cross-country game. One of the things which distinguished golf from every other pastime was that while other games were imitations of war in miniature golf was an imitation of life, in which the player had to thread his way among unexpected dangers and undeserved bad lies. Of golf almost alone among games it could be said that a man's worst enemy was himself.

That is still true, but we have been so anxious, in the sacred name of fair play, to take all the element of luck out of the game, that we have to a proportionate extent destroyed its value as a test of each man's ability to stand up to bad luck. Modern golf is a stiffer test of a player's skill, but it has robbed the game of something of its charm as an adventure of the spirit.

The Evolution of the Rules

PRIOR to the inauguration of the first competitions at Leith and St Andrews, there was no need for any established code of rules. At each golf centre the accepted procedure would be known to all the habitual visitors: disputed points would be referred to the amicable decision of one or two of the oldest players.   But both at Leith and St Andrews the Silver Clubs were originally offered for open competition.   Strangers competing for them might quite conceivably be coming from courses where the local procedure was slightly different.   So when the twenty-two Noblemen and Gentlemen of St Andrews met on 14th May 1754 to confirm the conditions and regulations governing the play for their trophy, they had already drawn up a series of 'Articles and Laws in playing the Golf.' The 'Conditions and Regulations' governing the competition are taken almost verbatim from those put out ten years earlier for the Silver Club of the City of Edinburgh, and it is probable that the 'Articles and Laws' were also adopted from a code in vogue at Leith.   They are so admirably brief that I need not hesitate to give them *in extenso*—shorn, however, of superfluous capitals:

1. You must tee your ball within a club-length of the hole.
2. Your tee must be upon the ground.
3. You are not to change the ball which you strike off the tee.
4. You are not to remove stones, bones, or any break-club for the sake of playing your ball, except upon the fair green, and that only within a club length of your ball.
5. If your ball come among water or any watery filth, you are at liberty to take out your ball and throw it behind the hazard six yards at least; you may play it with any club, and allow your adversary a stroke for so getting out your ball.
6. If your balls be found anywhere touching one another, you are to lift the first ball until you play the last.

7. At holing you are to play your ball honestly for the hole, and not to play upon your adversary's ball, not lying in your way to the hole.

8. If you should lose your ball by its being taken up or any other way, you are to go back to the spot where you struck last and drop another ball and allow your adversary a stroke for the misfortune.

9. No man at holing his ball is to be allowed to mark his way to the hole with his club or anything else.

10. If a ball is stop'd by any person, horse, dog or anything else, the ball so stop'd must be played where it lyes.

11. If you draw your club in order to strike and proceed so far with your stroke as to be bringing down your club, if then your club should break in any way, it is to be accounted a stroke.

12. He whose ball lyes furthest from the hole is obliged to play first.

13. Neither trench, ditch, or dyke made for the preservation of the links, nor the Scholars' Holes, nor the Soldiers Lines, shall be accounted a hazard, but the ball is to be taken out, teed, and played with any iron club.

(The Scholars' Holes refers to what would now be called a practice putting green near the present seventeenth, but the location of 'the Soldiers Lines' has defied modern research.)

The most illuminating of these rules is the first. What must have been the nature of the putting greens when golfers could make it a rule to tee their ball within a club length of the hole? It is true that a few years later we find that the 'Laws to be observed by the members of the golfing company [i.e. of Leith] in playing golf,' afford a meagre protection to the green immediately around the hole: 'You must tee your ball not nearer the hole than two club lengths, nor further from it than four,' and this is also the form of the rule in the St Andrews code as late as 1812. By 1851 St Andrews went a trifle further in the direction of preserving the putting surface, for Rule 2 of the revised code published in that year reads:

The ball must be teed not nearer (either in front or side of the hole) than four club lengths and not further from it than six....

The original Manchester (now Old Manchester) Club in 1860 provided its members with a wooden measure, wound with a length of cord. Upon the measure were printed the following directions:

> Balls may be removed if within six inches of each other.
> Balls must be teed within four club lengths of the hole.
> The putting ground extends six club lengths from the hole.
> The measure is six inches in length.
> The first knot on the cord represents four club lengths.
> The extreme length of the cord represents six club lengths.

The St Andrews code of 1754 was expressly framed to govern the play for the Silver Club, and it will be noted that the references to 'your adversary' in rules 5, 7, and 8 indicated that they refer to match play. Indeed rule 7 would be quite meaningless if it referred to stroke play. So far as they go, therefore, the code confirms my belief that the original method of deciding the competitions for the Silver Clubs was by drawing for opponents in matches, and contradicts Mr Everard's conception of an elaborately worked out stroke play computation, described in the next chapter.

In fact, it was because match play was still the accepted form of golf that these original rules, few and simple as they are, sufficed with slight modification for more than a hundred years. In a match the worst possible disaster, however little deserved, could only affect the result of a single hole, and the simple rule that the ball must be played as it lay or the hole given up provided an adequate solution for all occasions. Doubtful points could be decided by mutual agreement or reserved for decision by some friendly arbiter.

But as stroke play became more and more the accepted form of competition and contestants increased in numbers, decisions by mutual agreement or by an umpire specially appointed for the meeting, as was done for the first Open Championships, ceased to be a practical solution. Moreover, though players were accustomed to submit with a good grace to be robbed of a hole by an unplayable lie, they wanted rules for stroke play that would allow them to lift clear of the danger and go on. And so the code became more and more complicated by stipulations regarding the circumstances in which the player should be allowed to lift from a bad position, and the penalty (if any) to be paid.

For the full rigour of the game you have to go to the Aberdeen code of 1783, which laid it down that

> No stones, loose sand, or other impediments shall be removed when putting at the hole.
>
> No person shall be at liberty to vary or better his stance in playing, by breaking the surface of the green, placing or removing stones, sand, or any substance: damping his feet with water excepted.

Even in *chole* the possibility of a ball finding an unplayable lie was provided for in the rules, but who is to judge whether a ball is unplayable?   On various courses at various times the local code provided for a possible disagreement on the point.   At St Andrews from 1852 to 1856 the following rule was in force:

> When the ball lies in a hole or in any place that the player considers is not playable, he shall, with the consent of his adversary, lift the ball, drop it in the hazard, and lose a stroke.   Should the adversary say, however, that he thinks the ball playable, then he (the adversary) plays the ball; if he makes the ball playable in two strokes, the two strokes count as if the player had played the ball; the player then plays the ball as if he himself had played it out; but if the adversary does not get the ball out at the two strokes, then, as stated above, it is lifted and dropped, a stroke being lost.

This rule, however, was directly at variance with the traditional idea of golf as a game in which each side plays its own ball, free from any interference by its opponents, and moreover involved an obvious injustice in that a lie which is unplayable for one golfer might be playable by another.   So in 1856 Sir Robert Hay proposed and carried a motion to the effect that 'in match play every ball must be played where it lies or the hole be given up.'

These and similarly drastic regulations, such as the 'lost ball, lost hole,' which superseded the stroke and distance penalty in 1882 and remained in force until 1920, were all very well in match play, but they could not be applied to stroke competitions, and were a source of dissatisfaction to the growing number of newcomers to the game who recked nothing of its traditions and even in match play desired to keep a record of their scores.   One of the chief difficulties in the establishment of a universal code of rules was that while the St Andrews code was designed for match play, with an addendum of modifications for stroke competitions, the rest of the world regarded stroke play as the basis of the game and would have preferred a code of rules primarily designed for that.

Another factor in the demand for greater elasticity in the rules was the extension of the game to remote corners of the globe where conditions were entirely at variance with anything ever contemplated by Scottish legislators.   When the Duke of Windsor, as Prince of Wales, visited Jinga during his African tour, he had a round with Sir William Gowers, the Governor of Uganda, over the nine-hole course there.   In the course of the match the prince had the experience of finding his ball 'bunkered' in the footprint left by a hippopotamus, but to Uganda golfers, apparently, such an incident is one of the commonplaces of the round, so much so that they have provided for it by a 'local rule' which permits the player to lift his ball out of the print and drop it without penalty.   Such a rule, of course, is no different in legal theory from the old local rule adopted in many Scottish links allowing a player to lift his ball out of a rabbit scrape, but in some other overseas courses nature had made it inevitable that any attempt to play golf should involve a complete departure from the traditional spirit of the game.   For instance, I have in my possession some photographs of the courses at Rokko-san, in Japan, and at Wei-Hai-Wei, in which the greens appear as saucer-shaped depressions entirely surrounded by a ditch and low rampart, looking much more like bunkers than greens.   They were in fact made of brown clay, baked hard by the sun and kept in condition by the use of a heavy roller, and sprinkled with dry earth to give a grip to the ball.   They were all right to putt on, but anything of the nature of a pitch shot was clean out of the question. The ball could not possibly be made to stop on that asphalt surface, and a fairly accurate shot was required to drop within the rampart bank and run on into the little ditch on the inner side.   From there a local rule permitted the ball to be lifted without penalty on to the edge of the ditch *nearer the hole*, from which the player proceeded to putt out in the ordinary way.

As an extreme example of letting the duffer down gently I would select a local rule at the famous Cliff Hole on the Old Course at Biarritz, where the green stood high up on a shelf of the cliff, the tee being on the beach below.   The hole called for a shot of 108 yards up the face of the cliff, but if the ball failed to reach the green it was pretty sure to drop back into an unplayable lie on the beach. So the local rule permitted another attempt from the tee, the penalty being loss of distance only. But for stroke competitions the rule read: 'Medal play: Failure to get up after three shots: score of 7.' No doubt the object of the rule was to obviate the congestion and delay that might be occasioned by the persistence of some incorrigible optimist, but what a comforting thought to the long handicap brigade to know that at this hole nothing more deadly than 7 could appear on their card—unless, of course, they got up at a third attempt and proceeded to take five putts. It is said that a somewhat similar regulation used to be in force on a course in India where several holes called for tee-shots over an impenetrable belt of trees. At each hole a local rule permitted four attempts to clear the obstacle, but if after the fourth shot the player was still on the wrong side of the trees, the rule compelled him to debit himself with a 10 and pass sorrowfully on to the next hole.

Local rules of this type, of course, only served to emphasize the necessity for a universal code, and this was achieved as the result of a joint revision of the rules by the Royal and Ancient Golf Club and the United States Golf Association, at whose conference in 1951 one of the primary considerations was that 'the perspective was to be worldwide, to meet the varying conditions under which the game is now played.' The chief feature of the new code was the final establishment of loss of stroke and distance as the penalty for ball out of bounds, unplayable ball, and lost ball.

Unfortunately all these provisions for lifting from unplayable lies have tended to inspire members of the more unsophisticated golfing communities with the idea that on the fairway they are *entitled* to a fair smack at the ball, and so any tendency towards soft and soggy lies is made the excuse for the application of 'winter rules' to allow of the ball being teed up through the green. The original idea of 'winter rules,' of course, was not the advantage of the player but the protection of the turf. To prevent the fairway being cut up by iron shots from close lies, players were permitted by a temporary local rule to lift the ball and place it on the nearest spot of good turf. From a greenkeeping point of view, however, such a rule tends to defeat its own object, since it leads to the best spots of turf being destroyed in their turn by the iron clubs.   It may be necessary to have winter rules to provide for the possibility of plugged balls, but winter rules for the avoidance of bad lies are not to be encouraged, and in any case it should be clearly understood that no score made under winter rules can be accepted as a 'record' of any kind.

The modern golfer is inclined to want everything handed to him on a plate, but to the older school the negotiation of close and cuppy lies was all part of the game.   At Denham on one occasion, when the great James Braid had been called in to advise on the position of some new bunkers, an over-zealous green committee man drew his attention to one particular hole, saying: 'This is a bad hole.   A man who hits a good drive of say 230 yards, gets to about here, and has a hanging lie for his second shot.'   'If a man's a guid enough golfer to drive 230 yards,' Braid retorted, 'he ought to be a guid enough golfer not to care what sort of lie he gets for his second shot.' It is an observation which the advocates of wholesale teeing-up might do well to bear in mind.

The same conference of 1951 decided on the abolition of the stymie which had been a source of controversy from the beginning of time.   In September 1833 the Royal and Ancient Club itself adopted a 'no stymies' rule, but apparently did not regard the change as an improvement, for the stymie was restored in the following autumn.   It has always been unpopular in the United States, but in spite of the obvious unfairness of an important match being decided by the accident of the one ball lying in the path of the other, there have not been wanting advocates for the retention of the stymie as a 'sporting' feature of the game.

Cases in which a stymie altered the outcome of a big match are not few, but perhaps the most heart-breaking example, at any rate from the British point of view, was the stymie that decided the U.S. Amateur Championship of 1936 at Garden City.   That year the British Walker Cup team suffered an overwhelming defeat at Pine Valley, but Jack McLean, who is now professional at Gleneagles, did something to restore their lost prestige by taking Johnny Fischer to the thirty-seventh hole in the Championship.   Yet that final would never have gone to that extra hole had it not been for a stymie at the thirty-fourth.   The Scot had finished the first round of that final with two holes in hand.   He was three up at the turn

THE HOME OF THE FIRST ROYAL GOLF CLUB

The Perth Public Course on the North Inch, where golf has been played for 500 years and on which the Royal Perth Golfing Society still holds its meetings.

in the afternoon and still three up with eight holes to play. At this stage McLean's putting touch for a time deserted him, and by the time the match reached the tee of the thirty-fourth hole his lead had been cut to one. He had failed to ram home his advantage when he had the chance, but he still looked like winning when Fischer fluffed his chip. With his next shot, however, the American laid McLean a dead stymie, and though the Scot lofted it successfully the ball kicked out of the hole again. But for that stymie McLean would have won by 2 and 1, for the thirty-fifth was gloriously halved in a birdie 4. But now the American nerved himself for a final effort. McLean played the next two holes perfectly, but he lost them both, for Fischer squared with a 2 at the short home hole, and sank a ten-yard putt for a 3 to win the match at the thirty-seventh.

A stymie also helped 'Emperor' Bobby Jones to his only victory in the British Amateur Championship and the 'Grand Slam' of the four great championships in 1930. No man, it has been said, ever wins a championship without at least one 'let off,' and in that Championship at St Andrews Bobby's came in his fourth round match against Cyril Tolley. In his own report of the event written at the time Jones declared that Tolley held the edge all the way. 'I particularly regretted,' he added, 'winning at the nineteenth hole by the aid of a stymie which was almost impossible to negotiate.' It is only right to add, however, that Tolley laid himself that stymie.

Worst case of all, perhaps, was the final of the English Close Amateur Championship of 1951 at Hunstanton when G. P. Roberts, of Southport and Ainsdale, and H. Bennett, of Buxton, finished all square at the end of the thirty-six holes, and halved two more, only to have the issue decided in favour of Roberts by a hopeless stymie on the thirty-ninth green. The 'sportsmen' might argue that it was as good a way of deciding a drawn battle as any other, but it did more than anything else to turn opinion in England against the stymie.

CHAPTER TWENTY-EIGHT
(1744–1907)

Methods of Scoring

In the early days of golf the only form of play was the *match* between two opposing sides, decided by holes. What seems the simple and obvious plan of counting the number of each player's *strokes* had never suggested itself to the minds of the followers of the game, and even the tally of strokes at each hole was kept by a purely *relative* method of computation.

When King James IV went out 'to play at the Golfe with the Erle of Bothuile' on the third day of February 1504, in the first match of which any record has come down to us, the method of scoring was as follows. At the first hole the earl, let us suppose, had the longer drive, and the king would therefore be the first to play the next shot. In so doing, he would play *the odd*—one shot more than his opponent. The earl, let us imagine, had put his drive into a bunker a few yards further on. When he in his turn came to play his second shot he would be playing *the like*—the same number of strokes as his opponent. If he failed to get out, it would still be his turn to play, and this time it would be he who was playing *the odd*. If he still failed to get clear he would have to make yet another attempt, and this time he would be playing *the two more*. Say that with this shot he got clear of the bunker but still short of the other, and then put his ball safely on the green in *the three more*, the king, on coming up to play his approach, would be playing *one off three*, and so on. At every point at which the opponents had played an equal number of strokes for any hole, they would describe the position as being *like as we lie*.

That this method of counting goes back to the historic days of the game appears to be established by a reference in a quite unexpected place, a sermon delivered at Cambusnethan by Michael Bruce, who was a notable preacher in Scotland at the time of the religious troubles in the middle of the seventeenth century. 'The soul-confirmed man,' he says, 'leaves ever the Devil at the two more,' which suggests that even three hundred years ago the two more represented a leeway which no man could be expected to make up.

This method of reckoning, which was still in familiar use in my boyhood, gradually passed out of fashion as stroke play came more into vogue, and as golfers adopted the habit of keeping a note of the number of strokes taken for each hole, even in match play. But when golfers first conceived the idea of holding *competitions* for more than two opposing sides, the idea of stroke play was still unknown. Competitors were drawn in pairs by lot, and the player who scored the biggest win over his own particular opponent was declared the winner of the competition. The conditions of play for the Silver Club of the City of Edinburgh in April 1744, the first golf *competition* of any kind, provided that the candidates were to be matched into parties of two—'or of threes if their number should be great'—by lot; that the player who should have won the greatest number of *holes* should be the victor; and that if two or more should have an equal number, they should play round by themselves in order to determine the match.

It is obvious that under such conditions 'the luck of the draw' would be apt to have a disproportionate bearing upon the result. The best player in the field might be matched against another almost as strong as himself and finish only a hole or two to the good, while quite a moderate performer might, if he had the fortune to be drawn against a sufficiently weak opponent, finish with a pocketful of holes in hand, and find himself at the top of the list. The element of luck in such a method of deciding the result is indeed so obvious that one would hesitate to accept it as the true interpretation of the conditions quoted, were it not for the fact that the same principle is in vogue even to the present day in Scottish bowls tournaments. Rinks are matched against one another by lot, and the rink which is the greatest number of shots up on its opponents—or alternatively the Club whose rinks have the best average of shots up on their opponents—is declared the winner.

In practice, however, the plan probably did not work out so badly, for it must be remembered that the contest for the Silver Club was in effect a championship event, in which the players were competing for the honour of being 'Captain of the Golf.' Only a few of the best players would take part, and between these there was probably no serious discrepancy of playing ability. Actually, there were only twelve entrants for this first competition, of whom two apparently scratched, and the fact that John Rattray—the 'Rattray for skill renowned' of Mathison's poem—who was the first winner, was successful again the following year, suggests that there was no great element of luck in his case.

It is only right to add that the interpretation of the above conditions which I have adopted is not the only possible one. Mr H. S. C. Everard, the historian of the Royal and Ancient Golf Club, takes an entirely different view. The St Andrews golfers in 1754 subscribed for a Silver Club as a trophy for an Open Competition on the same lines as the Edinburgh one, and the conditions of play laid down by them contain the following clause:

After the figures are drawn, the set or match beginning with No. 1, etc., shall go out first, with a clerk to mark down every stroke each of them shall take to every hole; then by the time they are at the Hole of Leslie, the second set, beginning with No. 3, shall strike off; and so, all the rest in the same order, each set having a clerk. And when the match is ended . . . then a scrutiny of the whole clerks' books or jottings is to be made, and the player who shall appear to have won the greatest number of holes shall be declared the winner. . . .

It is clear from Mr Everard's remarks that he had no tradition of the meaning of this rule to guide him; he is only putting his own interpretation on the actual wording of the text, and he frankly admits that the interpretation is open to question. His view, however, for what it is worth, is that if A holed out in 4 at a hole at which five other competitors took more than 4, A was counted as winning 5 holes, and so on for every hole and every competitor, the winner being the player who had the largest number of points— ascertained by this method—over the twenty-two holes (as the St Andrews round then was). Mr Everard himself ridicules the arithmetical complications, and condemns the unfairness, of such a method of counting. On the score of scientific fairness I think there is actually a good deal to be said for it, but it seems to me to be too complicated ever to have had any existence outside of the brain of a mathematician. The phrase 'a scrutiny of the whole

The Apple-tree Gang

The earliest known photograph of golf in the United States. The players are Messrs. Harry Holbrook, Alexander P. W. Kinnan, John Upham, and John Reid, members of the St. Andrews Club of Yonkers, on whose course the photograph was taken by S. Hedding Finch in 1888. The two caddies are sons of Mr. Holbrook.

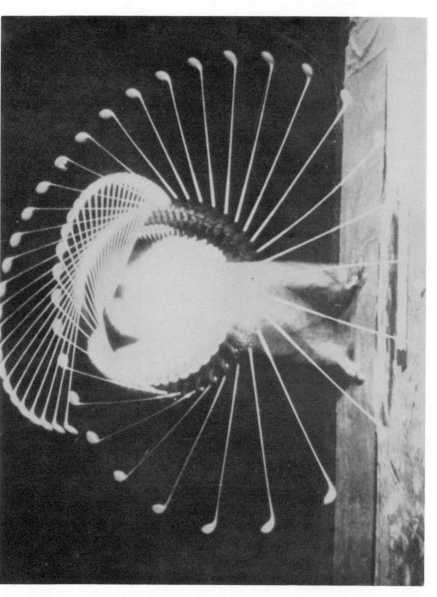

A 'multiple flash' photograph of a drive by Bobby Jones. The interval between pictures is one-hundredth of a second, the exposure of each picture one-hundred-thousandth of a second. Measured by this picture the velocity of the club head before impact is 166 feet per second, after impact 166 feet per second. The ——— of the clerks' jottings is to be made' seems hardly applicable to such a cumbrous process of calculation. It is so cumbrous in fact that I find it quite impossible to believe that such a system was ever in use at all. I see nothing more in the St Andrews rule than a provision that a marker should be sent out to keep the score of each match, in order that there might be no doubt how many holes each player was up or down. The 'scrutiny' was merely to make sure how many holes each player had won—as we would now say, how many he was 'up'—in his own particular match. And the man who had scored the biggest win was adjudged the winner of the Silver Club.

If my interpretation of the condition is the correct one, the biggest objection to this method of deciding the competition was the possibility that a comparatively mediocre performer, if he were drawn against an opponent who happened to be completely off colour, might win by a pocketful of holes and carry off the trophy. That the Edinburgh golfers made no change in the course of fifteen years was probably due to the fact that there had been no such noticeable injustice in the result of any of the contests. But the St Andrews golfers did not put up with it so long. The first contest for their Silver Club had been held in 1754. In a minute dated 9th May 1759 it is laid down that:

> In order to remove all disputes and inconveniences with regard to the gaining of the Silver Club, it is enacted and agreed by the captain and the gentlemen golfers present, that in all time coming whoever puts in the ball at the fewest strokes over the field, being 22 holes, shall be declared and sustained victor. And in case a ball shall be driven into a hole, or road, so that it cannot be played out, then in that case it shall be at the option of the player, to play the ball where it lyes, or to take it up and throw the ball back at least six yards, and to allow his adversary one stroke for his so doing.

Stroke play had been invented at last.

The difficulty which our great-grandsires experienced in getting away from the idea of match play is exemplified even in the rule just quoted, 'to allow his adversary one stroke for his so doing.' Why 'his adversary'? We should now say 'to be penalized one stroke for doing so.' Another curious phrase is 'whoever puts in the ball at the fewest strokes' in place of 'whoever holes out in the fewest strokes.' The language of the links has changed a good deal since 1759!

When the Royal and Ancient Club inaugurated its two handicap knock-out tournaments for the Calcutta Cup, first played for in 1885, and the Jubilee Vase, instituted in 1887, the method of handicapping was by a start in holes up, but this idea has never commended itself elsewhere. In the middle of last century serious differences of form in friendly matches were balanced, as appears from *Golfiana*, by slapdash allowances of a half (i.e. a stroke every second hole) or a third (a stroke at the second hole of every three). Later on handicaps seem to have been given by dividing the players into classes and allotting so many strokes difference between the classes. At North Berwick in the early days we find a minute dividing the competitors by name into five classes, with a couple of strokes difference between each. In the Edinburgh Burgess Society in 1862, members were divided into six classes, with a difference of four strokes between the classes. Even when this system was superseded by the simpler plan of giving each player a handicap of so many strokes, the chief defect of the system still remained that each Club tended to adopt as its scratch standard the normal performance of its best players, and that standard varied to an amazing degree from Club to Club.

An important step towards uniformity in this matter was the invention of the bogey score. In 1890 the late Mr Hugh Rotherham, of the Coventry Club, conceived the idea of a competition in which each competitor would be invited to play a match under handicap against a hypothetical opponent playing perfect golf at every hole. In those days the Coventry Club were still playing over the course at Whitley Common which had been the home of the Club since its formation in 1887. Mr Rotherham's first job, therefore, was to fix what he called the 'ground score' of the Whitley course, the score that a scratch player would take for each hole playing perfect golf. The first competition against this 'ground score' was played on 13th May 1891, and in the autumn of the same year the Coventry Club presented a silver challenge cup, to be played for annually under the same conditions.

The new fashion of competition became well known and popular among other Clubs, and attracted the attention of, among others,

Dr Thomas Browne, R.N., the honorary secretary of the Great Yarmouth Club, who introduced it in that club. It happened that at that time the famous music-hall ditty, with the refrain of

Hush! hush! hush!
Here comes the bogey man!

was just coming into vogue, and a friend to whom Dr Browne was explaining the new form of play jocularly remarked that the imaginary opponent was a regular bogey man. Dr Browne at once seized upon this suggestion, and so at Yarmouth and everywhere else the new score began to be called the bogey score. In the spring of 1892, in the course of a tour of the South Coast courses, Dr Browne introduced the idea of bogey play to Captain Seely-Vidal, of the Royal Engineers, the honorary secretary of the United Services Club at Gosport. Captain Vidal was greatly taken with the idea, and forthwith proceeded to work out a bogey score for his own club. But in making Mr Bogey a member he reminded his visitor that every member of the Club had to have service rank. He considered that nothing less than the rank of Colonel would befit the dignity of a player so steady and accurate, and 'Colonel' Bogey he became ever after.

It must be emphasized that in its original conception 'bogey' was the same as the modern 'par,' the score which a first-class golfer would take for each hole. But as golf balls continued to travel further and further and standards of play improved, bogey scores were not always revised as rapidly as they ought to have been. Old Club members were apt to be shocked to find that a hole at which they had always been proud to hole out in 5 was in future to be a par 4, and could with reluctance be persuaded to accept the change, so that on many courses there were two or three holes at which the bogey was allowed to remain a stroke more than par. The result was that by the time Colonel Bogey had attained his diamond jubilee his game had gotten a little into disrepute and he was no longer regarded as an absolutely top-class performer, so that in England, as in the States, 'par' is now substituted as the criterion of perfect play and the basis of all handicapping.

It is curious that in team contests, now invariably decided by the number of matches lost and won, opinion long vacillated between scoring by strokes, by holes, or by matches. The first inter-Club match of which I have been able to discover any record was fought out between the Edinburgh Burgess Golfing Society and the Bruntsfield Links Golf Club on 4th June 1818. As both Clubs at that time played at Bruntsfield, such a contest called for no elaborate arrangements. Mr J. Cameron Robbie refers to some earlier 'meetings' of the two Clubs, beginning in 1803, and rather rashly assumes that these references are to matches. I think it is clear from the terms of the minutes he quotes that the 'meetings' were purely convivial, and indeed the joint report on the proposal to hold the match of 1818 seems to make it clear that it was a new idea. The match was intended to celebrate the opening of a new hole at the south end of the links, but there is no record of the outcome either of this contest or of that of the following year. The contest of 1820, however, ended in favour of the Burgess by 5 matches to 2—play being by foursomes. After that year it would seem that there were no more matches until 1854.

This method of determining the result—by the majority of matches—would seem to modern golfers to be the simple and natural one, but it was soon superseded by the system of counting by the aggregate of holes up, which was still in vogue when the first amateur international between England and Scotland was played in 1902. A minute of the Musselburgh Club in 1830 shows that as a result of a challenge from the Bruntsfield Links Club, a six-a-side match was played at Musselburgh, the visitors winning by three holes; but a return match three weeks later, also played at Musselburgh, went to the local men by one hole.

Curiously enough, when the Edinburgh Burgess and Bruntsfield Links golfers in 1854 subscribed for a trophy for an annual match between the two Clubs, they agreed to decide it by medal play. Ten players a side took part in the first competition, which was won by the 'Burgess' players with 675 strokes to their opponents' 688. The scoring looks good, but is not in fact particularly so, play being over two rounds of a six-hole course. The Bruntsfield Club migrated to Musselburgh a few years later, and after that we find the annual contest with the Burgess Club being decided by the aggregate of holes up, which remained the usual method of deciding team encounters until the famous debacle in the University Match of 1907

King George VI, as Duke of York, playing in the exhibition match to celebrate the opening of the new course at Ton Pentre in 1924.

WHERE THE FIRST INTERNATIONAL GOLF MATCH BETWEEN GREAT BRITAIN AND THE UNITED STATES WAS PLAYED

The Royal Cromer course, where a Ladies' International Match between the two countries was played as long ago as 1905. The photograph shows the holes in the lee of Target Hill, with the sea in the background.

—already described—led to the general adoption of the system of scoring one point for each match, which is adopted in international encounters on both sides of the Atlantic.

When foursome play began to be introduced into inter-Club matches, its purpose was often purely social. The match would be decided by the singles in the morning, and the foursomes after lunch gave everybody a chance to take things easy. Then some genius discovered that the result of the foursomes ought to count in the final aggregate, and that if you play the singles first the score at that stage may be so one-sided that it does not matter what happens in the foursomes. So, with the idea of maintaining everybody's interest to the bitter end, it has become the established custom to play the foursomes first—a plan which has the additional merit of greater fairness to a visiting team, who have the opportunity in the foursomes of making themselves familiar with the strange course, and to that extent better equipped for decisive battle in the singles.

CHAPTER TWENTY-NINE
(1914–1939)

Between Two Wars

THE impact of the First World War was more severely felt in Great Britain than in the United States, where the new stars were just coming along. Nevertheless the first season after the war found British golfers still sitting on top of the world. Vardon and Ray paid a return visit to the States in 1920, and this time it was Ray's turn to carry off the U.S. Open. When he won the British Open in 1912, he set a new fashion by using his niblick as an approach club, sticking the ball time and again right up against the pin from anything up to 150 yards, and it was his niblick that won him the U.S. title at Inverness, Ohio. That Championship had a singular finish, for it is perhaps the only instance on record of a player being helped to victory by false information as to what he required to do to win. Here is the story as Ted himself told it to me on his return home. With nine holes to go, he was a stroke behind Harry Vardon, who was playing three holes in front of him. In the squall of rain which overtook them at that point, both dropped some strokes, and when he came to the seventeenth tee Ted was told that he had two 4's to win. His second to the seventeenth was a beautiful brassy shot with a little cut—a shot that Ted could play to perfection—but it ran just over the green. He was afraid of getting a bump out of line if he putted up, and therefore chipped back to four feet or so from the hole—and then his putt just failed to go down—5! He now required to do the last hole in 3.

For Ted, the second shot to the home green was only a niblick approach, but the green was an island plateau, entirely surrounded by bunkers, and the hole was cut not more than four yards from the far left-hand corner. However, he determined that he was going to get his 3, and instead of playing for the centre of the green and safety, he pitched boldly for the hole, although that meant that if he were the least bit off the line to the left he would be trapped.

But the shot came off exactly, and the ball came to rest within a couple of yards of the hole. And to spoil it all Ted missed the putt again! Only then did he discover that Vardon's total was one more than he had been told and that he was still heading the list by a single stroke. Several players had still to come in, however, and more than one came to the last tee requiring a 3 to tie with Ted. But I remember him telling me that not one of them took the risk of pitching for the hole. They all went for the middle of the green, which left them an all but impossible putt for their 3. And so Ted's total remained unchallenged to the finish.

That victory of Ted Ray in its turn helped to make history, for it produced 'the Oath of Inverness' by which a small band of American professionals bound themselves to go over year after year to the British Championship until they had squared the account by bringing it to America. They did not have to wait long, for in 1921 at St Andrews, 'Jock' Hutchinson won the British title after a tie with Roger Wethered, then a young man of twenty-two, who had captained Oxford in the previous year. Hutchison's victory in that championship owed a little to Lady Luck. In his first round he did the eighth hole in one, and would not have tied at all but for an unexampled bit of ill fortune that overtook the amateur in the third round. Wethered actually finished in fewer strokes than any other player in the field, but he incurred a penalty stroke at the fourteenth hole in the third round through kicking his ball as he walked back after studying the line of his run-up. He had gone forward to examine the ground, and retired slowly towards the ball, still keeping his eye on the route which he meant the shot to follow, with the result that his heel came in contact with the ball before he realized that he had reached it. Curiously enough, although that penalty stroke is one of the most famous tragedies of the links, there are many divergent accounts of the hole at which it occurred. I have seen the incident variously referred to as having occurred at the thirteenth and sixteenth holes, and it is frequently spoken of as having occurred in the final round. Actually it occurred at the fourteenth hole, the famous 'Long Hole In' in the third round. In spite of the penalty Wethered did the hole in 5 and finished the round in 72, to lead the field at this stage by a stroke. His fourth round of 71 seemed to have put him in an unassailable position, but Jock Hutchison drew level with a marvellous fourth round of 70 and the pair tied at 296. In the play-off, over thirty-six holes, on the following day, the professional drew steadily ahead, and won by nine strokes, to take the Open Championship across the Atlantic for the first time.

The Scots, however, were not prepared to regard this as an American victory, for Hutchison was born in St Andrews, and throughout the Championship most of the townsmen had been 'rooting' for him.   The true beginning of American triumphs was Walter Hagen's great win at Sandwich in 1922.   That championship saw one of the most amazing finishes that the game has ever known.   It happened that the invaders were all drawn to go out among the first players on the final day, and early in the afternoon the scoreboard showed the leaders to be

Walter Hagen (U.S.A.)	300
Jim Barnes (U.S.A.)	301
Jock Hutchison (U.S.A.)	302

with never a British player within sight of catching them.   The news had already been flashed over the cables that Hagen was the new Champion.   Walter himself had been wiling away part of the afternoon by giving a few of us an imitation of Joe Kirkwood's trick shots—vastly entertaining, for he made a hopeless mess of them.   And at the tail end of the afternoon George Duncan, who had won the Championship at Deal two years before, went out in the last couple of the day.   He had to do a 68 to tie; the best score up to that point was Hagen's fourth round of 72; George's own score for the morning round had been 81.   But like Gallio he cared for none of these things.   Never have I watched such iron play.   At each of the first two holes he had a possible putt for a 3, but failed to get it down; at the third he chipped from a bunker and then missed a putt he certainly ought to have holed.   But at the fourth the 3's began to come.   A magnificent 2 at the short sixteenth left him two 4's to tie and he made no mistake about the first of them. But his second shot to the home hole swung off slightly to the left of the green, his chip was too short, and although he made a heroic effort to get down the putt, it hit the hole and stayed out.   Never was there a braver round in such a crisis, but though Duncan's 69 was the first score to break 70 at Royal St George's, it was just not quite good enough to save the day. All the same it shook Walter Hagen. He and George were to meet in match play two or three times after that, twice in international matches, once in the match-play stages of the *Yorkshire Evening News* Tournament, and Duncan won them all.

For a time Duncan's epic round seemed to be the swan-song of British professional golf. It is true that Arthur Havers won back the Championship at Troon in the following year, with Hagen a stroke behind him, but after that for ten lean years the Open Championship trophy made the journey across the Atlantic with monotonous regularity. Walter Hagen was the winner on four occasions, 'Emperor' Bobby Jones on three, but it was Hagen who started the landslide.

Hagen was the Crillon of the links, revelling in hand-to-hand combat. It is noteworthy that alongside his two American Open Championships he can claim five American Professional (match-play) Championships won in a space of seven years. He was the born match-winner just as Bobby Jones was the born stroke-player. Both, of course, have been successful in both forms of play, but they have arrived at their victories by entirely different roads. Bobby Jones won the American Open before he won the Amateur title. Indeed he had several years of disappointment in the match-play event before he learned to convert match play into medal play, and found that 'if you keep shooting par at them, they all crack sooner or later.' Hagen's case was just the reverse. In the British Open his first two wins at any rate were obtained by wonderful recoveries that wrested holes from 'Ole Man Par' just as he would have wrested them from a human opponent. Players like Bobby Jones or Miss Joyce Wethered froze their opponents by the 'impersonal' way in which they set themselves to play for the figures. Hagen over-whelmed his adversary by the sheer impetuosity of his attack. After he had beaten Abe Mitchell in a famous seventy-two-hole match over Wentworth and St George's Hill, he told Francis Ouimet that in the crisis of the match he studied Mitchell's reflexes as a boxer does with an opponent in the ring to see how he was standing the strain. In a big match in which he defeated Bobby Jones he drove all day with his brassie in order always to have the odd to play with the second shots, because he knew he was at the top of his form with his irons and wanted to put Jones under the strain of continually trying to get 'inside' a perfectly played approach.   Did ever golfer think of such things until the master duellist of the links came along?

Even after he won his second British Open, players on this side were not quite certain whether to regard the newcomer to the golfing Olympus as a genuine demigod or as a mere adventurer.   The older heroes of the game were all distinguished for their skill with heroic weapons.   Braid was the mighty driver, Vardon the perfect iron player, Taylor the master of the mashie.   Hagen stands out as the wizard of the niblick and the putter.   And though every golfer will admit that the shots from the bunker and on the green are just as much a part of golf as the long game, yet it is only natural to imagine that the player who owes his success to his power of getting down from sand or rough with a niblick shot and a putt cannot really be a player of the highest class, in spite of all his victories. But the people who used to think of Hagen as gaining his championships by incredible recoveries after still more incredible mistakes were forced to recognize an immense change that 'Sir Walter' affected in his play in the four years that intervened between the winning of his second and third championships.   The man who played that record second round of 67 at Muirfield in 1929, the lowest score ever returned in the final stages of a British Open Championship up to that date, did so by wellnigh perfect golf. He was hitting the ball almost along a chalk line from tee to pin all the way, his only real mistake being a drive pushed out into a bunker at the difficult eighth.   There never was a more convincing round, for time and again his fours were really only three and a sixteenth, the fourth shot being no more than tapping the ball into the hole.   At Sandwich the year before he hardly made a real mistake in the whole of the four rounds, and there wasn't a single figure above a 5 on any of his cards.

The long run of American successes came to an abrupt end with the victory of Henry Cotton in the Open Championship of 1934 at Sandwich.   'Concentration Henry,' as Walter Hagen christened him, had schooled himself by years of hard work to a swing of mechanical perfection, and that year he reached the peak of his form. The Royal St George's on that occasion was stretched to 6,776 yards, and Cotton's scores for his first four rounds on it were 66 (in the preliminary qualifying stage), 67, 65, and 72. In a high wind in the fourth and final round of the Championship proper his intense concentration wavered a little and he hooked one or two long second shots, but his short game kept his score down and he finished in 79 for an aggregate of 283 to win by five strokes from S. F. Brews of South Africa.

The U.S. entry for that Championship was not numerically so strong as usual, but it included Gene Sarazen and Denny Shute, the winners in 1932 and 1933, Macdonald Smith, and Joe Kirkwood. But at Carnoustie three years later, when Cotton won for the second time, the field included the whole might of the U.S. Ryder Cup team, which a few weeks earlier had won a handsome victory in the professional international at Southport and Ainsdale—the first U.S. success in this event on British soil. So Walter Hagen and his merry men came to Carnoustie flushed with success, and maintained their challenge up to the last two rounds. Then suddenly, inexplicably, their effort petered out, and the championship resolved itself into a struggle between Cotton and Reg Whitcombe, with Cotton the eventual winner by two strokes. Reg, however, was to find consolation in a victory at Sandwich in the following year, when he showed himself a master of the art of controlling the ball in a tearing gale.

CHAPTER THIRTY
(1908–1954)

Sex Equality on the Links

ONE of the great attractions of golf is that it is every bit as good a game for women as for men. This is equally true of lawn tennis, but in tennis power and pace count for so much that the women can never hope to oppose the men on equal terms. In golf, skill counts for so much more than muscular strength that the difference between the standards of play of the two sexes is not immeasurable. One of the most notable developments of the last quarter of a century has been the way in which this gap has been gradually closing, until the margin between the top players of the two sexes is not more than three or four strokes per round. When Mrs Mildred ('Babe') Zaharias won the 1954 U.S. Women's Open Championship on the long and testing course of the Salem Country Club, at Peabody, Mass., she played the four rounds in 72, 71, 73, 75 for an aggregate of 291. That is within three strokes per round of the best that has ever been done by the men in the British or U.S. Opens.

The change in women's golf began in 1908 when Miss Cecil Leitch, 'the flapper from Silloth,' an unknown seventeen-year-old with her hair hanging down her back, reached the semi-final of the Ladies' Championship at St Andrews. Prior to Miss Leitch's day the ladies' swings tended to be much too ladylike! Miss Leitch's example taught the world that there was no reason why a girl should not put the same sort of punch into her shots as the men did. Then immediately after the First World War, when Miss Leitch was still the acknowledged queen of the links, came Miss Joyce Wethered (Lady Heathcoat Amory) to show us a new brand of women's golf, grinding out the par figures for hole after hole and for round after round with impeccable accuracy, and with a freedom from mistakes such as none of the men amateurs on her own side of the Atlantic could pretend to equal.

Even when Miss Wethered was at the height of her powers, however, the family estimate was that the handicap difference between her and her hard-hitting brother Roger varied from two to seven strokes according to the nature of the course; for distance counts, although they never pay off on the drive. And it is still true that length is the chief factor in the difference between the standards of women's golf and men's. No doubt Mrs 'Babe' Zaharias can hit a ball as far as any average scratch man can do, but not as far as the 'horizon drivers' like Chick Harbert or Jean Baptiste Ado, nor as far as the majority of men amateurs of international class. When the six leading U.S. women professionals took part in a 'Round Robin' Mixed Foursome Tournament along with six British men professionals at Ganton in 1951, Mrs Zaharias and her colleagues were consistently outdriven when opposed to the men, and when the women pressed their drives in an effort to keep up, the result was an immediate deterioration in the accuracy of their play.

Apart from the question of hitting power, however, it is a mistake to assume that in the short game the women ought to have no difficulty in proving themselves as good as the men. The assumption is based on the general idea that feminine perceptions are more sensitive and that this faculty should show to advantage on the greens. Unfortunately, although the experiments of the physiologists on the whole confirm the theory of superior sensitiveness of perception on the part of the female, the experiments indicate one important exception. The male of the human race is more sensitive than the female in the nice judgment of weight! And that faculty comes into play in a number of quite unexpected connections. Thus men make better pianists than women, and as a rule they have a more exact judgment of the strength of a chip or a long putt! My observation suggests that the women are steadier than the men in the actual holing out, but taking it by and large they are not so reliable in laying the ball dead from a distance of ten or fifteen yards.

In the years between the wars we had a regular series of 'Men v. Women' Test Matches at Stoke Poges. The women's team was almost invariably the more representative, most of their players being of international class, occasionally strengthened by the inclusion of distinguished visitors from overseas, while the men were not much more than a good London side. But over a considerable period of years the men fairly demonstrated their ability to concede the girls eight or nine strokes per round.   There were two good reasons for the men's success.   The first was that the Stoke Poges course was deliberately selected to give the harder hitting sex as big an advantage as possible, with more than half a dozen holes at which the men could count on getting up with a drive and a long iron while the girls couldn't quite get home with two woods.   As a proof of the extent to which length is the governing factor in this matter, it may be interesting to note that one of the few victories recorded by the girls' team was gained when a spell of exceptionally dry weather had baked the fairways hard, and the course in consequence was playing unusually short.   Under these conditions the girls also could get up in two at the 'tiger's two-shotters' and the men's advantage was gone.   The other reason was that, good as the ladies were, they were not so hardened to this type of test as to be entirely free from the strain of being regularly outdriven.   It is a disheartening job to play a hole perfectly and find that you lose it just the same because your opponent can reach the green in a stroke fewer than you require.   Even if a handicap stroke enables you to secure a half the inferiority complex still remains.

During the same period when the experiment was tried of playing a series of men v. women matches over a well-known pitching and putting course attached to a London golf school, the harder hitting sex were still successful.   The men were not asked to concede any odds, because the holes were too short for length to enter into the question, but the ladies were completely outclassed.   The shots at which all but the best of the women players seem to fail are what the old timers used to call the quarter shots.   Apparently most ladies have not the strength of wrists and fingers necessary to impart as much back-spin to these shots as the men do.   There is no more difficult shot in golf than the short pitch in which the ball has to be hit crisply in order to make it draw up quickly, and yet not too hard to suit the distance.   Unless a girl learns this shot when she is very young, it is the most difficult of all for her to acquire.

One event in which the ladies frequently appear to be every bit as good as the men is the annual Mixed Foursomes Tournament at Worplesdon, which is to all intents and purposes the Mixed Doubles Championship of the British Isles.   Again and again you find partnerships going round in scores which are as good, or almost as good, as the man could hope to achieve playing alone. This, however, is a familiar feature of foursome play at its best, when a stronger player is partnered with a weaker. The stronger golfer tries to pull out his game a little in order to make up for the deficiencies of his partner. The other finds the second shots made unexpectedly easy by her partner's longer drive, and she in turn is encouraged to play a bit above her usual form. The strength of such a foursome is the strength of its strongest link! But though the 4's are still being earned at the long two-shotters, they are not being obtained with the same monotonous ease as the man would compass if he were playing alone. A curious result of this is that the ladies as a rule seem to play the steadier golf. It is of course the accepted tradition among both players and press to put all the blame for the partnership's failure upon the mistakes of the men. But it is in fact the men who are guilty of most of the major errors, hitting long drives out of line among the trees, hooking brassie shots into the bunkers guarding the left of the green. The weakness of the ladies is not so easy to appreciate, because it lies mainly in the fact that their game is on a smaller scale. None of them seem to have that little bit of reserve of length up their sleeve which most of the men can produce in an emergency. The men's mistakes are often the result of the little bit of extra effort to make up for the girls' lack of distance.

Every attempt at comparison works round to the same conclusion that though women's golf may equal the men's in skill it can never quite equal the men's in scale. And yet there are times when the gap seems to be shrinking almost into nothingness, for in the States at any rate the women have already begun to challenge the men's monopoly of scores in the 'middle 6o's.' When the Western Women's Open Championship was held at Oklahoma City in 1949, Grace Lenczyk, the holder of the American Women's Amateur title, headed the field in the preliminary stroke-play qualifying stage with a score of 66. Even this amazing total ought to have been one less, for she threw away a stroke by missing a putt of a few inches, playing a careless one-handed stroke to tap the ball into the tin. This is probably the greatest single round in the annals of women's golf, for the Oklahoma City course is 6,679 yards long, with a par of 75.

The previous 'women's record' was 71; the best score done in competition by a man, 63. That was by Charles Coe, who won the American Amateur Championship in that same year. Oklahoma City is Coe's home course, and if you take a line through his best and Miss Lenczyk's record, you get a difference between the top players of the two sexes amounting to only three strokes!

One result of the high standard of women's golf in the States has been the emergence of a strong field of women professionals competing in their own open tournaments with a scale of prize money less lavish than the men's but sufficiently attractive to tempt their best amateur players into the professional ranks. Of the field of thirty who took part in the Women's National Open of 1954, more than half were professional tournament players.

There has as yet been no similar development on this side of the Atlantic, although golf as a profession for women dates back to before the First World War, when Mrs Gordon Robertson was for several years professional to the Princes Ladies' Golf Club, on Mitcham Common. In 1911 Miss Lily Freemantle was appointed professional to the Sunningdale Ladies' Club, and this was quickly followed by the appointment of Miss D. M. Smyth as professional to Le Touquet Ladies' Club. Miss Freemantle was the daughter of a well-known professional; Miss Smyth had for some years been a member of the Barnehurst Golf Club, and must count as the first instance of the 'converted amateur' on the ladies' side of the game.

All these ladies, however, were instructors rather than players. I do not think that any of them could have stood up to the test of a public appearance in tournament golf. The distinction of being the first woman professional to compete in a men's open tournament belongs to a French girl, Mlle Genevieve le Derff, who for a time was one of the assistant professionals at the Fourqueux Club. When the French Open Championship was played at her home course in 1929 she was one of the competitors, but the result was not particularly encouraging. A more successful attempt was that of twenty-two-year-old Miss Margaret Farquhar in the Scottish Professional Championship of 1933 at Lossiemouth, where she had for a time been assistant to George Smith. Her first round of 79 was only seven strokes behind the leading return at this stage and she eventually finished with an aggregate of 331 for the four rounds, against the 296 of Mark Seymour, the winner.

Such a result, however, only confirmed the traditional estimate of nine strokes as the margin of handicap between men and women. To-day, no man living could concede anything near nine strokes per round to Mrs Zaharias. It is her performances and those of her nearest rivals, like Miss Louise Suggs and Miss Betsy Rawls, which inspire the women with the hope of some day seeing a full dress test on level terms between representative teams of the world's best players, men and women, if only the men—miserable cowards that they are—will have the honesty to face up to it!

CHAPTER THIRTY-ONE
(1754–1954)

Historic Trophies and Mounting Prize-money

IN the earliest golf competitions the honour of victory had to be
its own reward. The conditions of play for the first competition
of all, for the Silver Club presented by the City of Edinburgh, laid
it down that the trophy was always to remain the property of 'the
Good Town' and that every victor was to append to it a gold or
silver piece, whichever he pleased, as a memento of his success.
Neither of these provisions, however, was carried out quite to the
letter. The original Silver Club was presumably regarded as being
handed over to the Honourable Company of Edinburgh Golfers
in 1764 when the town council agreed to the request of the Honourable Company that the competition should cease to be an open one,
and should be restricted to the Company's own members, who from
that time onwards were to be admitted by election. And this, as
well as the duplicates which the City of Edinburgh has from time
to time presented to take its place, as the earlier trophies became
overloaded with mementoes, is now the property of the Honourable
Company. From the very first also, the gold or silver 'pieces'
attached to the trophy by the winners took the form of silver golf
balls. The only variation occurs in connection with the Silver
Club of the Royal and Ancient, to which one or two royal captains
have attached a golf ball of gold. It is interesting to note, also, that
in all such cases it was, and is, the practice to make the silver ball
which the winner attaches to the trophy as close a replica as can be
managed of the actual ball with which he won. The result is that
some of the older trophies, with their mementoes of victory, illus-
trate most realistically the progress of ball-making through the last
two centuries. A similar practice has been established by the Oxford
and Cambridge Golfing Society in connection with their annual
competition for the President's Putter. In this case the actual ball
used by the winner in the final is attached to the trophy by a silver
band and chain.

The Royal and Ancient Club's original trophy of 1754 was supplemented by a second silver club in 1819, by which date the first had become overloaded with balls attached by successive captains. Another came into existence as the result of a curious survivorship bet between Sir David Moncrieffe and John Whyte-Melville, of Strathkinness, made in 1820, by which it was stipulated that on the death of one of them the other should present to the Club a Silver Putter, with the arms of the two parties to the wager engraved upon it. On this trophy the gold medals won at successive autumn meetings are hung, in the same way as the silver golf balls are hung by successive captains on the Silver Club, which is in fact a driver. It is interesting to record that though the death of Sir David Moncrieffe decided the wager thirteen years after it was made, his friend survived him for another half-century. 'Mount-Melville' was elected captain of the Royal and Ancient Club when he was twenty-three, acted as deputy for King Edward VII when the latter as Prince of Wales became captain in 1863, and was again chosen captain for a second time just before his death in 1883. The trophy of 1819 in its turn became overloaded with silver balls attached by the winners, and when the Duke of Windsor, then Prince of Wales, became captain of the Club, in 1922, he presented them with another duplicate of the original trophy, to start a fresh series.

All the principal trophies of the premier Club are competed for by scratch play. The Gold Medal presented by King William IV and the Gold Medal presented by the Club in 1806 are now the first and second prizes at the Autumn Meeting. The Silver Cross presented by Colonel J. Murray Belshes, of Balnagask, and the Silver Medal presented by the Golfing Society of Bombay, are the first and second prizes for the best scratch scores at the Spring Meeting, while the George Glennie Medal, presented by the Royal Blackheath Club, goes to the player with the best scratch aggregate over the two meetings. The only prize for stroke play under handicap is the Silver Boomerang presented by the Royal Queensland Golf Club, which is won by the best net score at the Autumn Meeting, and that was first competed for in 1923.

It was not to be expected that the Spartan simplicity of the early days should be emulated by every new Club that came into being, and in modern times Clubs have vied one with another to put up trophies that range from the wondrous to the weird. You have costly trophies like the St George's Challenge Cup, which is reputed to have cost £500, beautiful trophies like the Thorpeness Club's Silver Frigate—perfect in every detail of build and rig, down to the gunners working at their guns and the sailors in the rigging—'appropriate' trophies like the silver model of Edinburgh Castle which Mr Edward Esmond presented for competition among the artisan golfers of East Lothian, or the 'Antlers' which Prince Arthur of Connaught presented to the Royal Mid-Surrey Club, whose home is in the Old Deer Park at Richmond.

The majority of golf prizes are challenge trophies, the winner or the Club from which he enters having the right to hold the prize for the year. A not uncommon arrangement in the early days of the golf boom was that the trophy was to become the absolute property of any player winning it thrice, but that idea has latterly fallen out of favour, and the more usual plan is to provide a small replica or other memento of victory each year. But it was not to be expected that all Clubs or all golfers would rest content with this.

A New South Wales Club wanted to offer a block of land adjoining the course as a prize; an English Club wanted to offer a car for competition; at Baden, before the Kaiser War, a noble and enthusiastic member offered, as a prize for the ladies' competition, a Paris model hat of the value of £40, to be chosen by the winner; and so on. Small wonder that authorities on both sides of the Atlantic began to take fright and have latterly felt themselves impelled to lay down definite limits on the value of prizes for amateur competition. Even that does not entirely meet the situation, for the appeal of the modern outrageous number of handicap competitions is to vanity rather than greed. The extreme example is one which I was told many years ago by the manager of a famous firm of silversmiths. Four players who were going off on an Easter holiday together came to him to purchase four silver cups, which they proposed to play for among themselves—subject, however, to a proviso that nobody was to be eligible to win more than one prize, so that each of the four would have a proof of his prowess to take proudly home with him.

A more remarkable development has been the value of the 'glit-

The present home of the world's oldest Golf Club: the links of the Honourable Company of Edinburgh Golfers at Muirfield. The photograph shows the thirteenth green, with the Firth of Forth in the distance.

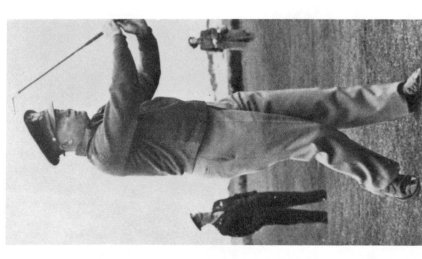

Photo: Topical Press

President (then General Eisenhower play-

Photo: Topical Press

Mr. (now Sir) Winston Churchill golfing at Cannes a year or

tering prizes for sharp swords' provided for professional golf.   In this matter, also, the United States has led the way, and the rest of the world has been forced to adopt something approaching the same standards.   The amazing increase in professional prize-money during the last hundred years is easily traced in the British Open Championship.   The eight professionals who in 1860 took part in the first contest for the title were competing purely for the honour and glory of wearing the Championship Belt; there was no other prize.   It was not until the fourth year of the Championship that money prizes were instituted—£5 for the runner-up, £3 for third, and £2 for fourth, the last being a special donation by the Edinburgh Burgess Society.   There was still no prize for the winner, who had to be content with the Championship Belt.   In 1864, however, a prize of £6 was provided for first place in addition to the Belt.   Six pounds was all the prize-money that 'Young Tom' Morris received when he won the Belt for the first time in 1868, and the first prize was only £8 when he won the first contest for the present Championship Trophy in 1872.

When Andrew Kirkaldy as a boy of fourteen made his first appearance in professional golf, in a tournament at Wemyss in 1874, he went over from St Andrews along with Bob Martin, Willie Fernie, Tom Kidd, and Tom Kirk, riding in a donkey-cart used for trade purposes by Fernie, who was a plasterer. (Most of the Scottish professionals of this date had a trade to turn to in the intervals of playing golf.)   The prize-money offered for this tournament, which drew thirteen competitors from St Andrews and North Berwick, barely exceeded as many pounds, divided into five prizes ranging from £6 to £1!

Slowly and fitfully the standards of prize-money rose.   When Harry Vardon and J. H. Taylor were winning their first Open Championships in the last decade of the nineteenth century, the prize list for the event totalled £100, of which £30 went to the winner, in addition to his gold medal.   After the First World War, when Hagen won his first British Open, his prize was no more than £75.   By 1931 the total had been increased to £500, of which £100 went to the winner, but it remained at this figure until after the Second World War, when it was increased to £1,000.   The total was raised to £1,500 a few years later, but in 1953 it was more than doubled. It was first increased to £2,500 for the Championship which Ben Hogan won at Carnoustie, and then at the end of the same year to £3,500 with a first prize of £750. If the ghosts of 'Young Tom' Morris and Harry Vardon were watching the play at Birkdale in 1954, I cannot but think that they must have felt just a little cheated when they saw the value of the cheque being handed to Peter Thomson, the first winner from Australia.

This enormous increase in tournament prize-money over the years has of course only been made possible by the growing popularity of golf as a spectacle. It is believed that the first time gate-money was charged at a golf contest in Britain was in 1892, on the occasion of a match between Douglas Rolland and Jack White at Cambridge, but in the British Open Championship gate-money was charged for the first time at Royal Lytham and St Anne's in 1926, the year of Bobby Jones's first victory. From the point of view of the looker-on golf has two attractions which distinguish it from almost every other sport. The spectator, if he so desires, and particularly if he decides to follow the fortunes of his own particular favourite among the contestants, gets almost as much exercise as the players themselves, with the additional advantage of being able to knock off when he likes and take a rest at some vantage point, looking down on the green of some particularly difficult hole, and watching the field go by. It is also one of the few sports in which a large proportion of the spectators nurse a not entirely illusory hope of applying their observation of the methods of the stars to the improvement of their own play. It is true that they often defeat this object by attempting to take in too many different points at one time, but even the dullest of beginners cannot watch player after player in a big tournament without carrying away some mental picture of the form of a well-grooved swing.

It is this feature of golf which attracts the huge gates of the stupendous series of big-money tournaments that make up the U.S. 'Gold Dust Circuit.' It is calculated that in a normal year in the States a hundred and fifty regular tournament professionals are contending in thirty-seven big events for a total prize-money of around $750,000. Yet Jimmy Demaret in *My Partner, Ben Hogan*, estimates that after paying their expenses not more than ten out of the hundred and fifty show a respectable profit at the end of the year, after playing hundreds of rounds of tension-filled golf. Imagine the nerve strain involved in a contest in which a player can win $25,000 with a single stroke, as Lew Worsham did by holing his pitch for a 2 at the last hole in the seventy-two holes World Championship tournament of 1953 at Tam o' Shanter, Chicago.

From the money point of view that was the most lucrative shot ever played. The home hole at Tam o' Shanter is 410 yards long. A par 4 would have earned Worsham the second prize of $10,000. A birdie 3 would have given him a tie for first place. His 'eagle' 2 made a difference of $15,000 for that one stroke. Everything combined to make that shot as dramatic as possible for ten thousand spectators gathered in the grandstands and on the slopes around the green as well as for the millions of viewers watching the finish of the tournament on their television sets. Owing to the numbers the players were playing in threes, and Worsham was in the last three to finish. When he dropped a stroke at the sixteenth he thought he had to get birdie 3's at each of the last two holes if he were to beat Chandler Harper, who was playing immediately in front of him, and he duly got his 3 at the seventeenth, holing an eight-foot putt to do it.

But word came back that Harper himself had cut a stroke from par at the eighteenth, laying his approach within a foot of the cup to finish with a 3. So Worsham came to the last tee knowing that he needed a 3 to tie and a deuce to win, and I have no doubt he concentrated his whole mind on bringing off the 3. His drive left him a little over a hundred yards from the hole and he took his wedge for the second shot. It was ruled on the pin all the way, pitched short of the hole, bounced forward, checked, skidded, and shot into the can—the wonder shot of all time! Can it be any matter for surprise that the successful players over a long series of similar events emerge from it 'tournament tough' to a degree that no other golfers can equal?

CHAPTER THIRTY-TWO
(1921–1954)

Golf as an International Sport

A DEVELOPMENT of far-reaching importance in the years follow-ing the First World War was the institution of the three great inter-national contests between Great Britain and the United States, the amateur international for the Walker Cup, presented by George H. Walker, who was president of the United States Golf Association in 1920, the professional international for the Ryder Cup, presented by Samuel Ryder, of St Albans, a keen supporter of British pro-fessional golf, and the ladies' international for the Curtis Cup pre-sented by the sisters Margaret and Harriet Curtis, both former holders of the U.S. Ladies' Championship. It was originally contemplated that the amateur and professional contests should be annual affairs, but latterly all have been held biennially. Although the amateur international was officially instituted on the course of the Royal Liverpool Club at Hoylake in 1921, the Walker Cup was not presented until the match on the National Links at Long Island in the following year. The professional matches for the Ryder Cup and the ladies' for the Curtis Cup were both preceded by earlier contests of a semi-official character.

Curiously enough it was the ladies who had the distinction of staging the first international golf match between Great Britain and the United States. The initiative, as usual, came from America. In 1905, when the British Ladies' Championship was to be played at Cromer, a remarkably strong contingent of the leading lady players in the States had got together for the first serious overseas attempt on the British title. What more natural than to suggest an international team match as a bit of useful practice for the Cham-pionship? So Cromer became the scene of the first golf inter-national with America. The British girls won that contest very handsomely by six matches to one, and were also successful in the Championship, which was won by Miss Bertha Thompson. It is

Photo: Bassano Ltd.

Miss Joyce Wethered (Lady Heathcoat Amory) whose championship career included four victories in the British Ladies' Championship, five in succession in the English event, and only two defeats.

Photo: Sport & General

Miss Cecil Leitch making her first appearance in championship golf, at the age of seventeen at St. Andrews in 1908, when she taught the world a new idea of women's golf style.

Photo: H. W. Neale

MRS. MILDRED ('BABE') ZAHARIAS
First American woman to carry off the British Championship and thrice
winner of the U.S. Women's Open Championship.

true that the Cromer match was 'unofficial' in the sense that it was not planned in advance, and it is also true that we had to wait a quarter of a century for this international rivalry to be revived. But the connection between that Cromer battle and the Curtis Cup Match is clear and unmistakable.   The sisters Margaret and Harriet Curtis, who were to be the successive holders of the American Championship in the next two years, played second and fourth respectively in the American team in that first international, and it is they who were the donors of the trophy which bears their name and is the guerdon of victory in the modern series of matches.   It is interesting to record that Miss Margaret Curtis, at the age of sixty-nine, was one of the competitors in the U.S. Women's Championship of 1949 at Merion.   She was knocked out in the first round by the reasonably close margin of 3 and 2, but her attempt set up a new 'high' in the matter of age in ladies' championship golf.

In all these international contests the difference in the character of the courses and in the weather conditions give a distinct advantage to the home players, for the miseries of a cold spell in an English spring were just as trying to the American golfers as the heat of a sweltering summer in the States to the British players.   The growing numbers of first-class players in America made it evident that British invaders had no hope of victory in either team or individual events in the States—though Jack McLean came near it when he took Johnny Fischer to the thirty-seventh hole in the final of the American Amateur Championship of 1936 at Garden City—and interest in the events has only been maintained by the partial success of British golfers on their own ground, for it is a remarkable fact that in the periods when British players seemed to be most hopelessly outclassed in individual events they managed to maintain a fair show in the internationals, and U.S. victories in the team matches coincided with British successes in the individual championships.

During the ten years from 1924 to 1933 when U.S. golfers monopolized the British Open Championship, British professionals remained undefeated in the international matches played on their own side of the Atlantic.   The U.S. professionals scored their first Ryder Cup win in England in 1934, and the British professionals have never got it back again, but during the last twenty years U.S. invaders have had small success in the Championship, their only victories being those of Sam Snead in the first championship after the Second World War and of Ben Hogan in 1953.

Among the amateurs it was the other way about. The earlier contests for the Walker Cup went all in favour of the U.S., but it was not until 1926 that Jesse Sweetser became the first American-born player to win the British Amateur crown, and 'Emperor' Bobby Jones in 1930 was the only other winner prior to 1934. Of the six championships played between 1934 and 1939 U.S. players won four, but it was in that period that Great Britain scored her only success in the Walker Cup Match.

In the matter of international exchange British ladies have always done better than the men. Miss Dorothy Campbell brought the U.S. Championship back to Scotland in 1909 and 1910. (As Mrs Hurd she won the title a third time in 1924, but by that date she was permanently resident in the States.) Miss Gladys Ravenscroft in 1913 and Miss Pam Barton in 1936 brought the tally of British successes in the States to four. On their own side of the Atlantic the British girls succeeded in holding off U.S. attacks on their title until Mrs Mildred Zaharias and Miss Louise Suggs, each on the eve of turning professional, won in 1947 and 1948 respectively. But here again the record of the Curtis Cup Match is in complete contradiction to that of the individual event. The British players indeed won that early international match at Cromer, and also a semi-official match at Sunningdale in 1930, but in the Curtis Cup contest their only success was a halved match at Gleneagles in 1936, and not until the U.S. had scored their first win in the Championship did Britain score her first win in the Curtis Cup—in 1952 at Muirfield.

CHAPTER THIRTY-THREE

History's Debt to Golf

ALTHOUGH golf doubtless owed some part of its popularity to the historical associations that earned it the title of the royal game, it has gone a long way to repay its debt by helping to preserve many ancient landmarks that would otherwise have passed into oblivion. One of the most famous instances is the course of the St Augustine's Club, at Ebbsfleet, not far from Ramsgate, where a Runic cross of stone a few yards from the clubhouse marks what is believed to be the spot where in A.D. 597 St Augustine first set foot on English soil, on coming over from the Continent to convert the heathen Saxons to Christianity. In the same field once stood St Augustine's oak—'Austin's Oak' by local tradition—under whose shade King Ethelbert is supposed to have received the missionaries. But the old tree was destroyed almost a century ago, and nobody was particularly interested in preserving a record of its position, so that the young oak planted in its place shortly before the First Great War not far from the eighteenth green only approximately indicates the site of the lost landmark.

On the course itself, not far from the fifth green and almost in the line of our tee-shot to the seventeenth, is 'St Augustine's Well,' a little spring of clear water which is said to have appeared miraculously to relieve the thirst of the saint. This is the scene of an annual pilgrimage by the Warden of St Augustine's College, Canterbury, who in his capacity of Bishop-Knight visits the spot and kneels down to drink the sacred water, his example being followed by the other officials and members of the college. Here is one historic spot which might long ago have been lost sight of or submerged under a sea of buildings, had it not been preserved by its position within the boundaries of a golf course.

Curiously enough, just as the oldest landmark connected with the founding of the English Church is preserved on a golf course at one

corner of England, so one of the oldest memorials of the still older
Celtic Church is to be found on a golf course at the opposite corner,
on the Atlantic coast of Cornwall.   Here the course of the Trevose
Golf Club is laid out in a typical stretch of sand-hill country, from
which even in the thirteenth century the encroachment of the sand
had forced the inhabitants to remove their church and their homes
farther inland to the high ground at St Merryn.   The ruins of the
original church, named after St Constantine, the first Christian
Emperor of Rome, stand within a few yards of the eighteenth tee.
A little further away is St Constantine's Well, which was redis-
covered less than half a century ago, and has since been completely
excavated.   The ruined church is a favourite object of pilgrimage to
visitors interested in the history of the Celtic churches, and for it,
too, the course is a guarantee of security for all time.

What may very probably be the oldest permanently established
course in the world is the public course of the North Inch (i.e.
island) of Perth.   It was here that James VI and I learned his golf
as a boy, and it is likely that this was the course where James IV
went a golfing, with the clubs he bought from 'the bowar of Sanct
Johnestown,' in 1502, though that is not quite certain because it is
not clear whether the North Inch or the South Inch was at that time
the usual golfing ground.[1]   Long before that the North Inch was
the recognized locale for sporting events.   It was the scene, for
instance, of the famous 'Battle of the Clans' between Clan Chattan
and Clan Kay, who here fought to the death a battle of thirty-a-side
in the presence of King Robert III, on 28th September 1396—an
adventure which forms one of the central episodes in *The Fair Maid
of Perth*.

The golfers on the North Inch are wont to boast that they once
kept their clubs on the site of a temple to Mars.   A marble slab on a
block of business premises at the junction of the Water Gate and
the High Street bears witness that:

Here stood the Castle of the Green, an ancient house in which golfers
used to keep their clubs and balls.   The house now occupying the site

[1] From 1592 onwards sundry kirk-session minutes record the thunders of
the Church against golfers found playing golf in sermon time in 'the meadow
inch of Muirton'—which makes it certain that by this date at any rate Perth
golfers were playing over the North Inch.

WALTER HAGEN WINS HIS THIRD BRITISH OPEN CHAMPIONSHIP, 1928
The ninth green at Royal St George's; Hagen lucky to find a good lie between the bunkers.

was built in 1788, and on clearing the site for its erection, two under-ground chambers were found ... the remains of an ancient British temple, said by Holinshed to have been founded at Perth by a grandson of King Lear, and traditionally reported to have preceded the Castle of the Green on its site.

Another of the Perthshire courses which is rich in historical associations is Pitlochry, where the Highland Tournament is played each year in August. The course occupies as picturesque a situation as can well be imagined, overlooking the valleys of the Tummel and the Garry, with Craiglunie rising steeply to the north of it. The short fourth hole is played to a green close to the remains of an old Pictish fort, where more than two thousand years ago a post of the Picts kept watch over their village of Moulin, and the seventh tee is actually on part of the site of the fort. Close by, giving its name to the sixth, are the 'Druid Stones' that mark all that remains of a Druidical circle, most of which was destroyed in the name of agricultural improvement over a century ago, an indication of how much safer such historical landmarks are in the hands of the golfers than in those of the farmers.

The second hole runs close by the site of the Old North Road, which for more than a thousand years was the main artery connecting the South of Scotland with the North, along which Robert Bruce withdrew his shattered forces after the disaster of Methven, and along which in 1689 General Mackay led the English forces to defeat at Killiecrankie. Mary Queen of Scots, passing along the same road to visit the Earl of Atholl, is supposed to have made a halt near the far end of the course, at a spot which gives to the fifth hole the name of Queen Mary's Rest.

The Leeds municipal courses at Templenewsam have several remarkable historical associations. Templenewsam takes its name from the Knights Templars, for it was one of the Preceptories of the Order, and under the name of Templestowe has been immortalized by Scott as the scene of the famous trial by combat between the Disinherited Knight and Sir Brian de Bois-Guilbert in *Ivanhoe*.

The most glorious period of its history, however, was the time of the Tudors. Its owner in the early part of the sixteenth century, named Darcy, was executed by Henry VIII in 1537 for complicity in the insurrection known as the Pilgrimage of Grace, and Henry granted Templenewsam to his niece, the Countess of Lennox. The mansion house, which overlooks the sixteenth fairway of the No. 2 course, has of course been rebuilt since then, but the present mansion is believed to incorporate the room in which was born the countess's son, Henry Stewart, Lord Darnley, the ill-fated husband of Mary Queen of Scots.

Further south in Nottinghamshire you will find a curious instance of a putting green that gives its name to a parliamentary division. The green in question is that of the fourteenth at Rushcliffe, a famous 'drop hole' calling for a mashie shot over a clump of oak and ash to a saucer green surrounded by a hollow of turf that was once a moat. The green itself is the site of Rushcliffe Hall, where the elections used to be held in the old days, and the name of the division still remains, although there is no such place as Rushcliffe and not a stone of the hall itself has been left standing.

The 'flying spur' that is the crest of the Highgate Golf Club commemorates the fact that part of the course still holds traces of the wall and moat that once enclosed a hunting lodge of the Bruces, whose English lands were at Tottenham. In 1305 Robert Bruce, disappointed of his expectation of being granted the Scottish crown after the defeat of Balliol at Dunbar, and forced by Edward to remain with the court in London, became aware that his correspondence with the Scottish patriot party was suspected by the king. He accordingly withdrew to the lodge at Highgate, where he was close to the great road to the north. The Duke of Gloucester, who was friendly to Bruce, discovered that Edward was meditating stronger steps against the latter, and not daring to commit himself by a more explicit message sent him a warning by means of a spur with feather attached. Bruce, of course, had no difficulty in reading the riddle, and rode at once for Scotland.

Older than almost any of the landmarks I have mentioned are the low ridges of turf that you can easily make out at the holes of the middle of the round at Laleham-on-Thames, still marking the site of what was once the fortified camp of the guard which the Romans maintained over the ford across the Thames—sixteen hundred years ago.

Golf does not always get the credit it deserves for the valuable work it has done in the preservation of many of the 'stately homes of England,' which would have had no chance of survival had they not been taken over as clubhouses. How many of the thousands who watch the play in the first big professional tournament of each season at Moor Park are aware that the park once belonged to Cardinal Wolsey, and that the clubhouse was the home of the ill-fated Duke of Monmouth? Henry VII gave Moor Park to the Earl of Oxford for his services at Bosworth Field. From Oxford it passed to Wolsey, whose memory is still preserved by 'the Cardinal's Oak,' and after Wolsey's fall it came to the earls of Monmouth, and later to the duke, who started the building of the present house. After the defeat of the duke at Sedgemoor and his execution on Tower Hill, his widow, Anne, Duchess of Buccleuch and Monmouth, caused many of the oaks in the park to be pollarded—in order, it is suggested, that they might never be used for the Navy of which James II was so proud. The Navy, however, had something to say in the development of Moor Park after all, for one of the two men whose riches were spent in preparing its magnificent portico and the enormous hall with five marble doorways and painted ceiling and panels was Admiral Anson, who circumnavigated the globe and collected half a million of Spanish treasure. Before him Benjamin Styles, who had made a fortune in the South Sea boom, is said to have spent £130,000 on the embellishment of what is now probably the most magnificent clubhouse in England.

Another clubhouse of special interest from an historic point of view is the home of the Rochford Hundred Golf Club, near Southend. Rochford Hall, as it was formerly named, dates from the beginning of the fourteenth century, and must be one of the oldest clubhouses in England. It was twice partially destroyed by fire, but the four main gables, one corner tower, and a number of the tall chimneys still represent the original building, which was a summer residence of Sir Thomas Boleyn, afterwards Viscount Ormonde and Earl of Wiltshire. Sir Thomas was the father of Anne Boleyn, who became the second wife of Henry VIII and the mother of 'Good Queen Bess.' No doubt Anne spent many of the summers of her girlhood at Rochford Hall, but I am afraid there is no foundation for the inevitable local legend that the amorous Henry did some of his courting there.

What is almost certainly the oldest building in the world to be used as a golf clubhouse, probably older than the game itself, is the home of the Chestfield Club at Shrub Hill, near Whitstable, which is believed to date from the reign of Edward II. The Manor of Chestfield is mentioned in the Domesday survey, and Hasted's *History of Kent* records the passing of the manor from one to another of three or four different families between 1307 and 1799. When the Chestfield course was opened in 1924, the clubhouse was the splendid old tithe barn, which stands close to the present house, and is itself a veteran among buildings, with a history that goes back for five hundred years or more. A few years later, however, the Club was able to acquire the 'Lower House,' which is believed to be almost as old as the manor, and appears to have been used as a 'guest house' in the days when the Canterbury pilgrims were wont to impose a continual strain upon the hospitality of this quarter of the world. A quaint, fascinating, crazy, picturesque old house it is, with its rough timbers and leaded windows, here a huge wooden pin holding two rafters together, there a tuft of dried grass in a patch of rude plaster bearing witness to the primitive methods of construction of bygone centuries. Of necessity a great part even of the walls of the house as it now stands is modern work, but great care has been taken in the work of repair and also in the furnishing arrangements to have everything in keeping with the venerable antiquity of the house.

On the Great North Road, in one of the most delightful parks in Hertfordshire, the Brookman's Park course is of historic interest because of the tradition that Sir Thomas More wrote his *Utopia* here. It seems that what is now known as Brookman's Park was originally two manors and two estates—More Hall, later known as Gobions or Gobeyns, and Brookman's. In the reign of Henry VIII, More Hall was owned by Sir John More, the father of England's famous chancellor, and on Sir John's death it became the jointure of his widow, who was his third wife. It is said that the famous group of the More family, which was Holbein's first work in England, was painted at More Hall. When Sir Thomas More was executed, Henry VIII turned the chancellor's stepmother out of the estate, which reverted to the Crown, but Queen Elizabeth removed the attainder and the manor became vested in Cresacre More, a son of Sir Thomas. The companion manor of Brookman's was held in 1400 by John Brookman, but the family died out in the next century. The original mansion house is supposed to have been pulled down in 1666, and the house that replaced it was destroyed by fire towards the end of last century. The present clubhouse was originally the stables, but was converted into the mansion house from the time of the fire. Some of its walls are three feet thick. It is interesting to note that the Great North Road formerly passed directly by the present clubhouse and on through the old farmyard into Bell Bar.

Interesting in another way is the clubhouse of the Upminster Golf Club, standing three-quarters of a mile from the centre of Upminster on the main road to Brentwood. Prior to the Reformation this ancient timbered mansion house with its mullioned windows and spacious staircase was a common residence of the abbots of Waltham Abbey. When Henry VIII confiscated the church lands, he handed over Upminster Hall to Thomas Cromwell, Earl of Essex, and after the fall of Essex it passed into the successive hands of the Latham and the Branfill families. Inevitably the transformation of the hall into a clubhouse called for a certain amount of alteration and enlargement, but the work has been carried out with uncommon taste and everything has been done to preserve the character of the lovely old building. The course is delightfully situated on the banks of the little River Ingrebourne, which comes in as a formidable hazard at three or four of the holes.

CHAPTER THIRTY-FOUR
(1833–1955)

Golf as a Royal Game Again

THE revival of the historic connection of the game of golf with the British royal line, which had been allowed to lapse under the House of Hanover, began with the creation of the first of the 'Royal' Golf Clubs by King William IV in 1833. The idea apparently came from Lord Kinnaird, who asked the king to confer this distinction on the Perth Golfing Society, which was formed in 1824, and played —indeed still plays—over the public course on Perth North Inch. There is no question that the Royal Perth Golfing Society was the first club to be so honoured, because in intimating the distinction to the Club, Lord Kinnaird speaks of it as 'an honour which no other Golfing Society could boast of.' The official confirmation is dated from Windsor, 4th June 1833.

The grant of this title to the Perth Society naturally aroused the envy of the St Andrews men, who felt that if honours of this kind were being handed out the St Andrews Society of Golfers had a better and prior claim, both as having been in existence from 1754 and on account of King William's official connection with the town as Duke of St Andrews. It was on this latter ground that Major Murray Belshes in January 1834 submitted a request that the king should be graciously pleased to become patron of the Club, and also since the Club was with the exception of the Edinburgh Club [*sic*] the oldest in Scotland, that His Majesty would permit it to be styled 'Royal and Ancient.'

The precedent thus set up was followed by Queen Victoria in numerous other cases. The Eastbourne Golf Club, whose first president was the Duke of Devonshire, became Royal Eastbourne within a few days of its formation. The Ashdown Forest Club was created Royal Ashdown on the occasion of a great review of troops

214

in the forest by the Duke of Cambridge, the royal field marshal coming over in full uniform to drive the first ball in celebration of the event. In many instances, such as the cases of Royal Jersey and Royal Guernsey, the distinction was conferred on pioneer Clubs in response to a humble request sent up from the members. Four of the Royal Golf Clubs possessed only a nine-hole links at the time the title was granted—Royal Musselburgh (which now, of course, has its own eighteen-hole course at Prestongrange), Royal Isle of Wight at Bembridge, Royal Worlington and Newmarket, and the now defunct Royal Cornwall Club at Bodmin. At the present time the number of Royal Golf Clubs is close on seventy, including three in Belgium and one in the Belgian Congo, on which the distinction was conferred by the King of the Belgians.

The granting of the title of 'Royal and Ancient' to the St Andrews Club had the happy result of awakening in William IV and his consort a fresh interest in the town from which they took their ducal title and in the game of which it was the headquarters. In 1837 the king presented to the Club 'a Gold Medal, with Green Ribband' to be played for annually (this has ever since been the principal prize at the Club's Autumn Meeting), and in the following year the widowed Queen Adelaide presented the Club with the Gold Medal bearing her name with the request that it should be worn by the captain of the Club on all public occasions.

These developments brought golf into royal notice, if not at once into royal favour, once more. King Edward VII as a boy in Scotland, and King George V in middle age, both tried their hands at the game without developing any great enthusiasm for it, and it was left to the younger princes of the House of Windsor to restore golf to its position as the royal game. Edward VIII and George VI had their first introduction to golf as boys on holiday at Newquay, and both became more than moderately good. A year or two before the death of their father, when the princes were competitors in the Household Brigade Tournament at Roehampton, they both played from a handicap of 11, and this I fancy just about represented the high-water mark of their golfing form.

King Edward VIII, now the Duke of Windsor, will always be remembered as one of the keenest golfers who ever struck a ball.

He was captain of the Royal and Ancient Club in 1922, played as a member of the Welsh Guards quartet competing in the Army Team Championship, was once runner-up and once a semi-finalist in the Parliamentary Handicap, has done three holes in one—at Royal Wimbledon, at Nassau in the Bahamas, and at Santos in Brazil— won handicap competitions playing off 11 or 12 at Sunningdale, Le Touquet, and Coombe Hill, and was runner-up in a match-play tournament of the Chiberta Club at Biarritz.   His greatest service to the game, however, has been as ambassador of golf's empire overseas.   Wherever he has gone, on tour to the Dominions, on holiday on the Continent, on visits official and semi-official, he has never missed an opportunity to spend any odd hours of privacy that he could snatch from the official programmes in a quiet round of golf.   He has played over scores of courses in the British Isles; he has played in the United States and Canada, in Brazil and in the Argentine, in South Africa, in Kenya and in Egypt, in India, in Japan and in Arabia, and in most of the continental countries. Even Joe Kirkwood, who has played over more than two thousand courses, probably cannot boast so wide a range.   To the long list of courses over which he played as Prince of Wales, the Duke of Windsor has since added many more to his original list in the United States.

The strange thing is that the proficiency which the then Prince of Wales only achieved by careful coaching and assiduous drumfire practice at Coombe Hill under the critical eye of Archie Compston came to his younger brother almost without effort.   King George VI followed his Tudor ancestors rather than the Stuarts in choosing as his favourite game lawn tennis, and in it he was first-class.   Along with Wing-Commander Sir Louis Greig, he won the Doubles Championship of the Royal Air Force in 1920, and got through a couple of rounds in the Men's Doubles at Wimbledon in 1926. But his skill at games seemed to be a natural gift, and at golf his easy and rhythmic swing made him completely at ease in playing before a gallery.   When he played himself in as captain of the Royal and Ancient Club—an ordeal which tests the nerve of even the most hardened of champions—he hit a 200-yard drive far and sure down the middle.   He was the only royal personage, so far as I am aware, who has ever taken part in an exhibition match to celebrate the opening of a new course. The occasion was the official opening in the spring of 1924 of the nine-hole course at Ton Pentre, constructed by the local miners in their spare time. The Duke of York, as he then was, and Captain Basil Brooke were opposed by Mr Frank Hodges, 'the Miners M.P.,' who was at that time Civil Lord of the Admiralty, and Mr Evans, the chairman of the Mining Association. The duke's side were not so successful as the earlier Duke of York and his shoemaker partner, for they lost the game by 2 and 1, but the match served very pleasantly to re-establish the old tradition.

The only player of what might fairly be called championship class among modern royal golfers was undoubtedly King Leopold of the Belgians. Immediately before the Second World War, when he was on holiday at Zoute, he competed in the Belgian Open Amateur Championship, which was being held there that year, got through the stroke play qualifying stage with ease, and also won through the first round of the match play stage before being beaten at the nineteenth hole in the last sixteen. In the Open Tournament at Ascona in 1946, which was won by Robert Lanz, then professional to the Zürich Club, King Leopold finished 'first amateur' with an aggregate of 155 for the thirty-six holes. In 1949 he got into the last eight of the French Open Amateur Championship at St Cloud. His attempt on the Belgian title at Zoute in 1939 was the first occasion on which a reigning monarch took part in a national championship and I am reasonably certain that his performance at Ascona was the first occasion on which any royal golfer was bold enough to compete in an open tournament against professional opposition on a strange course and in a foreign country.

On the other side of the Atlantic the popularity of golf has gone far to justify Mr Dooley's explanation that golf is known as the royal and ancient game 'because the Presidents of the United States have just took it up.' Between the wars, Presidents Wilson, Taft, and Harding all found their recreation on the links. It was President Harding who summed up the universal appeal of the game in one of his speeches with the statement that 'It used to be thought that golf was a game for the elderly, but the beauty of golf is that everybody can play it.' Franklin D. Roosevelt was quite a sound player till illness threw the stop sign on his golf. General Eisenhower was elected a member of the Royal and Ancient Club of St Andrews long before he became President of the United States.   At the other end of the social scale the immense development of public courses has helped to make golf as much the game of all classes as it is in its native Scotland.   But probably there is no one in whose way of life golf has wrought a bigger difference than that legendary figure the American business man.   At the beginning of the century, as the late Lord Birkenhead wrote in his book *America Revisited*, published soon after the First World War, the average American man of business 'was conceived of, and not altogether with injustice, as one who left home early and returned late, employing the long day in the feverish interests of Wall Street; he became dyspeptic at forty, and he very often died at fifty.   In the interval (if he were successful), he accumulated a vast fortune.   His wife and his beautiful daughters enjoyed it; but as far as he was concerned the rare alleviations of a hectic life coincided with a few hurried visits to Europe.'   But golf, Lord Birkenhead declared, has changed all this and has taught even the hustlers 'to realize that life is short, health vital, dollars incapable of transfer to the next world, and that therefore there is much to be said for a reasonable enjoyment of life in this.'

To members of those professions whose leisure comes at odd and irregular hours, notably to the actor and the vaudeville artist, golf has proved an inestimable boon.   It has also established a place for itself as the favourite recreation of followers of other sports.   And to the whole world, men and women, young and old, it offers a special attraction as the one sport whose recreational value depends not a whit on the skill of the performer.   In the words of the anonymous author of an oft-quoted ode to the game:

> They do not know what Golf may be
>   Who call it childish play,
> To drive a globule from a tee
>   And follow it away.
> They do not understand who scoff
>   And all its virtues miss,
> Who think that this is all of Golf,
>   For Golf is more than this.

For Golf is Earth's ambassador
   That comes to haunts of men,
To lure them from the banking floor,
   The counter and the pen,
To lead them gently by the hand
   From toil and stress and strife,
And guide them through the summer land
   Along the path of life. . . .

'A good journey to you,' said the Belgian golfers to the wheel-wright of Coq, as they parted from him in the dusk of the evening, 'and may St Anthony, the patron of golfers, preserve you from meeting the devil on the way.' That is my parting message to every reader of these pages.

APPENDIX

A Chronological Table of Leading Events

1353   Earliest reference to the cross-country game of *chole* as a popular sport in Flanders.

1415   Battle of Agincourt. The English invasion overruns northern France.

1420   Charles VI of France sends ambassadors to ask for help from Scotland.

1421   Battle of Baugé. The Scottish expeditionary force inflicts a decisive defeat on the English forces under the Duke of Clarence, the English surprise attack being discovered by a small band of Scots 'playing at ball' (? *chole*) towards the river crossing.

1424   Football forbidden by an Act of the Scots Parliament of James I, as interfering with military training.

1457   Golf joined with football by a similar Act under James II, banning both these popular sports in the interests of national defence.

1470   A similar enactment repeated under James III.

1491   —and again under James IV.

1502 [1]   Treaty of perpetual peace between Scotland and England signed by James IV in Glasgow Cathedral.
       (To a certain extent this treaty achieved its object. The two countries were still to meet in numerous battles, few of which brought much credit to Scotland, but there were no more wars of conquest.)

1502   James IV buys golf clubs and balls from the bow-maker of St Johnstoun (i.e. Perth).

1503   'The Marriage of the Thistle and the Rose'—James IV and Margaret Tudor, daughter of Henry VII of England—celebrated at Holyrood.

1504   James IV goes to golf with the Earl of Bothwell.

1513   Battle of Flodden and death of James IV.

[1] At this date the old Julian calendar was still in force, the year beginning 25th March. The Treaty of Glasgow was signed on 22nd February 1501 (old style) but to avoid confusion this and similar dates are quoted in terms of the modern calendar.

1527   Sir Robert Maule described as a regular player on Barry (Carnoustie) links.

1553 [1]   John Hamilton, Archbishop of St Andrews, confirms the communal right of playing golf over the links at St Andrews.

1567   Murder of Lord Darnley: Queen Mary accused of playing golf and pall-mall in the fields of Seton House within a fortnight of her husband's death.

1570   Story of the Earl of Cassilis's match against the Abbot of Crossraguel on the links at Ayr, the stake being the Abbot's nose!

1589   Playing of golf, carrick, and shinty forbidden in the Blackfriars Yards, Glasgow, 'Sunday or week-day.'

1592   The town council of Edinburgh issues a proclamation against playing golf at Leith on Sunday 'in tyme of sermonis.'

1600(?)   Kennedy of Bargany injured while playing golf on the links at Ayr.

1603   Union of the Crowns; King James VI of Scotland succeeds to the throne of England.

1608(?)   Henry, Prince of Wales, at golf in the park of the royal manor at Greenwich.

1618(?)   Introduction of the 'feathery' ball.

1618   King James VI and I issues a proclamation in favour of Sunday sports.

1621   First record of golf being played in the King's Park, Stirling.

1629   James Graham, Marquis of Montrose, recorded as playing frequently at Leith, Montrose, and St Andrews.

1630   Sir Robert Gordon describes Dornoch as the fairest and largest links in any part of Scotland. 'Fitt for archery, golfing, ryding, and all other exercises, they doe surpass the fields of Montrose or St Andrews.'

1633   Charles I renews his father's proclamation about Sunday sports.

1641   Charles I playing golf at Leith when the news is brought to him of the breaking out of the Irish rebellion.

1642   The town council of Aberdeen license John Dickson as golf-ball maker for the burgh.

1646   Charles I surrenders to the Scots at Newcastle, and while he is a prisoner there he and his suite are allowed to play golf in the Shield Field outside the city walls.

1649   Execution of Charles I.

1650   Charles II plays golf during his brief residence as king in Scotland.

[1] See footnote on page 221.

1658   Record of golf being played in 'Up-Fields' (Vincent Square), Westminster.

1660   Restoration of Charles II to the throne of England.

1672   The household accounts of Sir John Foulis of Ravelstoun show that golf at this date was a popular amusement of the Scottish nobility and gentry.

1682   First International Golf Match.   The Duke of York (afterwards James II) and a shoemaker named John Patersone defeat two English noblemen in a match at Leith.

1688   The Revolution. William of Orange becomes King of England as William III.

1690   Battle of the Boyne, to which William's forces sail for Ireland from Hoylake.

1707   Union of England and Scotland under one Parliament.

1711   Death of Maggie Johnstone, keeper of a 'howff' or tavern favoured by golfers coming to Bruntsfield Links, subject of a poem by Allan Ramsay.

1721   Earliest documentary reference to golf on Glasgow Green.

1724   Match at Leith between Captain Porteous of the Edinburgh Town Guard and Arthur Elphinstone, attended by a vast mob of spectators.

1728   Duncan Forbes of Culloden, Lord President of the Scottish Court of Session, records in his diary getting the better of his son in a match at Musselburgh, 'after a very hard pull.'

1744   First attempt to hold a golf meeting.   The golfers playing over Leith links persuade the City of Edinburgh to offer a Silver Club as a challenge trophy for open competition.

1744   John Rattray, surgeon in Edinburgh, becomes the first winner of the Silver Club.

1746–7 Play for the Silver Club abandoned during the troubles of the Jacobite Rebellion.

1754   Twenty-two golfers of St Andrews subscribe for a Silver Club to be played for in open competition in the same way as the Edinburgh one.   First winner: Bailie William Landale, merchant, St Andrews.

1758   Mention of golf being played at Molesey Hurst.

1759   First mention of stroke play (at St Andrews).

1764   The round at St Andrew's reduced to eighteen holes.

1764   The Leith golfers petition the town of Edinburgh to allow them to form themselves into a Club and restrict the competition for their trophy to the members of that Club (the Honourable Company of Edinburgh Golfers).

1766   Mr Henry Foot presents a Silver Driver for annual competition among the golfers at Blackheath.

1773   The St Andrews golfers begin to restrict their competitions to members of 'their own and the Leith Society.'

1773   The Edinburgh Burgess Golfing Society (the Royal Burgess Golfing Society of Edinburgh) takes formal shape.

1774   Thomas McMillan, Esq., of Shorthope, presents a Silver Cup for competition among the Musselburgh golfers and is himself the first winner of it.

1779   Golf played by Scottish officers quartered in New York during the American Revolutionary War.

1780   Formation of the (Royal) Aberdeen Golf Club.

1783   First record of the Glasgow golfers competing for their Silver Club.   The Club formally instituted in 1787.

1786   Earliest reference to the game in the United States: formation of the South Carolina Golf Club at Charleston.

1786   Formation of the Crail Golfing Society.

1787   The Bruntsfield Links golfers decide to form themselves into a Club.

1797   Formation of the Burntisland Golf Club.

1806   The St Andrews golfers make the captaincy of the Club elective, and substitute a Gold Medal for the Silver Club as the trophy for the Club championship.

1810   First mention of a ladies competition; held by the Musselburgh Golf Club for the local fisherwomen.

1818   Manchester golfers (Old Manchester Club) begin playing on Kersal Moor.

1824   Formation of the Perth Golfing Society.

1829   Formation of the Calcutta, afterwards Royal Calcutta, Golf Club.

1832   Formation of the North Berwick Golf Club.

1833   The Perth Golfing Society becomes the first of the 'Royal' Golf Clubs, created 'Royal Perth' by William IV.

1834   William IV confers the title of Royal and Ancient upon the Golf Club of St Andrews.

1836   The Honourable Company of Edinburgh Golfers removes from Leith to Musselburgh.

1842   Formation of the (Royal) Bombay Golfing Society.

1848   Introduction of the gutta-percha ball.

1851   Formation of the Prestwick Golf Club.

1856   Royal Curragh Golf Club founded in Kildare.

1856   First Golf Club on the Continent of Europe founded at Pau.

1857   Publication of the first book of golf instruction, *The Golfer's Manual*, by 'A Keen Hand' (H. B. Farnie).

1857   The Prestwick Club institutes the first Championship Meeting (Inter-Club Foursomes), played at St Andrews and won by George Glennie and Lieut. J. C. Stewart for Blackheath.

1858   The Championship Meeting changed to an individual event and won by Robert Chambers, of Bruntsfield Links, the famous publisher.

1859   The Amateur Championship won by George Condie of Perth.

1859   Death of Allan Robertson, the first of the great professionals.

1860   The Prestwick Club offer a Championship Belt for an annual Professional Championship—won by Willie Park.

1861   This tournament is thrown open to amateurs as well as professionals and becomes 'the Open Championship'—won by 'Old Tom' Morris.

1864   The (Royal) North Devon Golf Club formed at Westward Ho!

1865   The London Scottish Golf Club formed at Wimbeldon.

1867   Formation of the first Ladies' Golf Club, at St Andrews.

1869   The (Royal) Liverpool Golf Club formed at Hoylake, and Alnmouth Golf Club at Alnmouth.

1870   'Young Tom' Morris, at the age of nineteen, wins the Open Championship for the third year in succession and thereby makes the Belt his own property.

1870   Formation of the Royal Adelaide Golf Club, the first Golf Club in Australia.

1872   After a lapse of a year the Prestwick and St. Andrews Clubs and the Honourable Company of Edinburgh Golfers combine to provide a new trophy for the Open Championship, to be played for in rotation over Prestwick, St Andrews, and Musselburgh. The new trophy won by 'Young Tom,' who thus gains the Championship four times in succession.

1873   Formation of the Royal Montreal Golf Club, the first Golf Club in Canada.

1875   Oxford University and Cambridge University Golf Clubs formed.

1878   First University Match played on the course of the London Scottish Golf Club at Wimbledon: won by Oxford.

1880   The Glasgow Club inaugurates the oldest surviving Open Meeting, the annual competition for the Tennant Cup.

1881   Formation of the Royal Belfast Golf Club, at Holywood.

1884   Formation of the Oakhurst Golf Club at White Sulphur Springs, Virginia.

1884   Golf played on a nine-hole course in Phoenix Park, Dublin.

1885   Formation of the Royal Cape Golf Club at Wynberg, South Africa.

1885   Amateur Championship inaugurated by Royal Liverpool Club at Hoylake.   Won by A. F. Macfie, a Scottish member of the home club.

1888   Formation of the St Andrews Golf Club, of Yonkers, New York ('the Apple Tree Gang').

1891   Formation of the Shinnecock Hills Golf Club at Long Island.

1893   Formation of the Ladies' Golf Union and inauguration of the Ladies' Championship, won at St Anne's by Lady Margaret Scott.

1894   The Open Championship, for the first time played for on an English course, results in the first victory for an English-born professional, J. H. Taylor.

1894   Formation of the United States Golf Association.

1896   The Open Championship won for the first time by a Channel Islander, Harry Vardon.

1900   Harry Vardon tours the United States and wins the U.S. Open Championship.

1901   Invention of the rubber-cored ball by Coburn Haskell.

1902   First Amateur International Match between England and Scotland played at Hoylake.   Scotland victorious by 32 holes to 25.

1903   An Oxford and Cambridge Golfing Society team makes a tour of the United States.

1904   Walter J. Travis scores the first U.S. victory in the British Amateur Championship at Royal St George's, Sandwich.

1905   First International Golf Match between Great Britain and the United States.   British ladies beat U.S. ladies at Cromer by 6 matches to 1.

1907   The Open Championship at Hoylake won for the first time by a continental professional, Arnaud Massy.

1907   The Prince of Wales and the Duke of York take up golf as schoolboys on holiday at Newquay.

1908   Miss Cecil Leitch introduces a new masculine style into women's golf swing.

1911   The U.S. Open Championship won for the first time by a 'home-bred' professional, J. J. McDermott.

1913   Francis J. Ouimet at the age of twenty scores the first amateur victory in the U.S. Open, beating Harry Vardon and Ted Ray in a famous play-off.

1919   Management of the Open and Amateur Championships taken over by the Royal and Ancient Club.

1920   Miss Joyce Wethered at Sheringham wins the first of five consecutive victories in the English Ladies' Championship.

1920   Ted Ray becomes the second Channel Islander to bring back the U.S. Open Championship to the British Isles.

1921   The Royal and Ancient Club introduces the first limitation on the size and weight of the ball.

1921   Jock Hutchison takes the British Open Championship trophy for its first trip across the Atlantic.

1921   First Amateur International Match between Great Britain and the United States played at Hoylake.   The U.S. team victorious by 9 matches to 3.

1922   Walter Hagen becomes the first American-born player to win the British Open Championship and ushers in a long series of American triumphs which remains unbroken, except for Arthur Havers's win in 1922, until 1934.

1922   The Prince of Wales, afterwards King Edward VIII and now Duke of Windsor, captain of the Royal and Ancient Club.

1923   The Duke and Duchess of York (King George VI and Queen Elizabeth) play golf on the private course at Polesden-Lacey durying their honeymoon there.

1924   The Duke of York plays in an exhibition match at Ton Pentre.

1926   Jesse Sweetser at Muirfield records the first victory for an American-born player in the British Amateur Championship.

1926   The first (semi-official) Professional International Match between Great Britain and the U.S.A. played at Wentworth. Great Britain victorious by $13\frac{1}{2}$ matches to $1\frac{1}{2}$.

1926   Bobby Jones wins the British Open Championship.

1929   Walter Hagen wins the British Open Championship for the fourth time.

1930   Bobby Jones scores the 'grand slam,' by winning the British Open and Amateur and U.S. Open and Amateur Championships in the same year.

1930   The Duke of York (afterwards King George VI) plays himself in as captain of the Royal and Ancient Club.

1932   First official Ladies' International Match between Great Britain and the U.S.A. played at Wentworth.   Won by the U.S. by $5\frac{1}{2}$ matches to $3\frac{1}{2}$.

1933   The Prince of Wales (Duke of Windsor) reaches the final of the Parliamentary Handicap Tournament.

1934   Henry Cotton at Sandwich scores the first of his three victories in the Open Championship and puts an end to the long run of U.S. successes in this event.

1937   American professionals for the first time victorious in a Ryder Cup Match played in Britain. (Since then the U.S. players have retained the trophy undefeated).

1938   British Amateurs score their first (and so far their only) victory over the U.S. in the Walker Cup Match at St Andrews.

1939   King Leopold of the Belgians gets into the last sixteen of the Belgian Amateur Championship at Zoute.

1939–45 Golf interrupted by the Second World War.

1946   General Eisenhower elected an honorary member of the Royal and Ancient Club.

1946   King Leopold of the Belgians finishes 'first amateur' in the Swiss Open Championship at Ascona.

1947   First victory for an American player (Mrs Mildred Zaharias) in the British Ladies' Championship (at Gullane).

1948   Ben Hogan wins his first U.S. Open Championship (at Los Angeles).

1949   King Leopold of the Belgians reaches the last eight of the French Open Amateur Championship at St Cloud.

1949   First victory for a Commonwealth professional (Bobby Locke) in the British Open Championship (at Sandwich).

1951   Francis Ouimet elected the first American captain of the Royal and Ancient Club.

1952   British ladies gain their first (and so far their only) win over the U.S. in the Curtis Cup International Match, at Muirfield.

1952   Bobby Locke wins the British Open Championship for the third time in four years.

1953   Ben Hogan wins both the British and U.S. Open Championships, the latter for the fourth time in six years.

1954   Australia's banner year. Peter Thomson wins the British Open Championship at Royal Birkdale; Australian amateurs carry off the Amateur Championship at Muirfield and the Commonwealth Tournament at St Andrews, and finish 'first amateur' in the Open.

1955   Joe Conrad, the U.S. Air Force Champion, wins the British Amateur Championship at Royal Lytham and St Anne's—the sixth American victory in the ten years since the war.

Index

ABERDEEN Golf Club, Royal, 44, 46, 49, 173
Accounts of the Lord High Treasurers of Scotland, 1
Acts of Parliament, Scottish, 1–2
Adair, Miss Rhona, 158
Adams, Jamie, 168–9
Adelaide Golf Club, Royal, 163
Ado, Jean Baptiste, 193
Agincourt, Battle of, 12
Ailsa, Marquis of, 32
Allen, M. T., 99
Allen, Matthew, 87, 167
Amateur Championship, Beginning of the, 75–8, 101–6
Anderson, Jamie, 85–6
Anderson, Willie, 133
Anstruther, Sir Ralph, 55, 56, 58, 140
Apple-Tree Gang, 118
Aragon, Catherine of, 2
Arbuckle, James, 43
Architecture, Development of golf, 165–9
Art of Golf, 7
Ashdown Forest Golf Club, Royal, 125, 214
Australia, Beginning of golf in, 163
Avercamp, Hendrick, Dutch artist, 15
Ayr links, 32

Bachli, Douglas, 164
Baffing-spoon, Method of using, 144-5
Baillie, George, 157
Baird, Sir David, of Newbyth, 46, 47, 55–7
Balfour, A. J. (Lord Balfour), 107–9, 143
Balfour-Melville, Leslie M., 140
Ball, John, 88, 103–6, 151
Ballantine, James, 22
Balls, feathery, 135–40
——, gutta-percha, 140–1
——, rubber-cored, 135, 141–2

Bangalore Golf Club, 161
Bangkok Golf Club, Royal, 161
Barnes, Jim, 188
Barton, Miss Pam, 206
Battle of the Clans, 208
Baugé, Battle of, 12
Bavaria, Albert Duke of, Edict by, 16
Baxter, Peter, 138
Baynes, A. H., 97
Belfast Golf Club, Royal, 157
Belgians, Leopold, King of the, 215, 217
Belshes, Colonel J. Murray, of Balnagask, 199, 214
Belt, Open Championship, 79, 81–3
Bennett, H., 177
Berg, Miss Patty, 123
Berwick, Harry, 164
Berwick, William, 136, 138
Beverley Country Club, 134
Biarritz Old Course, local rule, 174
Birkdale Golf Club, Royal, 202
Birkenhead, Lord, 147, 218
Blackheath Golf Club, Royal, 4, 39–40, 45, 54, 61–2, 75, 77, 89–90, 93, 138, 199
Bogey, Meaning of the term, 27
——, Method of play against, 182–3
Boleyn, Anne, 211
Bombay, Golfing Society of, Royal, 160, 199
Book of Hours, Flemish, 17
Bothwell, Earl of, 1, 2, 30, 178
Boyne, Battle of the, 102
Bradshaw, Harry, 158
Braid Hills golf course, 10
Braid, James, 110–11, 158, 159, 176, 190
Brews, Syd, 191
Bride of Lammermoor, The, 122
Bril, Paul, Flemish artist, vi, 9
Brongers, J. A., Dutch writer, vi, 16
Brookline Country Club, 132

Brookman's Park Golf Club, 212–13
Brown, Mrs Charles S., 128
Brown, David, 88
Browne, Dr Thomas, R.N., 183
Bruce, Hon. C. N., Lord Aberdare, 99
Bruce, King Robert, vii, 209–10
Bruce, of Melbourne, Viscount, 164
Bruen, James, 158
Bruntsfield Links Golf Club, 41–2, 49, 75, 77, 83
Bulwell Common, Golf on, 166
Bunker, Derivation of word, 23, 25
Burgess Golfing Society of Edinburgh, Royal, 40–1, 49, 75, 77, 83, 166, 182, 184
Burke, Jack, 168–9
Burns, Jack, 88

Caddie, Derivation of word, 64
——, Duties of, 65–8
Calamity Jane, 149
Calcutta Golf Club, Royal, 160–1
Cambridge, Beginning of golf at, 95–6
Cambridge, Duke of, 215
Campbell, Miss Dorothy, 206
Campbell, John, of Glensaddell, 47, 55–7, 66, 72
Campbell, John, of the James River Country Club, vii, 113–14
Canada, Beginning of golf in, 162–3
Cape Golf Club, Royal, 163
Carlyle, Dr Alexander, of Inveresk, 40, 89
Carnegie, Claud Cathcart, 96
Carnegie, George Fullarton, 56, 67, 70
Carnoustie links, 31
Carr, Joe, 158
Catriona, References to golf in, 26
Cerda, Antonio, 164
Chambers, Robert, 78
Championships, Start of the, 75–80
Charles I, 4, 30
Charles II, 5, 37
Charles V of Germany, 17
Charlie, Bonnie Prince, 6
Chaume, Mdlle Simone Thion de la, 159
Chestfield Golf Club, 212
China, Beginning of golf in, 161

Chole, 8, 13, 14, 18, 173
'Choleur, Le Grand,' 8, 10
Clapham Common Golf Club, 92
Clarence, Thomas, Duke of, 12
Clark, Robert, v, 2, 78, 136
Cleek, Derivation of word, 23
Clubhouse, Oldest, 212
Clubs, Formation of the first, 35–44
Coe, Charles, 196
Colombo Golf Club, Royal, 161
Competitions, Institution of, 36 et seq., 179
Compston, Archie, 147, 153
Condie, George, 73, 78
Condie, James, 73
Continent of Europe, Beginning of golf in the, 158–60
Cotton, Henry, 158, 190–1
Course, Original meaning of the word, 27
Coventry Golf Club, 182
Crawford, 'Big,' 67
Crécy, Battle of, 18
Cromer Golf Club, Royal, 204–5
Cross-country Game, Golf as a, 7 et seq.
Cuchullain, Legend of, 7
Curragh Golf Club, Royal, 157
Curtis Cup International Match, 204–6
Curtis, Miss Harriet, 204–5
Curtis, Miss Margaret, 204–5

Daly, Fred, 158
Darnley, Henry Stuart, Lord, 3, 120, 210
Darwin, Bernard, 100
Davis, Robert H., 118
Demaret, Jimmy, 202
Denham Golf Club, 176
Derff, Mdlle Genevieve le, 196
Deulin, Charles, 8
Devil's Round, The, 9
Devonshire, Duke of, 214
Dibman, William, 162
Dickson, Andrew, 64, 143
Dirleton Castle Golf Club, 75, 77
Donck, Flory van, 160
Dougall, Captain W. H. Maitland, 66, 140

Driver, Derivation of the word, 23
Drives, Length of, 138–9
Dublin Golf Club, Royal, 107
Duncan, George, 188–9
Dunedin, Viscount, 95–6
Dunn, Jamie, 72
Dunn, Tom, 108
Dunn, Willie, 57, 71–2
Durham, James, of Largo, 55

Eastbourne Golf Club, Royal, 25, 214
East Lake Golf Club, 149
Edinburgh Golfers, Honourable Company of, 21, 36–8, 49, 59, 75, 76, 83, 198
Edward VII, 199, 215
Edward VIII (see Windsor, Duke of)
Eisenhower, President, 217
Elcho, Lord, 49, 90
Elphinstone, Alexander, 33
Erskine, Hon. Ruaraidh, 8
Evans, 'Chick,' 114–15
Everard, H. S. C., 21 note, 180

Fairlie, Major J. O., of Coodham, 76, 79, 81
Farnie, H. B., 23, 150
Farquhar, Miss Margaret, 196
Farrer, Guy B., 102
Ferguson, Bob, 85–7
Fernie, Willie, 87–8, 201
Fischer, Johnny, 176, 205
Fisherwomen golfers of Musselburgh, 121-2
Flodden, Battle of, 1, 3
Foot, Henry, 39
Forbes, Lord Duncan, of Culloden, 36
Fore, Origin of the word, 24
Formby Ladies' Golf Club, 125
Fort Orange and Beverwyck, Court of, 113–14
Foulis, Sir John, of Ravelstoun, 31, 65, 137
Four-ball play, 27
Foursome play, 27
Freemantle, Miss Lily, 196
Furgol, Ed., 153

Gaisgeach na Sgeithe Deirge, 8
Galloway, Bishop of, 31
Ganton Golf Club, 112, 153–4
Garden City Golf Club, 176
Garrick, David, at Hampton Court, 89
Gatheral, J. D., 152
George V, 215
George VI, 215–17
Germinal, 8
Gibson, John, 139
Glasgow Golf Club, 42–4, 49, 139
Glasgow Green, Golf on, 42–4
Glasgow, Treaty of, 1, 2, 29
Glennie, George, vi, 55, 76, 165–6
Gloucester Cathedral, 18
Goff, The, 36, 64, 69
Goldberg, Isaac, 20
Golf and Golfers, 78
Golf: a Royal and Ancient Game, v, 78, 122
Golf (Badminton Library), v, 8, 27, 39, 123, 150
Golf Book of East Lothian, 35, 137
Golf, Derivation of name, 20, 26
Golfer's Manual, The, 23
Golfiana, 56, 67, 139, 182
Golf Illustrated, vi
Golfing, vii
Golf in Perth and Perthshire, 78, 138
Gosset, George, 96
Gossett, Rev. J. H., 93
Gourlay, ball-maker, 140–1
Graham, Dr William, 139
Green, original meaning of the word, 22
Greenbrier Golf Club, 117
Greenkeeping, evolution of, 165–7
Grierson, Dr James, 53
Grimm's Law, 20–1

Hagen, Walter, 71, 72, 153–6, 188–90
Hamilton, John, Archbishop of St Andrews, 60
Handicapping, Methods of, 126
Harbert, Chick, 193
Harding, President, 217
Harper, Chandler, 203
Harris, Robert, 106
Hartley, Rex, 68

Haskell ball, 141–2
Havers, Arthur, 189
Hay, Sir Robert, 76, 78, 85, 173
Heart of Midlothian, The, References to golf in, 26, 33
Henley's Telegraph Works Co., 140
Henry V, 12
Henry VII, 2, 3, 211
Henry VIII, 2, 3, 209, 211–13
Henry, Prince of Wales, 3, 4, 17
Herd, Sandy, 66, 88, 110, 142
Herreshoff, Fred, 106
Hezlet, Lt-Colonel Charles, 158
Hezlet, Miss May, 158
Highgate Golf Club, 210
Hilton, Harold H., 88, 104–6, 148
History of the Royal and Ancient Golf Club, 53
Hogan, Ben, 71, 202, 206
Holderness, Sir E. W. E., 100
Home, John, 89
Hong Kong Golf Club, Royal, 161
Honourable Company (*see* Edinburgh Golfers)
Hooch, Pieter de, Dutch artist, 17
Hooge, Romayn de, Dutch artist, 15
Hughes, W. E., 62
Hulton, Miss Blanche, 124
Hunt, Bernard, 168–9
Hutchings, Charles, 104
Hutchinson, Horace G., 54, 93–4, 97–8, 100, 104, 150
Hutchison, Jock, 187–8

India, Beginning of golf in, 160
Innerleven Golfing Society (*see* Leven Golf Club)
Innes, William, of Blackheath, 50
Inverness, Oath of, 187
Ireland, Beginning of golf in, 7, 157
Iron play, Introduction of, for approaching, 145
Isle of Wight Golf Club, Royal, 215

James II of England, 5, 64, 102, 135, 211
James II of Scotland, 2, 12
James IV of Scotland, v, 1, 2, 30, 137, 143, 178

James V of Scotland, 3
James VI and I, 3, 30, 60, 89, 135–7, 143
James River Country Club, Golf Museum, vi, 113
Japan, Beginning of golf in, 161
Jinga (Uganda) golf course, 174
Johnstone, Maggie, 42
Jones, Bobby, 105, 149, 177, 189–90, 206

Kellner, Cecil George, 95–6
Kennedy, Hugh, 13
Kennedy of Bargany, 32
Kerr, J. Bruce, vi
Kerr, Rev. John, 46
Kidd, Tom, 201
Kingsley, Charles, 93–4
Kinloch, Captain, 23
Kinloch, Sir David of Gilmerton, vii. 157
Kipling, Rudyard, 94
Kirk, Bob, 86, 87
Kirkaldy, Andrew, 67, 88, 201
Kirkaldy, Hugh, 67
Knox, John, 24, 30
Knuckle Club, Blackheath, 39
Kolven, 14–17
—— in America, 113–14
—— on the ice, 14
Kroll, Ted, 168–9

Ladies' Competitions, Earliest, 121–2
—— Golf Clubs, First, 123
—— Golf Union, Formation of, 124 et seq.
Laidlay, John E., 103–4, 151
Laleham Golf Club, 210
Landale, Bailie William, 38
Lang, Andrew, v, 8, 39, 135, 137
Lawful sports, Declarations concerning, 30
Layamon: *Roman de Brut,* 19, 23
Le Blan, Mdlle Manette, 160
Lees, Charles, R.S.A., 55
Leitch, Miss Cecil, 128, 192
Leith links, 5, 29, 33, 35, 36, 45, 52–3, 59, 61, 64, 69, 86
Leland, O. M., Dean, vi, 9

Lenczyk, Miss Grace, 195
Leopold, King (*see* Belgians, King of the)
Leven Golf Club, 49, 75, 77, 78
Links, Meaning of the term, 25
Linskill, W. T., 95, 97–8
Liverpool Golf Club, Royal, 101–3
Lloyd George, David, 109
Locke, Arthur D'Arcy ('Bobby'), 163
Lockhart, Robert, 117
Logan, Halbert, of Restalrig, 32
London, Coming of golf to, 89–92
London Scottish Golf Club, 62, 90–2
Lost ball, Rule regarding, 173
Low, John L., 100, 106, 130
Lytham and St Anne's Golf Club, Royal, 124, 202

McCready, S. M., 158
McDermott, J. J., 132
Macdonald, Charles B., 168
MacFie, A. F., 103
Mackenzie, Dr Agnes Mure, 12, 17
Mackenzie, C. K. (Lord Mackenzie), 97
McLean, Jack, 176, 205
McMillan, Thomas, of Shorthope, 40, 121
Macnair, J. F., 160
Macpherson, Dr J. G., 71, 74, 78, 150, 165–6
Manchester, Old, Golf Club, 90, 93, 171–2
Margaret, Princess, daughter of Henry VII, 2, 3
Martin, Bob, 84–5, 201
Mary, Queen of Scots, 3, 64, 120, 209, 210
Mashie, Derivation of the name, 23
Massy, Arnaud, 159–60
Mathison, Thomas, 36, 64, 69
Maule, Sir Robert, of Panmure, 30
Maxwell, Robert, 105
Mayne, William, 'bower burgess of Edinburgh,' 3, 143
Melvill, Andrew, 31
Melvill, James, 135–7
Messieux, Samuel, 139
Minehead Golf Club, 54
Mitchell, Abe, 189

Molesey Hurst, Golf at, 89
Molesworth, Arthur, 145
Molesworth, Captain, R.N., 93–4, 148
Moncrieffe, Sir David, 199
Monmouth, Duke of, 211
Montgomery of the Ards, Viscount, 157
Montreal Golf Club, Royal, 162
Montrose links, 31, 61, 75, 77
Montrose, Marquis of, 31, 65
Moor Park Golf Club, 211
More, Sir Thomas, 212
Morris, 'Old Tom,' 72–3, 81, 141
Morris, 'Young Tom,' 82–3, 87, 145, 201–2
Muirfield links, 105
Mure, William J., 55
Mure-Ferguson, S., 104
Murray, Andrew Graham (*see* Dunedin, Viscount)
Musselburgh Golf Club, Royal, 40, 46, 75, 77, 121, 184, 215
Musselburgh links, 71, 72, 83, 87, 88, 121, 145, 166

Naarden, Edict of, 16
Nagle, Kel, 164
Nassau Country Club, 129, 149
National Links, American, Long Island, 168
New Zealand, Beginning of golf in, 163
Niblick, Derivation of name, 24
North Berwick Golf Club, 46–8, 57, 62, 75, 77, 108, 151, 182
North Devon Golf Club, Royal, 54, 90, 93–4
Nose, Golf match for an abbot's, 32
Notts Golf Club, 166

Oakhurst Golf Club, of White Sulphur Springs, 117
Odds, Methods of giving, 182
Oklahoma City Golf Club, 195–6
Oldest Clubhouse in England, 211–12
Open Championship, institution of, 78–80
—— ——, first English winners of, 88, 94
—— ——, first French winner of, 159

Open Championship, first U.S. winner of, 188
Orr, Miss E. C., 128
Oswald, Eric, vi
Oswald, John, of Dunnikier, 158
Ouimet, Francis J., 131–4, 149
Oxford and Cambridge Golfing Society, 198
—— —— American tour, 129
Oxford University, Beginning of golf at, vii, 95–7

Panmure Golf Club, 76
Park, Willie (junior), 105, 149, 151, 153–5
Park, Willie (senior), 71, 81, 153
Parrish, Samuel L., 118–19
Patersone, John, 5, 64
Pau Golf Club, 159
Pearson, A., 97
Pearson, Miss Issette, 125, 127
Perth Golfing Society, Royal, 75, 77, 214
Perth North Inch course, 1, 3, 208
Philp, Hugh, 144
Phoenix Park, Dublin, Golf in, 107, 158
Pine Valley Golf Club, 176
Pitlochry Golf Club, 209
Playfair, Sir Hugh Lyon, 55–6, 71
Porteous, Captain John, 26, 33
Prescott-Decie, Colonel R., vii, 167
President's Putter, 198
Prestwick Golf Club, 62, 75, 77, 78–80, 81–3
Prize-money, Growth of, 201
Purvis, Dr W. Laidlaw, 125
Putt, Derivation of the word, 22

Quebec Golf Club, Royal, 162
Queensland Golf Club, Royal, 199

Ramsay, Allan, 42
Rangoon Golf Club, 161
Rattray, John, 36, 37, 180
Ravenscroft, Miss Gladys, 206
Rawls, Miss Betsy, 197
Ray, Ted, 132–3, 186–7
Redgauntlet, References to golf in, 25–6
Reid, John, 117

Rivington's Royal Gazette, 114
Robbie, J. Cameron, 41, 42
Robert III of Scotland, 208
Roberts, G. P., 177
Robertson, Allan, 68, 70–4, 78, 141, 145, 148
Robertson, David, 68, 70
Robertson, Mrs Gordon, 196
Rochford Hundred Golf Club, 211
Rokkosan (Japan) golf course, 161, 174
Rolland, J. E. Douglas Stewart, 105, 202
Roosevelt, President, 217
Ross, Dame Margaret, of Balneil, 122
Rotherham, Hugh, inventor of bogey play, 182
Rough, Original meaning of the word, 27
Royal Golf Clubs, First, 214
   (Individual 'Royal' Clubs are indexed under the rest of their name)
Royal golfers, 1, 215–17
Royston Golf Club, 96
Rules of golf, Development of, 170–7
Rushcliffe Golf Club, 210
Ryder Cup International Match, 204–6
Rye golf course, 99

St Andrews Archers' Club, 39
St Andrews Golf Club, of Yonkers, N.Y., 117–18
St Andrews links, 29, 45, 59–63, 69, 71, 72, 82, 109, 165, 187
St Andrews, The Royal and Ancient Golf Club of, 22, 38–9, 48, 53, 65, 75, 77, 84, 170–3, 175, 180–2, 198–199, 214–15
St Anthony, 9, 219
St Augustine, 207
St Clair, William, of Roslin, 54–5, 123, 150
St Constantine, 208
St Cuthbert's Church, Kensington, 19
St George's Golf Club, Royal, 99, 110, 131, 188, 190
St Johnston (see Perth)
St Saveur, Vicomtesse de, 160
Sarazen, Gene, 133, 191

Sargent, Miss N. C., 128
Savannah Golf Club, 116
Sayers, Ben, 67
Scoring, Methods of, 99, 178–85
——, Terms used in, 178–9
Scott, Lady Margaret, 127
Scott, Sir Walter, 25–6
Shinnecock Hills Golf Club, 118–19
Shute, Denny, 191
Simpson, Gordon, 126
Simpson, Sir W. G., 4, 7
Singapore Golf Club, 161
Smale, John, of Aberdeen, 13
Smith, Eric Martin, 100
Smollett, Tobias, 33
Smyth, Miss D. M., 196
Snead, Sam, 206
South Africa, Beginning of golf in, 163
South Carolina Golf Club, 115–16
Spoon, Derivation of word, 23
Starkie-Bence, Miss A. M. M., 126
Steel shafts, Coming of, 146–8
Stevenson, Robert Louis, 26
Stewart, Allan, 32
Stewart, Captain J. C., of Fasnacloich, vi, 55, 76
Stewart, Robert, of Ralston, 13
Stoke Poges Golf Club, 193–4
Strath, David, 82, 84–5
Stroke play, Introduction of, 181
Stuart, Alexander, 97–8
Stuart, Prof. James, 139
Stymie, Derivation of word, 24
Stymies in famous matches, 176–7
Suggs, Miss Louise, 123, 197, 206
Sunday golf, Ban on, 29, 208 note
Sunningdale Golf Club, 167
Surgeon's Daughter, The, 25
Sutherland, Old, 23, 66
Sweetser, Jesse, 206

Taft, President, 217
Tait, Lieut. Freddie, 104–5, 139
Tam o'Shanter Golf Club, 203
Taylor, John Henry, 94, 110–11, 145, 159, 190, 201
Team Matches, Beginning of, 183–5
Tee, Derivation of the word, 21–2

Templenewsam courses, 209
Thomson, Mrs Anstruther, 9
Thomson, Peter, 164, 202
Tolley, Cyril J. H., 100, 177
Tollygunge Golf Club, 161
Toogood, Peter, 164
Toronto Golf Club, 163
Travers, Jerome D., 134
Travis, Walter J., 130–1, 142
Trevelyan, G. M., 5, 14
Trevose Golf Club, 208
Troon Golf Club, 143
Trophies, Historic, 198–200
Tuxedo Golf Club, 119
Tytler of Woodhouslee, 64

Uniforms, obligatory in early Clubs, 48
Union Club, St Andrews, 39
United States, Beginning of modern golf in, 117–19
—— ——, Early golf in, 113–19
United States Golf Association, 175
Unplayable ball, Rule regarding, 173
University Golf Match, 95–100, 184
Upminster Golf Club, 213
Utopia, 212

Vardon, Harry, 105, 110–12, 129, 132–133, 142, 151–2, 186–7, 190, 201–2
Vardon, Tom, 112
Vicenzo, Roberto de, 164
Victoria, Queen, 214
Vidal, R. W. Sealy, 96

Walker Cup International Match, 204–206
Wallace, D., of Leven, 78
Walton Heath Golf Club, 167
Wei-hai-wei course, 174
Wentworth Golf Club, 168
Westminster, 'Upfields,' Golf in, 89
Westward Ho! course, 90, 92–4, 110
Wethered, Miss Joyce, 123, 128, 189, 192–3
Wethered, Roger, 100, 123, 187, 193
Whitcombe, Charles, 133, 155
Whitcombe, Reg., 133, 191

White, Jack, 153–5, 202
Whyte-Melville, John, of Mount Melville, 22, 47, 66, 76, 199
William III, 6, 102
William IV, 199, 214
Wilson, President, 217
Wimbledon Common golf course, 62, 90–1, 98
Wimbledon Golf Club, Royal, 91–2
Wimbledon Park course, 16

Windsor, Duke of, 50, 174, 199, 215–16
Wirral Ladies' Golf Club, 125
Witchcraft on the links, 122–3
Wolsey, Cardinal, 2, 211
Worcestershire Golf Club, vii, 167
Worsham, Lew, 203

Zaharias, Mrs Mildred ('Babe'), 123, 192–3, 197, 206
Zola, Émile, 8

Afterword

by S. L. McKinlay

It was with a mixture of relish and reverence that I approached the re-reading of Robert Browning's fine history of golf—relish because I remembered the enjoyment it gave me when first I read it, reverence because Robert Browning was for me a very special person. We met rarely, but our lives were linked in many ways. We had been at the same school, Whitehill, a co-educational public school, in the American sense, in the East End of Glasgow. It had something more than local renown for producing scholars and sportsmen, including Scottish international soccer players, at least one sprinter of Olympic calibre, and two Walker Cup players.

Browning went to Glasgow University a generation before me, took an honours degree in mathematics and natural philosophy (modern physics, I suppose) in 1904 when only twenty, and three years later he graduated in law, with distinction. So he was probably just about as well educated as any man who spent his life editing a golf magazine and writing about the game he had loved since he was a boy playing on a local public course in Glasgow park where I played my own first strokes. He dabbled briefly in the law, like Bernard Darwin, but he had developed a taste for journalism while a student, writing humorous articles and light verse for the university magazine, which he edited for a year while preparing for his second degree. He went to Manchester for a short time but went on to London, where he soon became editor of the magazine Golfing *and remained in the chair for virtually the rest of his life.*

Browning came from a notable family. His father Daniel, a dealer in fine arts, had Parliamentary ambitions but these were squashed in the election after World War One when he succumbed to one of the "Red Clydesiders", the Rev. Campbell Stephen. One of Browning's brothers, Andrew, went on to become Professor of History at Glasgow University, where he was one of my teachers. The other brother, David, was a brilliant Classical scholar at Glasgow University, where he won the Snell Exhibition to Balliol College, Oxford, the highest scholarship award any Glasgow undergraduate could win.

Oddly, David's path and mine also crossed. After leaving Oxford he became a leader-writer (editorial pundit) on the Glasgow Herald, *Scotland's most prestigious paper (despite the claims of the more grandly named* Scotsman*). My first newspaper job was as a fledgling sub-editor on the* Herald, *and there I came to know and like David Browning, a quiet, shy man, like his brothers, with an impish sense of fun. He left the* Herald *for the oddest and best of reasons: he came into money—not very much, though £500 in 1930 was a sizeable sum. But it was how he did it that was fun. A chocolate company offered that amount for a slogan in reply to a supposed query by a bar of chocolate to a consumer—"Why do you like me?", and David Browning, ex-Oxford don, scooped the pool with "Because we both have such good taste". And back he went to Oxford to live in a garret and become one of the great lexicographers and compilers of this century. His one-volume "Everyman Dictionary" is the best of its kind, his edition of "Roget's Thesaurus" is unsurpassed, and his "Dictionary of English and American Literary Biography" should be on every bookshelf.*

It was small wonder, I suppose, that Robert Browning, with that ancestry and such talented brothers, shoud become an editor of great distinction. He was the first editor I ever wrote for—in the beginning un-

solicited, later on a regular monthly basis for many years. He was always uniformly kind and helpful, possibly at the start because I was an old Whitehill boy but afterwards because that was the nature of the man. Nor was I the only young writer to benefit from his support. Just after World War Two, I came across a Manchester man newly out of the R.A.F. after a spell as a prisoner in the notorious Stalag Luft lll at Sagan. He was Flt. Lt. P.A.W. Thomas and he had no occupation, having been a regular in the R.A.F., which he was now leaving. He was a pretty good golfer and desperately keen to write about the game. He told me about the makeshift golf course the prisoners had built in the camp compound, and I suggested he write it up and send it to Browning, to whom I wrote outlining the circumstances. Browning promptly published the piece, and that was really the start of the writing career of Pat Ward-Thomas, later the famous golf correspondent of the Guardian.

If I have travelled some way from Browning's own work, it is because he led to so many alluring byways. There was, for example, his light verse, which he started writing as a student and which he continued to produce almost to the end of his life, often under the nom-de-plume Hara-Kari, probably because he had an almost too poetic name himself. He also had a wonderful sense of fun. One of his regular contributors to Golfing was called Clayton Terriss, which sounds like a character from "Dallas". He was a very knowledgeable and skillfull writer, but I was probably one of the few readers of the magazine who penetrated his identity. Browning was brought up in a handsome house in the Dennistoun district of Glasgow, one of a row called Clayton Terrace.

One good critic thought Browning's light verse among the best of his generation, but it was so widely scattered among different periodicals as to defy any attempt at collection. I have, however, a copy of one of his

longest, and best, poems, "The Pilgrims' Progress",
which describes in rhymed couplets the exploits of four
London golfers who set out "to golf all August around
the North." There are some lovely lines—

> Then off through Dirleton, cool and shady,
> To Muirfield, Archerfield, Aberlady.
> They golfed at Gullane, on 'One' and 'Two',
> They played Longniddry and Luffness New.

One could go on and on. For example, at St. Andrews, they

> Laughed in the 'Beardies', despaired in 'Hell',
> But played the first and the last quite well.

But, being a West of Scotland man myself, my favorite lines are

> Troon and Prestwick—Old and 'classy'—
> Bogside, Dundonald, Gailes, Barassie.

There is a warmth in the lines that shows Browning
never lost his awareness of having been born and educated in Scotland. He never, in nearly fifty years, became anglified, and his handling of Scots dialect in his
history is impeccable. He never over-emphasizes, never
inserts an additional "r" to produce a phoney burr. His
story of the Scots caddie rebuking Rex Hartley at
Gleneagles is perfect. It reminds me of a Muirfied caddie only a few years back whose master, playing with a
spoon from the tee for security, had got into the "safe"
position of dormie two. Flushed with pride, on the
seventeenth he asked for his driver. The caddie refused
to hand it over. Instead, he thrust forward the trusty
spoon with the cautionary words, "This is nae time tae
be buggerin' about wi' a driver".

Maybe, however, I should translate at least one Scottish word in the history for the benefit of alien ears.
Browning says King Charles's experience of golf was of
a nature to give him what the Scots call a "scunner" for

the rest of his life. I can do no better than give brother David's definition of this near indefinable word from his dictionary: "scunner—loathing; object of disgust".

Robert Browning was himself "scunnered" at times by what he with rare asperity calls the barrow-boys of Fleet Street—the glib writers on sport who don't check their references or dig out facts for themselves. He himself was punctilious in his research, and the early chapters of his book, which from another hand might have been so dull, are marvels of lightness and enlightenment. I think I detected only one error when first I read the book, at the behest, if you please, of no less than the author himself. In September, 1955, Browning sent me a copy with the modest request that "I should be very grateful if you could make your article for the October issue a review of the book. Don't be shy about pointing out my grosser errors. And your petitioner will ever pray . . ."

The error I found concerned the birthplace of Young Tom Morris. Browning says he was born in St. Andrews, in 1851, but in that year his father went to Prestwick to be keeper of the green, and I think young Tom was born there. Even St. Andrews experts I consulted at the time could not authenticate the place of birth, but doubtless some more diligent and inspired new reader of the book will prove me wrong and Browning, as he deserves to be, right.

It is certainly a pleasing thought that a hundred years after Robert Browning was born his splendid book will now gain a new and wider currency. Like the jolly golfers, he "played the first and the last quite well".